M000086988

PRIVATE RACISM

Usually, when we discuss racial injustice, we discuss racism in our public or political life. This means that we often focus on how the state discriminates on the basis of race in its application and enforcement of laws and policies. This book draws on the synergy of political theory and civil rights law to expand the boundary of racial justice and consider the way in which racial discrimination happens outside the governmental or public sphere. "Private racism" is about recognizing that racial injustice also occurs in our private lives, including the television and movie industry, cyberspace, our intimate and sexual lives, and the reproductive market. Professor Sonu Bedi argues that private racism is wrong, enlarging the boundary of justice in a way that is also consistent with our Constitution. A more just society is one that seeks to address rather than ignore this less visible form of racism.

Sonu Bedi is the Joel Parker 1811 Professor in Law and Political Science, Associate Professor of Government, and the Hans '80 and Kate Morris Director of the Ethics Institute at Dartmouth College. He has published three books: *Political Contingency* (2007), *Rejecting Rights* (Cambridge University Press: 2009), and *Beyond Race, Sex, and Sexual Orientation: Legal Equality without Identity* (Cambridge University Press: 2013).

Private Racism

Sonu Bedi

Dartmouth College

CAMBRIDGE
UNIVERSITY PRESS

University Printing House, Cambridge CB2 8BS, United Kingdom

One Liberty Plaza, 20th Floor, New York, NY 10006, USA

477 Williamstown Road, Port Melbourne, VIC 3207, Australia

314–321, 3rd Floor, Plot 3, Splendor Forum, Jasola District Centre, New Delhi – 110025, India

79 Anson Road, #06–04/06, Singapore 079906

Cambridge University Press is part of the University of Cambridge.

It furthers the University's mission by disseminating knowledge in the pursuit of education, learning, and research at the highest international levels of excellence.

www.cambridge.org
Information on this title: www.cambridge.org/9781108415385
DOI: 10.1017/9781108233507

© Sonu Bedi 2020

This publication is in copyright. Subject to statutory exception and to the provisions of relevant collective licensing agreements, no reproduction of any part may take place without the written permission of Cambridge University Press.

First published 2020

Printed in the United Kingdom by TJ International Ltd. Padstow Cornwall

A catalogue record for this publication is available from the British Library.

Library of Congress Cataloging-in-Publication Data
Names: Bedi, Sonu, author.
Title: Private racism / Sonu Bedi, Dartmouth College, New Hampshire.
Description: Cambridge, United Kingdom ; New York, NY : Cambridge University Press, 2020. | Includes bibliographical references and index.
Identifiers: LCCN 2019019740 | ISBN 9781108415385 (alk. paper)
Subjects: LCSH: Racism. | Discrimination. | Equality.
Classification: LCC HT1521 .B394 2020 | DDC 305.8–dc23
LC record available at https://lccn.loc.gov/2019019740

ISBN 978-1-108-41538-5 Hardback
ISBN 978-1-108-40134-0 Paperback

Cambridge University Press has no responsibility for the persistence or accuracy of URLs for external or third-party internet websites referred to in this publication and does not guarantee that any content on such websites is, or will remain, accurate or appropriate.

To my students

CONTENTS

ACKNOWLEDGMENTS

It was an intellectual pleasure to write this book. This is largely because I had the opportunity to discuss the book with a range of individuals who provided such generous and insightful feedback.

I presented earlier versions and parts of this book at the conferences for the American Political Science Association and the Society for Business Ethics, as well as Yale's Legal Theory Workshop, Boston University's Gender, Law and Policy Colloquium, Notre Dame's Political Theory Colloquium, and the 2nd Annual Moral and Political Philosophy Workshop at Dartmouth's Ethics Institute.

I thank Jed Rubenfeld for inviting me to Yale's workshop. That workshop, early in the writing process, proved crucial in encouraging me to clarify and revise the argument. I had the privilege of receiving feedback from many in the Yale Law School community. I thank Eileen Hunt Botting for inviting me to Notre Dame's Political Theory Colloquium where I received invaluable comments on an earlier version of the argument in Chapter 5. I thank Linda McClain for inviting me to Boston University's Colloquium. I had the good fortune to present to Linda's class later in the writing process, receiving incisive comments while completing the book. I also thank Brandon Terry for providing thoughtful and encouraging comments at the Moral and Political Philosophy Workshop at Dartmouth. I thank all the participants at these venues for engaging my overall thesis so rigorously and thoughtfully. I was also lucky to have a conversation with Christopher Parker about framing the argument.

I also benefitted from many long and fruitful discussions about the book with Monu Bedi, Suneal Bedi, Brian Bowden, Victoria Kennedy,

Elvin Lim, Vincent Mack, Tim Nguyen, Timothy Spruill, and Craig Sutton. I also thank the anonymous reviewers for their constructive guidance.

I am lucky to be a member of the Department of Government and a member of the larger Dartmouth community where I have such supportive colleagues. It's a pleasure to be a faculty member here. I also benefitted from a senior faculty fellowship and sabbatical in 2015–2016 which provided me time to work on the book.

I am also lucky to be teaching at Dartmouth. The first time I taught my own course here was in January 2007. Since then, I have been fortunate to have such great students to teach and learn from. My teaching influences my scholarship and vice versa. In that spirit, I dedicate this book to my students. It was also a pleasure to present parts of the book to meetings of the *Dartmouth Law Journal* and the Dartmouth Minority Pre-Law Association. I received encouragement and instructive feedback from the students who attended. Students in my spring 2017 seminar entitled "Race, Law, and Identity" read earlier chapters also providing thoughtful comments. Connie Lee provided research assistance for Chapter 3.

An earlier version of Chapter 4 was published in the *Journal of Politics*, Vol. 77 (4) (2015) ("Sexual Racism: Intimacy as a Matter of Justice").

I'm grateful to John Berger, my editor extraordinaire at Cambridge University Press, for his support and commitment. John has been a senior editor at the Press for over fifteen years, where he has dedicated so much of his time to advancing knowledge. I thank him for that. John is leaving the Press in 2019, so this will be one of his final books at the press. I'm fortunate to be one of John's authors.

INTRODUCTION

This book is about enlarging the boundary of racial justice by recognizing and addressing private racism. This book defines "private racism" as racial injustice that happens in the private sphere. By focusing on racial injustice that happens outside the governmental or public sphere, we expand the scope or boundary of racial justice. Usually, when we discuss racial injustice, we discuss racism in our public or political life, namely public racism. This means that we often focus on how the state discriminates on the basis of race in its application and enforcement of laws and policies. This book draws on the synergy of political theory and civil rights law to expand the boundary of racial justice and consider the way in which racial discrimination happens outside the governmental or public sphere.

In particular, this book discusses racial injustice that happens in the television and movie industry, cyberspace, our intimate and sexual lives, and the reproductive market. I argue that these are some of the places where racial injustice happens in private.

In drawing on political theory, this book takes a methodologically diverse approach to understanding racial justice. The focus of methodology may be a familiar one in other subfields in political science. Political theorists also care about methodology. Like other political scientists, we too deploy tools, instruments, and frameworks to study a particular issue. Our tools are often conceptual and evaluative in nature rather than empirical. But they are tools nonetheless, representing different and often contrasting ways of arriving at our normative conclusions.

One such conceptual methodological difference, and the focus of this book, is the distinction between ideal and nonideal theory,[1] or what this book will call for clarity purposes "the ideal society approach" and the "actual society approach" respectively. These represent two distinct methodologies of justice. There are of course other such methodologies. I draw on these two because they strike me as two prominent ways of understanding or thinking about racial justice.

Put in general terms, the "ideal society approach" says that in an ideal society race would not matter. Racial discrimination would not occur. The ideal society approach is most often associated with John Rawls's *A Theory of Justice*, so the book will treat Rawls's argument as a representative of this approach. According to this approach, racial discrimination is wrong, because society should treat race as something that is "arbitrary from a moral perspective."[2] The ideal society approach defines racial injustice in terms of racial discrimination. It's wrong for society to discriminate.

This methodology of justice also has political and legal significance. The Republican Party's 2016 platform references it:

> We reaffirm the Constitution's fundamental principles: limited government, separation of powers, individual liberty, and the rule of law. We denounce bigotry, racism, anti-Semitism, ethnic prejudice, and religious intolerance. Therefore, we oppose discrimination based on race, sex, religion, creed, disability, or national origin and support statutes to end such discrimination. As the Party of Abraham Lincoln, we must continue to foster solutions to America's difficult challenges when it comes to race relations today. We continue to encourage equality for all citizens and access to the American Dream. Merit and hard work should determine advancement in our society, so we reject unfair preferences, quotas, and set-asides as forms of discrimination.[3]

Taking the ideal society approach seriously means that racial discrimination is wrong, and society should seek to prohibit it. This approach finds "quotas," "set asides," and other kinds of remedial policies based on race to be unfair. Merit and hard work, not race, should be all that matters. As a representative of the ideal society approach, Chief Justice

---

[1] See, e.g., Farrelly 2007, Geuss 2008, Valentini 2012, Wiens 2012.
[2] Rawls 1999 [1971]: 64.
[3] www.gop.com/the-2016-republican-party-platform/

John Roberts says: "The way to stop discrimination on the basis of race is to stop discriminating on the basis of race."[4] This means that he and those jurists who favor this approach will likely strike down race-based affirmative action policies, because these policies discriminate on the basis of race.

Put also in general terms, the "actual society approach" says that in our actual society, race does matter. This approach draws attention to racial inequality and stereotypes that exist in our actual society. We can associate this kind of approach with a range of work by scholars such as Elizabeth Anderson, Charles Mills, Martha Nussbaum, and Iris Marion Young. This book will treat arguments by these scholars as representative examples of the actual society approach. According to this approach, racial inequality or stereotypes are wrong and therefore society should do something about this. There may be disagreement about what society should do under the actual society approach. (Disagreement that I discuss in more detail in Chapter 1.) At the very least, it's wrong for society to further racial inequality or stereotypes under this approach.

This approach also has political and legal significance. The Democratic Party's 2016 platform references it:

> Democrats will fight to end institutional and systemic racism in our society. We will challenge and dismantle the structures that define lasting racial, economic, political, and social inequity. Democrats will promote racial justice through fair, just, and equitable govern-ing of all public-serving institutions and in the formation of public policy. Democrats support removing the Confederate battle flag from public properties, recognizing that it is a symbol of our nation's racist past that has no place in our present or our future. We will push for a societal transformation to make it clear that black lives matter and that there is no place for racism in our country.

Taking the actual society approach seriously means that society should seek to recognize and address racial inequality, transforming society to be more equal in terms of race. As a representative of the actual society approach, Justice Sonia Sotomayor says: "The way to stop discrimination on the basis of race is to speak openly and candidly on the subject of race,

---

[4] *Parents Involved in Cmty. Sch.* v. *Seattle Sch. Dist. No. 1* (2007) at 748.

and to apply the Constitution with eyes open to the unfortunate effects of centuries of racial discrimination."[5] This means that she and those jurists who favor the actual society approach will likely uphold race-based affirmative action policies, because these policies seek to remedy racial injustice.

Those who reject affirmative action policies often do so by deploying the ideal society approach. They view such policies as instances of racial discrimination, discrimination that is otherwise unjust or wrong. Those who favor such policies often do so by deploying the actual society approach. They view such policies as seeking to remedy racial injustice. And jurists and legal scholars also deploy these approaches in either defending or rejecting affirmative action policies. This is why we usually view those who adopt the ideal society approach as ideologically conservative and those who adopt the actual society approach as ideologically liberal in matters of race.

In a methodological diverse fashion, this book will draw on both approaches. I argue that both methodologies of justice support the conclusion that private racism is a form of injustice. Both support the book's core normative claim that we should enlarge the boundary of racial justice. I use both to create an overlapping moral consensus that will underwrite this claim. In *Brown* v. *Board of Education* (1954), these approaches also formed an overlapping moral consensus that recognized that racism in the public or governmental sphere is wrong. In *Brown*, Chief Justice Earl Warren asks: "Does segregation of children in public schools solely on the basis of race, even though the physical facilities and other 'tangible' factors may be equal, deprive the children of the minority group of equal educational opportunities?" He concludes it does. Warren's opinion references both the ideal and actual society approaches. In a reference to an ideal society, *Brown* focuses on the idea that discrimination "solely on the basis of race" is wrong. "Separate but equal" is, as *Brown* famously says, "inherently unequal."[6] In an ideal society, society would not separate or discriminate against individuals on the basis of race, because society would treat race as morally irrelevant. In a reference to our actual society, *Brown* makes clear that this policy also deprives "the children of the minority

---

[5] *Schuette* v. *BAMN* (2014) at 381, dissenting.
[6] *Brown* (1954) at 495.

group of equal educational opportunities."[7] Segregation "generates a feeling of inferiority as to their status in the community that may affect their hearts and minds in a way unlikely ever to be undone."[8] *Brown* recognizes that racial inequality and stereotypes exist in our actual society and that segregation only contributes to and furthers this injustice. It is no wonder that *Brown* is considered by most, if not all, of us, regardless of ideology or methodology, as the iconic "symbolic" case that condemns racism in our public life.[9]

In drawing on this moral consensus, this book argues that we should also condemn racism in our private life. Both approaches or methodologies of justice enlarge the boundary of racial justice by supporting that moral conclusion. Because this argument draws on both approaches, it makes an argument that cannot be characterized as either ideologically liberal or conservative.

I will argue that the ideal society approach expands the boundary of racial justice by treating racial discrimination as the relevant injustice. If we should treat race as a morally irrelevant characteristic, it does not matter whether racial discrimination happens in public or private. I show that according to the ideal society approach, individuals who discriminate on the basis of race in private also act unjustly. This provides us moral reasons for enlarging the boundary of racial justice.

I will argue that the actual society approach expands the boundary of racial justice by treating racial inequality and stereotypes as the relevant injustice. If we treat racial inequality as the moral wrong, it does not matter whether this inequality or these stereotypes happen in public or private. I show that according to the actual society approach, individuals who further this inequality or these stereotypes in private act unjustly. This also provides moral reasons for enlarging the boundary of racial justice.

We need not look just to political theory. Civil rights law also expands this boundary. The legal part of this book will draw on landmark civil rights statutes such as the Civil Rights Act of 1964 and the Fair Housing Act of 1968 and the cases that importantly interpret these statutes, such as *Jones* v. *Mayer* (1968), to flesh out this expansive view of the boundary of racial justice. The book's legal argument will work in

---

[7] *Brown* (1954) at 493.
[8] *Brown* (1954) at 494.
[9] See generally Rosenburg 2004.

tandem with the ideal and actual society approaches. That synergy between political theory and civil rights law will be an important feature of the book.

We can see this synergy at work in *Jones* where a white homeowner refused to sell his house to Joseph Lee Jones, because he was black. The US Supreme Court held that this violates Section 1982 passed by the Reconstruction Congress after the Civil War. The Court references both the ideal and actual society approaches in doing so. It concludes that Section 1982 "bars all racial discrimination, private as well as public, in the sale or rental of property, and that the statute, thus construed, is a valid exercise of the power of Congress to enforce the Thirteenth Amendment."[10] In reference to discrimination, the conclusion draws on the ideal society approach that says racial discrimination is wrong. In reference to the Thirteenth Amendment, the conclusion draws on the actual society approach that says racial inequality and stereotypes – the "badges and the incidents of slavery"[11] – are wrong. In that one sentence, *Jones* references both. This book will do the same by discussing both approaches in each chapter.

In drawing on both methodologies, *Jones* makes clear that these laws sought to combat racism in public and private.

> For the same Congress that wanted to do away with the Black Codes also had before it an imposing body of evidence pointing to the mistreatment of Negroes by private individuals and unofficial groups, mistreatment unrelated to any hostile state legislation.[12]

The Court goes on to reference various kinds of private injuries, injuries that are not part of the public or political sphere but the private one.

> "Accounts in newspapers North and South, Freedmen's Bureau and other official documents, private reports and correspondence were all adduced" to show that "private outrage and atrocity" were "daily inflicted on freedmen . . ." The congressional debates are replete with references to private injustices against Negroes – references to white employers who refused to pay their Negro workers, white planters who agreed among themselves not to hire freed slaves without the

[10] *Jones* (1968) at 413.
[11] *Jones* (1968) at 440–441.
[12] *Jones* (1968) at 427.

permission of their former masters, white citizens who assaulted Negroes or who combined to drive them out of their communities.

Indeed, one of the most comprehensive studies then before Congress stressed the prevalence of private hostility toward Negroes and the need to protect them from the resulting persecution and discrimination.[13]

By referencing "private hostility" and "private injustices," *Jones* acknowledges and repudiates racism that happens outside the governmental or public sphere. This book will do the same, devoting each chapter to a different instance of private racism.

The book makes claims that are descriptive, normative, and legal in nature. I show that racism does take place in our private lives (the descriptive claim), that this kind of racial discrimination is wrong under both the ideal and actual society approaches (the normative claim), and that the law already prohibits certain instances of private racism (the legal claim). This book argues that racial injustice happens in private. So, just as we care about racial equality in public, we should enlarge the boundary of racial justice and also care about racial equality in private. The moral consensus provided by the ideal and actual society approaches to racial justice supports that conclusion or so I argue. In doing so, these methodologies of justice affirm an expansive view of the boundary of racial justice.

In positively commenting upon Justice Sotomayor's words from above, former Attorney General Eric Holder warns that we should not focus solely on the "high-profile expressions of outright bigotry."[14] For if we do

we are likely to miss the more hidden, and more troubling, reality behind the headlines.

These outbursts of bigotry, while deplorable, are not the true markers of the struggle that still must be waged, or the work that still needs to be done – because the greatest threats do not announce themselves in screaming headlines. They are more subtle. They cut deeper. And their terrible impact endures long after the headlines

[13] *Jones* (1968) at 427–28.
[14] www.washingtonpost.com/politics/transcript-attorney-general-eric-holders-speech-to-morgan-state-university-graduates/2014/05/17/d6b72284-ddd0-11e3-b745-87d39690c5c0_story.html

have faded and obvious, ignorant expressions of hatred have been
marginalized.[15]

Holder is correct that racism can sometimes be "more hidden" or more
"subtle." One way this can happen, and the focus of this book, is when
racial injustice happens in the private sphere. This book takes seriously
the idea, most often associated with feminist political theory, that the
personal is the political. In doing so, it expands the boundary of racial
justice by showing that racism happens in private. This book has five
chapters followed by a conclusion.

The first chapter ("Enlarging the Boundary of Racial Justice") elaborates upon the moral consensus that will drive the rest of the argument, drawing on the synergy of political theory and civil rights law to
expand this boundary. This consensus draws on both the ideal and
actual society approaches to explain that racism which occurs outside
the governmental or public sphere is also unjust. According to the ideal
society approach, racial discrimination is unjust, because society should
treat race as a morally irrelevant characteristic. Racial discrimination that
occurs in our private lives is wrong. According to the actual society
approach, racial inequality and stereotypes are the relevant injustice,
because these inequalities make it more difficult for racial minorities to
find various goods and services. Furthering or facilitating this inequality
or these stereotypes in our private lives is wrong. Both frameworks will
form the overlapping moral consensus that will motivate the book's
argument.

I also show that civil rights law enforces this consensus by prohibiting racial discrimination and racial steering. Racial discrimination may
be the more familiar practice that occurs in private like the discrimination Joseph Lee Jones faced in finding housing. Racial steering occurs
when individuals, most notably real estate agents or brokers, "steer or
channel a prospective buyer into or away from an area because of
race."[16] Steering can facilitate racial discrimination and therefore
further racial inequality or stereotypes. The ideal and actual society
approaches justify the law's ban on racial discrimination and steering,

---

[15] www.washingtonpost.com/politics/transcript-attorney-general-eric-holders-speech-to-
morgan-state-university-graduates/2014/05/17/d6b72284-ddd0-11e3-b745-
87d39690c5c0_story.html
[16] *Zuch* v. *Hussey* (E.D. Mich. 1975) at 1047.

respectively. The ideal society approach says that racial discrimination in private is wrong. The actual society approach says that encouraging or furthering racial inequality or stereotypes in private is wrong. These acts of discrimination and steering will figure prominently in the book.

The second chapter ("Casting Racism") considers the injustice of racial discrimination by television and movie studios in their casting decisions. I argue that casting racism is a form of employment discrimination. This chapter argues that this kind of private racism is wrong and unlawful. I argue that casting racism violates formal equality of opportunity and furthers the harm of cultural imperialism. Both the ideal and actual society approaches repudiate it. Federal law also prohibits casting racism, making no exception for this kind of discrimination. This chapter then considers whether television and movie studios have a First Amendment right to expressive association that would permit them to engage in this kind of racial discrimination.

The third chapter ("Digital Racism") considers racism in our private, digital lives. According to a 2018 Pew Research poll, one quarter of adults in the United States say they are "almost constantly" online.[17] This means that we conduct much of our private lives online or digitally. This chapter discusses two kinds of digital racism, digital discrimination and digital steering. Digital discrimination occurs when users on websites and platforms discriminate on the basis of race. I show that although discrimination is a well-documented phenomenon, it is difficult to hold websites responsible for it. This is because, as a matter of law, they are not held responsible for what their users do. This chapter argues we can more effectively combat digital racism by banning digital steering. Digital steering occurs when websites and platforms encourage or direct us to discriminate on the basis of race. This chapter argues that we should hold websites responsible for steering. In doing so, this chapter draws on the ideal and actual society approaches to treat websites and platforms as digital public accommodations. These sites structure how we interact, communicate, and transact in the world. As such, this chapter argues that it's wrong

[17] www.pewresearch.org/fact-tank/2018/03/14/about-a-quarter-of-americans-report-going-online-almost-constantly/

for websites to encourage or direct their users to discriminate on the basis of race. We should ban them from doing so.

The fourth chapter ("Sexual Racism") considers racism in our intimate or sexual lives. I show that racial discrimination, stereotyping, and intersectionality happen in our intimate lives. This makes it more difficult for those who are not white to find intimacy, where intimacy is the opportunity to be in a romantic or sexual relationship. I argue that this is a form of racial injustice, because it denies individuals an important social primary good under the ideal society approach and a capability central to human dignity under the actual society approach. The chapter suggests how society can address sexual racism by banning websites and platforms from steering us to discriminate on the basis of race in our intimate lives.

The fifth chapter ("Reproductive Market Racism") argues that racism is a prominent aspect of the market for gametes, because in selling sperm and ova, reproductive banks also provide buyers the option to exclude donors on the basis of race. Reproductive banks provide this option by discriminating against potential donors on the basis of race and steering buyers to do the same. Most notably, these banks engage in racial steering by disclosing the race of the donor. In doing so, they provide buyers the option to form a biological family that is racially homogenous. This allows buyers the option to avoid racially integrating their families. This is how banks sell segregation, or so this chapter argues. Drawing on both the ideal society and actual society approaches to racial justice, this chapter argues that selling segregation is wrong.

The conclusion ("Private Injustice") acknowledges that we may face other kinds of private injustices besides private racism. As a way to spur further conversations about enlarging the boundary of justice in other ways, the concluding chapter will consider private homophobia and private economic injustice. Treating these as two types of private injustice also stands to enlarge the boundary of justice. I focus on these two, because the Court has recently discussed the first and because political philosophy, in particular G.A. Cohen's article "Where the Action is: On the Site of Distribute Justice,"[18] discusses the latter.

---

[18] Cohen 1997.

1 ENLARGING THE BOUNDARY OF RACIAL JUSTICE

Racial justice is often about addressing racism in our public or political lives. We focus on the way in which the government discriminates on the basis of race by denying individuals opportunities to participate in the democratic process, to access a fair criminal justice system, and to find public education, police protection, and other such goods. This book enlarges the boundary of racial justice by focusing on private racism, on racism that happens in private, outside the governmental or public sphere. Each chapter will present another instance where we can enlarge this boundary by addressing racial injustice in our private lives.

This chapter provides the moral consensus that will motivate the book and each of the individual chapters. This moral consensus draws on the ideal and actual society approaches or methodologies of justice. I argue that both these approaches support an expansive view of the boundary of racial justice by recognizing that private racism is wrong. I show that civil rights law enforces this consensus by prohibiting racial discrimination and steering in our private lives.

This chapter is in four sections. First, I elaborate upon both the "ideal society" and "actual society" approaches in political theory to explain why racism in private, outside the governmental or public sphere, is wrong. The ideal society approach affirms a moral principle that says we should not discriminate on the basis of race in our private lives. The actual society approach affirms a moral principle that says, at the very least, we should not further racial inequality and stereotypes in our private lives. Second, I argue that both methodologies of justice provide an overlapping moral consensus that supports the conclusion that private racism is unjust. In doing so, they both motivate us to expand the boundary of racial justice and address racial injustice that happens in the private sphere. Third, I show that civil rights law enforces this consensus by prohibiting a range of individuals from discriminating and steering on the basis of race. Fourth, I discuss the historical resistance to adopting an expansive view of the boundary of racial justice.

TWO METHODOLOGIES OF JUSTICE

There are a number of moral perspectives that could support the conclusion that private racism is wrong. This book looks at two such approaches or methodologies: "an ideal society approach" and "an actual society approach." The ideal society approach promulgates moral principles by asking what an ideal society would look like. The actual society approach promulgates moral principles by looking at what our actual society looks like. Scholars often describe this distinction as one between ideal and nonideal theory.[1] I adopt the terms "ideal society" and "actual society" as a clearer way to state the difference.

Laura Valentini instructively treats this distinction as a methodological one, where the ideal society approach "may be taken to mean 'full-compliance theory'" and an actual society approach "may be understood as 'partial compliance theory.'"[2] The motivating question under this rubric is "what duties and obligations apply to us in situations of partial compliance" (actual society) as opposed to "situations of full compliance" (ideal society). I realize that there may be other ways to understand this distinction between ideal and nonideal theory. For purposes of this book, I assume that an ideal society approach is about what justice demands of us in situations of full compliance and an actual society approach is about what justice demands in situations of partial compliance.

I follow Valentini in also viewing these frameworks as methodological ones. By drawing attention to these approaches as distinct frameworks for understanding justice, I hope to show that like other subfields in political

---

[1] See, e.g., Farrelly 2007, Geuss 2008, Valentini 2012, Wiens 2012.
[2] Valentini 2012: 654.

science, political theory is also methodologically diverse. Making these two methodological assumptions or frameworks explicit more clearly captures the way political theorists often discuss and debate justice. Rather than treating the ideal and actual society methodologies as antagonistic, this book will treat them as distinct but complementary ways of enlarging the boundary of racial justice. I draw on both to explain why private racism is wrong. Again, these may not be the only ways to support this moral conclusion. I focus on these two because they are prominent ones in debates about racial justice.[3] For instance, Charles Mills describes the distinction in the following way:

> Both ideal and non-ideal theory are concerned with justice, and so with the appeal to moral ideals. The contrast is that ideal theory asks what justice demands in a perfectly just society while non-ideal theory asks what justice demands in a society with a history of injustice.[4]

I draw on both these approaches to explain why racism in private, outside the governmental or public sphere, is wrong. Some may prefer one methodology of justice over the other. For purposes of this book, it does not matter, because both approaches support the core moral claim that private racism is wrong. This section works out each of these approaches and then explains how both would include opportunities beyond the commercial sphere within the boundary of justice.

The Ideal Society Approach

John Rawls's *A Theory of Justice* is a prominent representative of the ideal society approach.[5] Before formulating his theory of justice, Rawls makes clear that he assumes a society that is fully complying with the principles of justice. For him, "[e]veryone is presumed to act justly and do his part in upholding just institutions."[6] He explicitly treats this assumption as a form of "strict compliance as opposed to partial compliance theory."[7] "The latter studies the principles that govern how we are to deal with injustice."[8]

---

[3] See Anderson 2013 [2010], Mills 1999 [1997], 2017.
[4] Mills 2017: 34.
[5] Rawls 1999 [1971].
[6] Rawls 1999 [1971]: 8.
[7] Rawls 1999 [1971]: 8.
[8] Rawls 1999 [1971]: 8.

s that the "problems of partial compliance theory are the
:nt matters ... that we are faced with in everyday life."[9]
"reason for beginning with ideal theory is that it pro-
, the only basis for the systematic grasp of these more
."[10] This is why he also assumes that "the principles of
justice would regulate a well-ordered society."[11] The idea of a "well-ordered society" and one where there is "strict compliance" to principles of justice motivates the ideal society approach.

Rawls states that in this well-ordered society where everyone is presumed to act justly, there are "no arbitrary distinctions ... between persons in the assigning of basic rights and duties."[12] One such distinction, relevant here, is race. "For example, none would urge that special privileges be given to those exactly six feet tall or born on a sunny day. Nor would anyone put forward the principle that basic rights should depend on the color of one's skin or the texture of one's hair."[13] Rawls goes on to say:

> From the standpoint of persons similarly situated in an initial situation which is fair, the principles of explicit racist doctrines are not only unjust. They are irrational. For this reason we could say that they are not moral conceptions at all, but simply means of suppression. They have no place on a reasonable list of traditional conceptions of justice.[14]

According to this ideal society approach, racism is both unjust and irrational. From the standpoint of those persons in an initial fair situation (what Rawls calls the "Original Position"), race is a characteristic that is "arbitrary from a moral perspective."[15] This is why those in the Original Position abstract away from "their race and ethnic group, sex, or various endowments."[16] In fact, Rawls even says that persons in the Original Position also do not know "their own social position, their place in the distribution of natural attributes, or their conception of the good."[17]

[9] Rawls 1999 [1971]: 8.
[10] Rawls 1999 [1971]: 8.
[11] Rawls 1999 [1971]: 8.
[12] Rawls 1999 [1971]: 5.
[13] Rawls 1999 [1971]: 129.
[14] Rawls 1999 [1971]: 129–130.
[15] Rawls 1999 [1971]: 64.
[16] Rawls 2001: 15.
[17] Rawls 1999 [1971]: 172.

As a matter of racial justice, this means that an ideal society should not distribute rights and opportunities on the basis of race. That characteristic has no moral relevance in formulating principles of justice. Rawls defines a society as composed of major social institutions. He describes these institutions as the "basic structure of society." That basic structure is the important boundary of justice. He defines it in the following way:

> For us the primary subject of justice is the basic structure of society, or more exactly, the way in which the major social institutions distribute fundamental rights and duties and determine the division of advantages from social cooperation. By major institutions I understand the political constitution and the principal economic and social arrangements. Thus the legal protection of freedom of thought and liberty of conscience, competitive markets, private property in the means of production, and the monogamous family are examples of major social institutions. Taken together as one scheme, the major institutions define men's right and duties and influence their life prospects, what they can expect to be and how well they can hope to do. The basic structure is the primary subject of justice because its effects are so profound and present from the start.[18]

In so describing the boundary of justice in this way, Rawls takes an expansive view of it. Justice is not simply about our public or political life. Although the political constitution is part of the basic structure, he also speaks of the "family" and "the principle economic and social arrangements" as within the boundary of justice. This means that our public *and* private lives are within this boundary. Rawls's inclusion of social and not just political or legal institutions as part of the basic structure makes this clear. Justice is not only about our public opportunities, which include our opportunity to vote or to access a fair criminal justice system. Our opportunities to find housing, employment, accommodation, and access a range of other private goods and services are also within the boundary of justice, as Rawls defines it. In fact, as I argue in Chapter 2, Rawls even treats "formal equality of opportunity" as a constitutional essential, one that applies to our employment opportunities, both public and private.

---

[18] Rawls 1999 [1971]: 6–7.

This is why Arash Abizadeh defines the "basic structure" as including the institutions that "determine and regulate the fundamental terms of social cooperation" and "that have profound and pervasive impact upon persons' life chances."[19] These include not just political or public institutions but those institutions that concern our private lives.

G. A. Cohen also remarks:

> Yet it is quite unclear that the basic structure is always thus defined, in exclusively coercive terms, within the Rawlsian texts. For Rawls often says that the basic structure consists of the major social institutions, and he does not put a particular accent on coercion when he announces that specification of the basic structure ... [I]nstitutions belong to the basic structure whose structuring can depend far less on law than on convention, usage, and expectation: a signal example is the family, which Rawls sometimes includes in the basic structure and sometimes does not.[20]

Important for the argument of this book, Cohen goes on to say that

> once the line is crossed, from coercive ordering to the non-coercive ordering of society by rules and conventions of accepted practice, then the ambit of justice can no longer exclude chosen behavior, since the usages which constitute informal structure (think, again, of the family) are bound up with the customary actions of people.[21]

I will revisit Cohen's argument later in the book and then again in the concluding chapter. Once we realize that the ideal society approach cares about injustice outside the "political constitution," as Rawls says, this methodology of justice has the conceptual resources, as Cohen puts it, to enlarge the "ambit of justice." Again, for Rawls, racism is not just unjust but also irrational. According to the ideal society approach, society should treat race as a morally irrelevant characteristic. This means that in a fully just society, there would be racial equality of opportunity. Our opportunity to participate in the democratic process or the opportunity to access a fair trial, public education, police protection, and other public goods and services would not be limited on the basis of our race in a fully just society.

---

[19] Abizadeh 2007: 319.
[20] Cohen 1997: 19–20.
[21] Cohen 1997: 2.

This also means that our opportunity to find housing, employment, accommodation, and access a range of other private goods and services would also not be limited on the basis of our race in such a society. After all, according to the ideal society approach, everyone is "presumed to act justly and to do [their] part in upholding just institutions."[22] In an ideal society, there would be equality of opportunity in the private sphere as well. Again, for Rawls, the basic structure includes those opportunities that "influence [our] life prospects."[23] Opportunities that are outside the public or political sphere are also important ones, opportunities that make up the "economic and social arrangements" of society. These opportunities, including the opportunity to find housing, employment, and a range of other private goods, influence our life prospects. These opportunities, according to Rawls, are therefore within the boundary of justice.

A society that is fully complying with the principles of justice means not just that the political constitution is free from racial discrimination but that other major social institutions including "principal economic and social arrangements" are also free from it. That is what it means to take seriously the idea that society should treat race as a morally irrelevant characteristic. Put simply, in an ideal society, there would be racial equality in our public and private lives.

That means my opportunity to secure a job or find a house or a place to stay should not be limited simply because of my race. That is a form of injustice, because in an ideal society there would be equality of both public and private opportunities. Because this discrimination is based on a characteristic that an ideal society would treat as morally irrelevant, racial discrimination can be wrong no matter if it happens in private or public.

What, then, does justice require according to the ideal society approach? It requires that we not discriminate on the basis of race and deny individuals important private opportunities such as the opportunity to find housing, employment, and accommodation. In an ideal society, there would be no discrimination in accessing these kinds of private opportunities and goods. In each chapter, this book will show how the ideal society approach enlarges the boundary of racial justice in this way.

---

[22] Rawls 1999 [1971]: 8.
[23] Rawls 1999 [1971]: 6–7.

The Actual Society Approach

The actual society approach also supports the conclusion that racism in our private lives is wrong. It does not assume an ideal society where everyone is fully complying with the principles of justice. This methodological approach assumes partial rather than full compliance of these principles. In recognizing that our actual society contains racial inequality and stereotypes, this methodological approach to justice also supports expanding the boundary of racial justice to include our private lives. Once we focus on inequality or stereotypes as the relevant injustice, we realize that this injustice occurs in our private lives as well. Racism limits our opportunities to find housing, employment, and other private goods and services. A range of audit studies, for instance, show that discrimination and inequality exist outside the governmental sphere.[24] These studies inform the actual society approach, an approach that recognizes that racial inequalities can make it more difficult for those of us who are not white to find various goods and services in our private lives.

Elizabeth Anderson pursues an actual society approach, making clear that she does not seek to advance principles "for a perfectly just society, but ones that we need to cope with the injustices in our current world, and to move us to something better."[25] According to her, we must recognize the "persistence of large, systematic, and seemingly intractable disadvantage that track lines of group identity [in this case race], along with troubling patterns of intergroup interaction that call into question our claim to be a fully democratic society of equal citizens."[26] Her book draws on recent social scientific work that illuminates racial inequality and stereotypes in our private lives, including the opportunities to find employment, housing, health care, lodging, and other private goods and services. This actual society approach treats racial inequality and stereotypes (or "racial segregation" as Anderson describes it) as an injustice.

After all, Anderson is explicit about including civil society within the boundary of justice. She says that equal citizenship "involves

---

[24] For a summary of these audit studies, see generally Bertrand and Duflo (2017: 13–16).
[25] Anderson 2013 [2010]: 3.
[26] Anderson 2013 [2010]: 3.

functioning not only as a political agent – voting, engaging in political speech, petitioning government, and so forth – but participating as an equal in civil society."[27] She defines civil society broadly to cover our private life outside the governmental or public sphere:

> Civil society is the sphere of social life that is open to the general public and is not part of the state bureaucracy, in charge of the administration of laws. Its institutions include public streets and parks, public accommodations such as restaurants, shops, theaters, buses and airlines, communications systems such as broadcasting, telephones, and the Internet, public libraries, hospitals, schools, and so forth.[28]

What, then, does justice require according to the actual society approach? In her book *The Imperative of Integration*, Elizabeth Anderson argues that justice demands racial integration in our actual society. For Anderson, the actual society approach generates a moral imperative of racial integration, requiring the "the full inclusion and participation as equals of members of all races in all social domains."[29] It is not enough, for Anderson, that we desegregate. According to her, desegregation is "necessary but far from sufficient."[30] Anderson argues that society must directly encourage integration in "all social domains." She considers integration an imperative of justice. In fact, she makes clear that society should directly pursue this kind of policy in our public and private lives with a wide variety of affirmative action programs.[31]

Others may be more skeptical that racial integration is the moral solution. In a symposium on the *Imperative of Integration*, Lawrie Balfour suggests that there could, in fact, be moral costs to racial integration. These costs "might include forms of secondary marginalization, distinctions within marginalized groups that enable the integration of the most respectable members of the group at the expense of the most vulnerable (Cohen, 1999);[32] they might also involve

---

[27] Anderson 1999: 317.
[28] Anderson 1999: 317.
[29] Anderson 2013 [2010]: 112.
[30] Anderson 2013 [2010]: 113.
[31] Anderson 2013 [2010]: ch. 7.
[32] Cohen 1999.

heightened antagonism toward immigrants, non-citizens and anyone seen as 'foreign.'"[33] According to Balfour, "racial segregation is clearly wrong, but there may be reasons still to ask whether integration is as obviously right as Anderson contends."[34] Tommie Shelby also registers some skepticism with Anderson's argument – in part, because he thinks we should not forget that principles that do "less good" may still be "imperatives of justice." He says:

> The thesis that integration would shake the foundations of racial oppression is an interesting social-theoretic claim. And, if true, perhaps we should give integration greater practical priority over other imperatives of justice, because were these integration efforts successful, this could potentially make achieving racial justice much easier. But these other measures, such as vigorous antidiscrimination enforcement and a more equitable distribution of wealth, would remain imperatives of justice. A similar thing is true of the claim that integration would have a greater positive impact on black life chances and black-white relations than other measures. We should surely prioritize actions that would do more good over those that would do less. Yet the ones that do less good may still be imperatives of justice. I will therefore leave aside the question of which imperatives of racial justice should have practical priority and treat the linchpin thesis as asserting that ending segregation is an important necessary condition for realizing social justice.[35]

For purposes of this book, I assume that the actual society approach requires that society not further or perpetuate segregation. This may be one of those "less good" imperatives. After all, this imperative only requires that society not further or perpetuate segregation. I adopt this principle because it is one that we can all agree upon from the actual society approach. Anderson and Shelby both seek to end segregation. They agree that this is a necessary condition for racial justice. This book takes that necessary condition seriously in enlarging the boundary of racial justice from the actual society approach. That approach requires that society not make it easy for, as Balfour puts it, "structures of opportunity and power" to perpetuate racial inequality. In turn, she

---

[33] Balfour 2014: 350.
[34] Balfour 2014: 349.
[35] Shelby 2014: 263.

calls for an "imperative of desegregation" that "may enable American citizens to revive *both* the utopian energies *and* the bitter insights that animated the Civil Rights Movement."[36]

If we care about desegregation or ending segregation in our actual society, we must first stop furthering it. I assume that the actual society approach requires at least that. This means that we should not make it easy for individuals to discriminate on the basis of race in a way that would facilitate or further racial injustice. I argue that this "less good" imperative actually turns out to be quite strong in combatting private racism. This book explains why. Once we fully enforce this moral imperative, we can always consider adopting one that would demand more, such as Anderson's imperative of integration. For purposes of clarity and to motivate an argument that more of us can accept, this book adopts a principle that demands less. In each chapter, this book will show how the actual society approach enlarges the boundary of racial justice in this way.

Beyond the Commercial Sphere

Both the ideal and actual society approaches, then, would include opportunities beyond the commercial sphere within the boundary of justice, something I consider explicitly in Chapter 4. Consider, for instance, that there may be a range of networks, connections, and social opportunities that are important in our private lives. In so far as those too are limited by race, this matters from a perspective of justice. Even if these are not commercial in nature, they may be important to us. For instance, a study by Katherine L. Milkman, Modupe Akinola, and Dolly Chugh found that discrimination and racial inequality may exist in our informal mentoring networks for graduate school.[37] They conducted an audit study of over 6,500 professors at top universities and from a range of disciplines. In their experiment, the authors acted as fictional prospective students seeking to discuss research opportunities prior to applying to a doctoral program. The authors found that when students sought to request a meeting in a week, "Caucasian males

---

[36] Balfour 2014: 352.
[37] Milkman, Akinola, and Chugh 2012.

were granted access to faculty members 26% more often than were women and minorities; also, compared with women and minorities, Caucasian males received more and faster responses."[38]

As graduate students we know how important these opportunities can be. And we know they often don't take place in the office but at conferences, informal get-togethers, symposia, and dinners. If race did limit one's opportunity to access important social networks, to receive feedback, or to be mentored, this inequality would be wrong according to both the ideal and actual society approaches. The ideal society approach says that in a fully just society, race would not matter. Discriminating against potential mentees on the basis of race would therefore be wrong. It denies individuals equality of opportunity. After all, society should treat race as morally irrelevant. The actual society approach says that racial inequality still exists. If individuals assume that racial minorities are less capable than their white counterparts, these stereotypes stand to further racial inequality. Discrimination based on such stereotypes makes it more difficult for those who are not white to find these important networking and mentorship opportunities. Racial injustice can arise in our social opportunities as well.

AN OVERLAPPING MORAL CONSENSUS

I draw on both these approaches to provide an overlapping consensus that will motivate the book's core moral argument for expanding the boundary of racial justice. Both methodologies of justice recognize that private racism is wrong. In doing so, they recognize that race can also limit important social opportunities.

One way to understand this idea of an overlapping consensus is to reference Rawls's discussion of it in *Political Liberalism*. There he says that such a consensus of "reasonable comprehensive doctrines" endorses society's conception of justice "from [their] own point of view."[39] We can see this idea at work here. Whereas the ideal society approach focuses on racial discrimination as the relevant injustice, its

---

[38] Milkman, Akinola, and Chugh 2012: 710.
[39] Rawls 1996 [1993]: 134.

actual society counterpart focuses on racial inequality or stereotypes as the relevant injustice. Taken together, both doctrines support the conclusion that private racism is wrong. Both recognize that racial injustice can happen in private. This book will define the relevant practice in each chapter as unjust by drawing on both the ideal and actual society methodologies of justice. This will represent the moral consensus that will underwrite the book's normative claims.

I am not the only one who sees the value in drawing on both the ideal and actual society approaches simultaneously. Tommie Shelby also sees the value in doing so (he describes the actual society approach as nonideal theory):

> Ideal theory and nonideal theory are complementary components of an endeavor to devise a systematic account of social justice. In fact, nonideal theory logically depends on ideal theory, and the aims of nonideal theory give ideal theory its practical significance. For example, Rawls's famous principles of justice (equal liberty, fair equality of opportunity, and the difference principle) are the product of ideal theorizing and as such … provides evaluative standards for judging when a social order is seriously unjust and an objective to strive for in our resistance to oppression … Thus, charges of injustice presuppose ideals of justice, which particular individuals, institutions, or whole societies can and often depart from.[40]

Jack M. Balkin and Reva B. Siegel also recognize the importance in thinking about these moral principles or frameworks together. They argue that "American civil rights jurisprudence vindicates both anticlassification and antisubordination."[41] The anticlassification "principle holds that the government may not classify people either overtly or surreptitiously on the basis of a forbidden category, for example, their race."[42] This informs the ideal society approach with its focus on race as a morally irrelevant or forbidden category of classification. The antisubordination principle holds that the "law should reform institutions and practices that enforce the secondary social status of historically oppressed groups."[43] This informs the actual society approach

---

[40] Shelby 2016: 11–12.
[41] Balkin and Siegel 2003: 10.
[42] Balkin and Siegel 2003: 10.
[43] Balkin and Siegel 2003: 9.

with its focus on racial inequality. Balkin and Siegel instructively analyze the way in which the Court has drawn on both anticlassification
and antisubordination to hold that racism in public is unconstitutional.

I too argue that we should consider the ideal and actual society
approaches alongside one another. This book draws on two important
moral frameworks about what makes racism wrong. It treats these
frameworks as methodologies of justice. The ideal society approach
affirms the moral principle that racial discrimination is unjust, because
society should treat race as a morally irrelevant characteristic. In
a perfectly just society, there would be no racial discrimination. The
actual society approach affirms a moral principle that society should
not further racial inequality or stereotypes. In a society that is only
partially just or in partial compliance of the principles of justice, we
should not further racial injustice by making it easy for us to discriminate on the basis of race. I argue that both these frameworks support the
conclusion that private racism is wrong.

These frameworks do not always generate a moral consensus.
Most notably, we can use these frameworks to arrive at different
moral conclusions about remedial, affirmative action programs
based on race. Some of us may find affirmative action unjust.
Others may see it as a way to remedy injustice. This will likely depend
on whether we adopt the ideal society approach or an actual society
one. Those who object to such programs can draw on the ideal society
approach to support their claims. Because racial discrimination is the
relevant injustice for this approach, programs that discriminate on the
basis of race can be seen as forms of injustice. The fact that these
programs have a remedial purpose would not make a moral difference
to those who draw on the ideal society approach. After all, that
approach says that society should treat race as a morally irrelevant
characteristic.

In contrast, those who support affirmative action programs can
draw on the actual society approach to justify the legitimacy of these
programs. Because racial inequality is the relevant injustice for this
approach, programs that discriminate on the basis of race may be
permissible, even necessary in certain situations. These programs
seek to remedy racial inequality and challenge racial stereotypes. The
fact that these programs have a remedial purpose does make a moral

difference to those who draw on the actual society approach. After all, that approach says that society should address rather than ignore racial inequality or stereotypes in our actual society.

This means that there may not be a moral consensus about remedial, affirmative action programs. It depends on what methodology of justice one adopts. This has political and legal ramifications as well. Republicans, who are more likely to voice the ideal society approach, argue against affirmative action whereas Democrats, who are more likely to voice the actual society approach, argue for it. The same goes for justices on the Court. Justices like Justice Sotomayor are more likely to adopt the actual society approach and uphold affirmative action as a practice that is constitutional. Justices like Chief Justice Roberts are more likely to adopt the ideal society approach and treat affirmative action as constitutionally suspect.

As a result, some may be more inclined to adopt one approach rather than the other. For instance, Charles Mills is quite critical of the ideal society approach. He suggests that we must promulgate moral principles not for a well-ordered society, as outlined above, but rather for an "ill-ordered society."[44] We must interrogate what ills society. This line of reasoning sometimes views the Rawlsian project as having nothing interesting to say about racial injustice.[45]

By deploying both the ideal and actual society approaches to enlarge the boundary of racial justice, this book seeks to show the value of drawing on Rawls. In doing so, I argue that private racism is an important way of understanding some of our fundamental methodologies of justice. In expanding the boundary of racial justice, this book will show that to discuss racial justice is to discuss justice. Considering the issue of race is not peripheral to justice but central to it. I treat private racism as a form of private injustice. By expanding the boundary of racial justice, we also expand the boundary of justice. For once we recognize racial injustice outside the public or governmental sphere, we are also likely to recognize other kinds of private injustice. I revisit this point in the concluding chapter by discussing private

---

[44] Mills 2015: 548.
[45] But see Shelby 2004.

homophobia and private economic injustice in light of the two methodologies of justice discussed in this book.

This book will not argue that one methodological approach is better
or more important than another. This may disappoint those who see
one approach as superior to the other. I draw on both to provide the
moral overlapping consensus that will motivate the book's core argument. That consensus is crucial, because it stands to strengthen the
argument that private racism is a form of injustice.

This book does not discuss affirmative action because it focuses on
what we agree on, not what we disagree about. Because I adopt both the
ideal and actual society approaches to advance my argument, my focus
is on the way in which both approaches agree on the conclusion that
private racism is wrong. That consensus will drive the remaining
chapters of the book, showing how both approaches would consider
the practice in question to be a form of injustice. Once we enlarge the
boundary of racial justice, we can always revisit the moral permissibility
of affirmative action afterwards. The primary aim of this book is first
and foremost to enlarge this boundary. To do that, I draw on the
overlapping moral consensus arising from the ideal and actual society
approaches.

ENFORCING THIS CONSENSUS

Civil rights law enforces this consensus by prohibiting racial discrimination and steering that happen in private, outside the governmental or
public sphere. I argue that the ideal and actual society approaches
justify these restrictions on discrimination and steering, respectively.
It is not just that these approaches are complementary as a matter of
political theory. I also show that civil rights law affirms the ideal society
approach by banning discrimination and affirms the actual society
approach by banning steering. I discuss each in turn.

Discrimination

The most obvious kind of legal restriction on individuals is the prohibition on racial discrimination. For instance, Titles II and VII of the Civil

Rights Act of 1964 covering "public accommodations"[46] and "employers"[47] respectively prohibit a range of individuals from discriminating on the basis of race. Title II states that "persons shall be entitled to the full and equal enjoyment of the goods, services, facilities, privileges, advantages, and accommodations of any place of public accommodation, as defined in this section, without discrimination on the ground of race, color, religion, or national origin."[48] This covers all kinds of places. Under Title II, these include hotels, restaurants, real establishments, gas stations, sports arenas, stadiums, and places of entertainment. In fact, by calling some of these private places, including movie theaters, hotels, and restaurants, "public accommodations," the law makes clear that even outside the governmental sphere individuals must not discriminate on the basis of race.

The Civil Rights Act of 1968 (sometimes referred to as the Fair Housing Act (FHA)) also prohibits sellers, landlords, and real estate agents from discriminating against a prospective homeowner or renter on the basis of race. The FHA also prohibits banks and lending institutions from engaging in racial discrimination. The ban on discrimination covers a wide variety of individuals. This ban on discrimination seeks to ensure equality of opportunity, so that we may find employment, housing, lodging, and other private goods and services without regard to race. Congress also passed a variety of civil rights statues after the Civil War, including the Civil Rights Act of 1866. This Act also combats racial discrimination by private individuals. The relevant statutes are codified as 42 U.S.C. Sections 1981 and 1982.

The Court interprets these statutes to make clear that Congress's purpose was, in fact, to enlarge the boundary of racial justice. This is why the Court in *Jones* holds that with regard to Section 1982:

> All citizens of the United States shall have the same right, in every State and Territory, as is enjoyed by white citizens thereof to inherit, purchase lease, sell, hold, and convey real and personal property.[49]

---

[46] Title II, 42 U.S.C. 2000.
[47] Title VII, 42 U.S.C. 2000.
[48] Title II, 42 U.S.C. 2000.
[49] *Jones* (1968) at 412.

The Court reasoned that "so long as a Negro citizen who wants to buy or rent a home can be turned away simply because he is not white, he cannot be said to enjoy 'the *same* right ... as is enjoyed by white citizens ... to ... purchase [and] lease ... real and personal property.'"[50] The statute restricts what individuals may do in private. The Court makes clear that on "its face, therefore § 1982 appears to prohibit *all* discrimination against Negroes in the sale or rental of property – discrimination by private owners as well as discrimination by public authorities."[51] According to the Court, "even the respondents [those challenging the statute] seem to concede that, if § 1982 'means what it says' – to use the words of the respondents' brief – then it must encompass every racially motivated refusal to sell or rent, and cannot be confined to officially sanctioned segregation in housing."[52] The Court goes on to say that the respondents acknowledged "what they consider to be the revolutionary implications of so literal a reading of § 1982."[53] The respondents objected that "Congress cannot possibly have intended any such result." The Court holds that "[o]ur examination of the relevant history, however, persuades us that Congress meant exactly what it said."[54] In short, Congress intended to prohibit a wide range of racial discrimination in private.

And in *Runyon* v. *McCrary* (1976), the Court held that Section 1981 also imposes a requirement on individuals not to discriminate on the basis of race in providing a range of private goods and services. That statute also affirms a broad view of the boundary of racial justice. It reads:

> All persons within the jurisdiction of the United States shall have the same right in every State and Territory to make and enforce contracts, to sue, be parties, give evidence, and to the full and equal benefit of all laws and proceedings for the security of persons and property as is enjoyed by white citizens, and shall be subject to like punishment, pains, penalties, taxes, licenses, and exactions of every kind, and to no other.[55]

---

[50] *Jones* (1968) at 421 (emphasis added by the Court).
[51] *Jones* (1968) at 421.
[52] *Jones* (1968) at 421–422.
[53] *Jones* (1968) at 422.
[54] *Jones* (1968) at 422.
[55] 42 U.S. Code § 1981.

In *Runyon*, a private nonsectarian secondary school denied admission
to a student on the basis of his race. This case was a set of consolidated
cases of various private schools discriminating in their admission policy. In one such case, the petitioner had asked about "nursery school
facilities for her son." She asked if the school was integrated, and the
answer was "no." And that "only members of the Caucasian race were
accepted."[56] These parents, in turn, argued that the school's actions
violated Section 1981. The Court agreed, reasoning:

> It is apparent that the racial exclusion practiced by the Fairfax-
> Brewster School and Bobbe's Private School amounts to a classic
> violation of § 1981. The parents of Colin Gonzales and Michael
> McCrary sought to enter into contractual relationships with
> Bobbe's School for educational services. Colin Gonzales' parents
> sought to enter into a similar relationship with the Fairfax-Brewster
> School. Under those contractual relationships, the schools would
> have received payments for services rendered, and the prospective
> students would have received instruction in return for those pay-
> ments. The educational services of Bobbe's School and the Fairfax-
> Brewster School were advertised and offered to members of the
> general public. But neither school offered services on an equal basis
> to white and nonwhite students.[57]

Here the relevant actor was a private school that refused to contract
with black parents simply because they were black. The school denied
the parents the private opportunity to send their child to the school.
The Court held that this violated the federal statute that prohibits racial
discrimination in the "mak[ing] and enforce[ing] of contracts."

Racial discrimination, moreover, can happen to those of any race.
In *McDonald* v. *Santa Fe* (1976), the companion case to *Runyon*, L.N.
McDonald and Raymond Laird, two white employees of a company,
were fired for violating company policy. The company said that they
were fired for that reason. McDonald and Laird suspected that they
had been fired for being white, because another employee, who was
black, also violated company policy but was not fired. They sued the
company. At first, the lower court held that they could not bring
a lawsuit, because they are white.

---

[56] *Runyon* (1976) at 165.
[57] *Runyon* (1976) at 172–173.

In reversing that decision, Justice Thurgood Marshall writing for the Court holds that Section 1981 "proscribe[s] discrimination in the making or enforcement of contracts against, or in favor of, any race."[58] And according to Marshall, there is "no indication that [this federal law] intended to provide any less [protection] ... regarding racial discrimination against white persons."[59] Denying a private opportunity on the basis of race is unlawful, no matter the racial group being discriminated against. The Court sent the case back to lower courts to figure out whether the discrimination had occurred. (There was no subsequent decision, so I couldn't determine whether the case had been settled or dismissed by one of the parties.) Regardless, *McDonald* makes clear that this kind of racial discrimination is wrong no matter what racial group is being denied the private opportunity.

We can draw on the ideal society approach to justify this ban on racial discrimination in our private lives. In a society where there is full rather than partial compliance, there should be equality of opportunity in our private lives. In denying a parent an opportunity to educate their child simply on the basis of race, the private secondary school violates principles of justice. This kind of racial discrimination in private is wrong. In fact, Section 1982 lists a number of private opportunities, including the opportunity to make and enforce contracts, to buy and sell, to inherit, purchase lease, sell, and convey real and personal property. If someone denies such an opportunity on the basis of race, they act unjustly under the ideal theory approach. After all, in a fully just society there would be equality of private opportunity. In an ideal society, no one would deny anyone a private opportunity based simply on race. In a fully just society, racism in private would not exist. This is because society would treat race as morally irrelevant.

Moreover, according to the ideal society approach, it does not matter what racial group is being discriminated against. In treating race as a morally irrelevant characteristic, racial discrimination against any racial group is likely to be wrong under this approach. In *Runyon*, a private school discriminated against someone black. In *McDonald*, a private employer discriminated against someone white. Both were

---

[58] *McDonald* (1976) at 296.
[59] *McDonald* (1976) at 296.

denied equality of private opportunity based simply on their race. That denial is still wrong, because in a well-ordered society, everyone would be treated equally without regard to race.

According to the ideal society approach, we can say that employers such as the one in *McDonald* may deny private opportunities on the basis of education or qualifications that would make someone a better employee. This is why the 2016 Republican Platform states that "merit and hard work should determine advancement in our society." These are characteristics that society may consider morally relevant. Similarly, a homebuyer may refuse to sell their house to someone, because the price is too low. A school may decide to reject a child, because there is no space or the child did not score high enough on some entrance exam. If the school in *Runyon* had rejected the black parents the opportunity to send their child to the school for one of these reasons, this may not have been wrong under the ideal society approach.

The ideal society approach justifies the ban on racial discrimination, because the discrimination is based on a characteristic that society should treat as morally irrelevant. In *Runyon*, there was no evidence that their son failed to meet other requirements imposed by the school. It's worth pointing out that in one of these cases the child was a toddler and the school was a daycare. So, it is clear that in that case, the denial of the private opportunity was based simply on the person's race. In an ideal society, this kind of racial discrimination is not only unjust but also irrational.

Steering

In addition to prohibiting discrimination, the Fair Housing Act prohibits racial steering that happens outside the governmental sphere.[60] This steering occurs when individuals such as real estate agents or brokers "steer or channel a prospective buyer into or away from an area because of race."[61] In *Gladstone Realtors* v. *Bellwood* (1979), the Court held that real estate agents may violate this provision of the FHA

---

[60] 42 U.S.C. § 3604.
[61] *Zuch* v. *Hussey* (E.D. Mich. 1975) at 1047.

by steering prospective black home buyers to one area and steering prospective white home buyers to another. The Court held that this type of steering is unlawful. A real estate agent violates the law by "directing prospective home buyers interested in equivalent properties to different areas according to their race."[62] This is the most blatant form of racial steering, one that is also a type of discrimination. Here, the real estate agent steers by discriminating against buyers, showing them fewer or different properties based on their race.

But, importantly, steering also occurs when an agent provides information to buyers in ways that make it easy for them to discriminate. George Galster and Erin Godfrey call this "information steering."[63] Galster and Godfrey analyze the National Fair Housing Alliance 2000 Study data to conclude that this kind of steering often takes the form of editorializing where in at least 12 to 15 percent of the cases "agents systematically provide gratuitous geographic commentary that provides more information to white homebuyers and encourages them to choose areas with more white and fewer poor households."[64] In this case, the agent is not discriminating against a similar situated black homebuyer. After all, she is not denying the black homebuyer the equal opportunity to buy or purchase in a particular area. Rather, the agent is simply providing additional commentary to her white client, either encouraging or discouraging her from moving to that area. Even if the real estate agent is providing accurate information, she may not inject race into a buyer's decision-making process.

Historically, real estate agents steered by stoking a seller's racial prejudices in order to make a profit by securing a quick sale. The FHA explicitly bans this kind of steering, called "racial blockbusting," by making it unlawful "for profit, to induce or attempt to induce any person to sell or rent any dwelling by representations regarding the entry or prospective entry into the neighborhood of a person or persons of a particular race, color, religion or national origin."[65] Here too the real estate agent is not discriminating against anyone. She is simply

---

[62] *Gladstone* (1979): 94.
[63] Galster and Godfrey (2005).
[64] Galster and Godfrey (2005): 255.
[65] 42 U.S.C. § 3604 (e).

providing information to a prospective seller to encourage them to sell. But in so doing, she engages in racial steering.

In one such often-cited district case of racial steering and blockbusting, *Zuch* v. *Hussey* (E.D. Mich. 1975), plaintiffs alleged that real estate agents encouraged white homeowners to sell their house because of the influx of black residents and to buy in other areas that were more racially homogenous.

> As a result of their tendency to exploit racial fear, solicitations [by real estate agents] have the effect of speeding up the exodus of white residents from the area ... these solicitations ... influence the recipients to sell their homes so that the [real estate agents] may thereby profit from such sales.[66]

And these agents would also steer buyers toward areas on the basis of race.

> It is the opinion of this Court that when a real estate agent actively undertakes an effort to influence the choice of a prospective home buyer on a racial basis, whether on his own initiative or in response to the buyer's initiative, the agent either directly or indirectly discourages the prospective home buyer from purchasing a home in a particular area.[67]

Whether an agent influences a buyer's decision in response to the "buyer's initiative" or on the agent's own initiative makes no difference to the charge of racial steering. Both are illegal.

A current Department of Housing and Urban Development public service announcement accordingly defines the following as a case of racial steering, depicting a mother and daughter who are racial minorities with the following paragraph:

> We found the home of our dreams, but the real estate agent said she thought we would be more comfortable in a different neighborhood. But I know it's illegal to steer prospective homeowners to or from certain neighborhoods based on race or national origin. Report racial steering and put an end to it. Like we did.[68]

---

[66] *Zuch* (E.D. Mich. 1975) at 1045.
[67] *Zuch* (E.D. Mich. 1975) at 1048.
[68] www.hud.gov/sites/documents/NFHAHUD14_STEERING_ENG.PDF

Here the racial steering involves discouraging a buyer or renter from moving into a certain neighborhood. This is why the Code of Ethics and Standards of Practice of the National Association of Realtors forbids a real estate agent from doing so. Article 10–1 states:

> When involved in the sale or lease of a residence, Realtors shall not volunteer information regarding the racial, religious or ethnic composition of any neighborhood nor shall they engage in any activity which may result in panic selling, however, Realtors may provide other demographic information.[69]

This means that a realtor is also not allowed to answer all the questions a buyer may want answered. Answering such questions could be another way that the agent turns out to steer buyers on the basis of race.

As reported in one case, Babs De Lay, an owner of a real estate agency in Salt Lake City, said that a prospective buyer had asked her for "the most Jewish, democratic neighborhood" in the area. De Lay replied that "You know I can't [point out that neighborhood] because of fair housing laws, so you're going to have to tell me where that is."[70] The prospective buyer ended up reaching out to a local synagogue and democratic groups to find out about what area best matched those demographics, and then told De Lay to look for houses within a certain radius of that area.[71]

In another article discussing what questions real estate agents may not answer, Praful Thakkar, an agent in Andover, MA, of South Asian descent, reported that he has many prospective buyers who are also of South Asian descent.[72] And they commonly ask him, "Can you tell us how many other Indian families live on this street?" Even though he believes they are simply asking "Are there people like us around?" he declines to answer. He provides the names of the current owners on the street and lets his buyers decide "whether the names are Indian or not."[73] If the real estate agent provides information that encourages

---

[69] www.nar.realtor/sites/default/files/documents/2018-Code-of-Ethics-and-Standards-of-Practice.pdf

[70] Thorsby, "What Your Real Estate Agent Can't Tell You," US News. 12/14/2105.

[71] Thorsby, "What Your Real Estate Agent Can't Tell You," US News. 12/14/2105.

[72] Harney, "Don't expect realty agents to answer loaded questions about neighborhoods," *Washington Post*. 3/6/2106.

[73] Harney, "Don't expect realty agents to answer loaded questions about neighborhoods," *Washington Post*. 3/6/2106.

buyers to discriminate on the basis race, the agent engages in steering. This is prohibited under the law, not to mention unethical according to the Real Estate Code of Ethics.

Donna Evers, president and broker of a real estate agency in Washington D.C., says if buyers ask discriminatory questions, she tells them there are many sources to find that information. "It's all on the Internet – crime rates, all sorts of data. We say, 'Go look it up.'"[74] The real estate agent may provide a prospective buyer a range of information about the area or property – including whether home values are likely to increase in that area, how close the home is to the subway or a bus stop, whether the neighborhood has many restaurants or coffee shops – but the FHA explicitly prohibits the agent from discussing the racial demographics of the neighborhood with a prospective home buyer.

According to a 2018 National Association of Realtors Profile, 87 percent of buyers purchased their home through a real estate agent or broker – a share that has steadily increased.[75] Additionally, over "half of buyers 37 years and younger (56 percent) and buyers aged 38 to 52 years (51 percent) found their home through the internet."[76] The Internet has a range of websites and applications such as Zillow, Redfin, Movoto, and Trulia. These technologies allow prospective buyers to search a wide range of properties for sale and rent.

Consider that the Fair Housing Alliance, the only national civil rights group dedicated solely to eliminating housing discrimination, threatened Movoto.com, a realty brokerage site, with a lawsuit in 2009 for racial steering. Movoto.com had included racial statistics for the neighborhood surrounding the property listing on its website. The Fair Housing Alliance "warned Movoto that the provision of racial statistics for the neighborhood surrounding a property listing 'may have the effect of steering prospective home buyers away . . .'"[77] Here, there is

---

[74] Harney, "Don't expect realty agents to answer loaded questions about neighborhoods," *Washington Post*. 3/6/2106.

[75] 2018 National Association of REALTORS® Home Buyer and Seller Generational Trends: 65. www.nar.realtor/sites/default/files/documents/2018-home-buyers-and-sellers-generational-trends-03-14-2018.pdf

[76] 2018 National Association of REALTORS® Home Buyer and Seller Generational Trends: 51.

[77] Harney, "Some realty sites describe neighborhoods' racial and ethnic makeup; is that legal," *Washington Post*. 6/20/2014.

no racial discrimination. Everyone is getting access to the same information. Movoto.com is not treating prospective buyers or its users
differently on the basis of race. Still, this is an instance of racial steering
that is prohibited under the law. Although Movoto denied violating the
law, it stopped including such demographic information once the
Alliance had threatened to file a complaint under the Fair Housing
Act.[78] In fact, to my knowledge, none of the real estate platforms or
websites I cite includes this kind of racial demographic information.

Under an actual society approach, racial steering is wrong, because
it facilitates or encourages racial inequality. This methodology of racial
justice focuses on inequality or stereotypes as the relevant racial injustice. By acknowledging that this kind of racial injustice exists in our
actual society, we can draw on this approach to justify the ban on
steering. Steering furthers the injustice by making it easy for us to
discriminate on the basis of race.

When real estate agents encourage homeowners to sell their house
because of the influx of a particular racial group, these agents are
facilitating or encouraging housing choices that will make it more likely
that neighborhoods, communities, and other social spaces remain segregated and racially homogenous. And at the same time, racial steering
will make it easier for buyers to make housing decisions based on racial
stereotypes. In *Zuch*, the real estate agents did just that by playing on
the racial fears of white residents:

> The testimony taken at the hearing indicates that there are white
> residents . . . who do in fact correlate the entry of black families with
> the incidence of lower class social pathology. From their testimony
> there emerges the following psychological equation: The quality of
> life in a community diminishes with the entry of minority families,
> particularly black families. It is these fears, and this action that the
> [real estate agents] in this action are alleged to have exploited or
> attempted to exploit.[79]

The district court makes clear that this kind of "trafficking . . . on the
fears of whites and the desperation of Negroes, clearly affects equality

---

[78] Harney, "Some realty sites describe neighborhoods' racial and ethnic makeup; is that
legal," *Washington Post.* 6/20/2014.
[79] *Zuch* (E.D. Mich. 1975) at 1032.

in housing and is abhorred by all citizens, regardless of their personal views on the racial question."[80] In fact, *Zuch* references the actual society approach by saying that "if there were no fear, there would be no need . . . for a Fair Housing Act. But we must proceed from what is reality."[81] Citing an earlier Supreme Court opinion, *Zuch* explains that the purpose of "our national housing policy is to 'replace the ghettos' with 'truly integrated and balanced living patterns' for persons of all race."[82] Racial steering is wrong, precisely because it facilitates rather than ends segregation.

This is why the Fair Housing Alliance "warned Movoto that the provision of racial statistics for the neighborhood surrounding a property listing 'may have the effect of steering prospective home buyers away . . . and undermining the promotion of racial integration, one of the purposes of the Fair Housing Act.'"[83] The Alliance was not suggesting that the website must encourage integration; only that it should not encourage racial *segregation*. Disclosing the race of the area did just that, allowing individuals who desired to segregate to do so easily through the information provided by the website. That information steering problematically facilitates or encourages homebuyers to live in areas that are racially homogenous.

And the Fair Housing Act has had a positive effect of banning the most egregious and blatant forms of private racism. According to sociologists Maria Krysan and Kyle Crowder, authors of *Cycle of Segregation: Social Processes and Residential Stratification*:

> Certainly, much has changed since 1968. Although it offered only feeble enforcement provisions, the Fair Housing Act officially outlawed discrimination by race and provided an important legal tool for dismantling de jure systems of American apartheid. Moreover, recent decades have seen dramatic softening of racial attitudes and the emergence of a significant black middle class. Populations in most metropolitan areas of the country have also become increasingly diverse, helping to at least complicate the traditional black-white systems of social stratification. All of these changes have helped to

[80] *Zuch* (E.D. Mich. 1975) at 1050.
[81] *Zuch* (E.D. Mich. 1975) at 1053.
[82] *Zuch* (E.D. Mich. 1975) at 1050, citing *Trafficante* v. *Metropolitan Life* (1972).
[83] Harney, "Some realty sites describe neighborhoods' racial and ethnic makeup; is that legal," *Washington Post*. 6/20/2014.

erode residential segregation in many metropolitan areas and led to the emergence of many stably integrated neighborhoods.[84]

These aforementioned ways demonstrate that society is at least in partial compliance with the principles of justice. Krysan and Crowder make clear that "[s]ince passage of the Fair Housing Act, the levels of the most overt forms of discriminatory treatment have declined."[85]

Yet, they also make clear that "barriers to residential access remain."[86] These sociologists draw on a perspective grounded in social structuring to explain the way in which these barriers of access facilitate racial segregation. They call this the "Social Structural Sorting Perspective."[87] Central to this perspective is explaining "how people end up living where they do." Krysan and Crowder "illuminate a broader set of factors that shape where people end up living and provide a complementary and more complete understanding of how discrimination, preferences, and economics operate to shape patterns of segregation."[88] They look to a range of factors that facilitate residential racial segregation, drawing on qualitative and quantitative data.

One such factor that they discuss, and relevant here, is the role of racial steering. Krysan and Crowder discuss a range of cases, including that of Alicia, a black woman, who wanted to move to a more racially diverse neighborhood in Chicago but ended up in a predominantly black one. Alicia told the interviewer that she had reservations about what the agent had showed her. According to Alicia:

> I just felt like we could have a broader search. Knew we were looking for things like that, but she [the real estate agent] only kept showing us Maywood, Bellwood. Kinda pushing us to those areas. It was already a black mix. We didn't like that ... And my daughter feels very, you know, she's like, "Why are there no white people here?" She's born and raised in [city in southern Illinois], where it's a mix in her schools down there. So, she was just like, it's a big cultural change.[89]

---

[84] Krysan and Crowder 2017: 3–4.
[85] Krysan and Crowder 2017: 10.
[86] Krysan and Crowder 2017: 10.
[87] Krysan and Crowder 2017: part II.
[88] Krysan and Crowder 2017: 42.
[89] Krysan and Crowder 2017: 173.

The authors draw from this and other interviews to conclude that a major reason Alicia

> ended up in a predominantly black neighborhood, is that her real estate agent steered her family toward such a neighborhood, though Alicia implied that this happened because the agent simply knew about more available units in these communities. In Alicia's case, the impact of steering was subtle – and the steering was ultimately successful – because of another factor: the time pressure on finding a place made it easier to take the agent's suggestions.[90]

This kind of steering may not be as obvious or as blatant as Movoto's practice of disclosing the racial demographics of communities or neighborhoods on its site. Nevertheless, this form of steering still encourages prospective buyers such as Alicia to move to an area that is racially homogenous. Alicia could have pushed her real estate agent to show her an area that was more racially diverse. But the agent's subtle steering still had an effect of directing or encouraging Alicia to move to a community that was predominantly black.

Steering is wrong, because over time these instances of encouragement or direction will keep communities racially homogenous. Steering makes it more likely that racial inequality in our actual society will remain. If individuals like Alicia are encouraged or directed, by real estate agents or other intermediaries, toward communities that are racially homogenous rather than racially diverse, this will facilitate and sustain this kind of spatial segregation in our actual society. Racial steering is wrong, because it facilitates and furthers this inequality.

HISTORICAL RESISTANCE TO ENLARGING THE BOUNDARY OF RACIAL JUSTICE

By combatting racism in private, civil rights law also takes an expansive, not narrow, view of the boundary of racial justice. Writing in the *New Republic* in 1963, Robert Bork objected to civil rights law for precisely this reason. He resisted the idea that society should enlarge

---

[90] Krysan and Crowder 2017: 175.

the boundary of racial justice, as defined by the overlapping consensus above. He argued:

> It is one thing when stubborn people express their racial antipathies in laws which prevent individuals, whether white or Negro, from dealing with those who are willing to deal with them, and quite another to tell them that even as individuals they may not act on their racial preferences in particular areas of life.[91]

For Bork, the boundary of racial justice had to stop at the public or political sphere. It could not be enlarged and encompass the private sphere. He agreed that it is wrong when "stubborn people express their racial antipathies in laws."[92] But "quite another to tell them that even as individuals they may not act on their racial preferences in particular areas of life."[93] This objection, articulated by Bork and others, sought to restrict the boundary of racial justice. According to it, the law may address public racism, but it shouldn't do anything about racism in private. This is why according to one judge who also believed in a limited boundary for racial justice:

> The *rights* and *privileges* of the fourteenth amendment . . . as treated in the segregation decisions and as understood by everybody, related to *public institutions* and *public utilities* for the obvious reason that no person, whether white, black, red, or yellow, has any right whatever to compel another to do business with him in his *private* affairs.[94]

Like Bork, this judge argued that whereas the law may combat racism in public, it may not do anything about racism in private. He resisted enlarging the boundary of racial justice to include what happens in our private lives.

In resisting, Bork's position rejects the overlapping consensus that is at the center of this book. On the one hand, he says that behind "that judgment [that racism in private is wrong] lies an unexpressed natural-law view that some personal preferences are rational, that others are irrational, and that a majority may impose upon a minority its scale of preferences."[95] Again, the ideal society approach proclaims the exact

---

[91] Bork 1963: 22.
[92] Bork 1963: 22.
[93] Bork 1963: 22.
[94] *Slenderella* (Wash. 1959) at 867 (dissenting).
[95] Bork 1963: 22.

opposite. Rawls says that racism is not just wrong but also irrational. For the ideal society approach it does not matter where racism happens. Denying someone an opportunity, public or private, on the basis of race is wrong. That denial is based on a characteristic that society should treat as morally irrelevant.

On the other hand, Bork says that this kind of legislation "means a loss in a vital area of personal liberty."[96] He views enlarging the boundary of racial justice as an attempt to coerce us "into more righteous paths." For him, that "itself is a principle of unsurpassed ugliness."[97] The actual society approach proclaims the opposite. That approach says that allowing individuals to act on their "racial antipathies" in private furthers the ugliness of racial inequality and stereotypes. We should seek to address and remedy this kind of inequality, not further it.

Others also resisted enlarging the boundary of racial justice. For instance, Senator Richard Russell, Jr., an avowed segregationist, participated in a filibuster against the Civil Rights Act of 1964, famously saying on the Senate floor: "We will resist to the bitter end any measure or any movement which would have a tendency to bring about social equality and intermingling and amalgamation of the races in our [Southern] states."[98] Christopher Schmidt discusses some of this historical resistance, pointing out how one restaurant owner even proclaimed that prohibiting private racism would be "the death of private property rights in America."[99]

Bork concedes that it "is necessary that police protect a man from assault or theft but it is a long leap from that to protection from the insult implied by the refusal of another individual to associate or deal with him."[100] Bork goes on to say that this long leap

> involves a principle whose logical reach is difficult to limit. If it is permissible to tell a barber or a rooming house owner that he must deal with all who come to him regardless of race or religion, then it is impossible to see why a doctor, lawyer, accountant, or any other professional or business man should have the right to discriminate . . . Why should the law not require not merely fair hiring of Negroes in

[96] Bork 1963: 22.
[97] Bork 1963: 22.
[98] Loevy 1990.
[99] Schmidt 2013: 418.
[100] Bork 1963: 22.

subordinate positions but the choice of partners or associates in
a variety of business and professional endeavors without regard to
race or creed?[101]

Bork resisted civil rights law, because he did not want to enlarge the
boundary of racial justice to cover all these instances where individuals
can discriminate in private.

Some even went so far as to use religion to resist enlarging this
boundary. In *Newman* v. *Piggie Park Enterprises, Inc.* (1968), a case concerning the constitutionality of public accommodation laws, one of the
restaurant owners argued that his faith held that "racial intermixing or any
contribution thereto contravenes the will of God."[102] The Court
summarily dismissed that claim in a footnote, reasoning that this "free
exercise" defense is "patently frivolous."[103]

Some even saw this effort at combatting private racism as a form of
"involuntary servitude" forbidden by the Thirteenth Amendment. In
elaborating upon their objection in a legal brief before the Court, these
detractors

> recognized that one might reply by pointing out that the barber,
> porter restaurateur, waiter, etc. is always free to disengage from his
> occupation, and hence the servitude is not "involuntary."[104]

But as they go on to say:

> First of all, [this reply] ignores the fundamental and even inherent right
> of any free person to obtain a living in any of the common occupations
> of society ... To deprive a person of this basic right to pursue his
> calling, a right just as fundamental to his life and liberty as such other
> high priority freedoms, to wit, freedom of speech and freedom of
> religion, unless he furnishes labor or services for certain individuals
> for whom he does not desire to work is obviously coercion if not
> outright punishment. When an individual is either coerced into work-
> ing for another or punished for failure to do so, the inescapable con-
> clusion is that such employment amounts to involuntary servitude.[105]

---

[101] Bork 1963: 22.
[102] *Newman* v. *Piggie Park Enterprises* (1968), Supreme Court Transcript of Record,
Appendix at 9a, ¶2 (reproducing Bessinger's February 5, 1965, Answer to the Complaint).
[103] *Piggie Park* (1968) at 403.
[104] 1964 WL 81380 Appellate Brief, *Heart of Atlanta* v. *U.S.* (1964).
[105] 1964 WL 81380 Appellate Brief, *Heart of Atlanta* v. *U.S.* (1964).

This objection sought to characterize an expansive view of racial justice as a form of involuntary servitude. In *Heart of Atlanta Motel* v. *U.S.* (1964), the Court rejects this objection as well:

> We find no merit in the remainder of appellant's contentions, including that of "involuntary servitude." As we have seen, 32 States prohibit racial discrimination in public accommodations. These laws but codify the common law innkeeper rule, which long predated the Thirteenth Amendment. It is difficult to believe that the Amendment was intended to abrogate this principle. Indeed, the opinion of the Court in the Civil Rights Cases is to the contrary as we have seen, it having noted with approval the laws of "all the States" prohibiting discrimination. We could not say that the requirements of the Act in this regard are in any way "akin to African slavery." [citations omitted][106]

Heart of Atlanta makes clear that there is nothing unconstitutional about laws that enforce an expansive view of the scope or boundary of racial justice. Such laws are not even novel:

> There is nothing novel about such legislation [Title II]. Thirty-two States now have it on their books either by statute or executive order, and many cities provide such regulation. Some of these Acts go back four-score years. It has been repeatedly held by this Court that such laws do not violate the Due Process Clause of the Fourteenth Amendment.[107]

It is worth pointing out that Justice Hugo Black in his concurrence even dispenses with the Thirteenth Amendment in a footnote saying that this argument "is so insubstantial that it requires no further discussion."[108] In rejecting the objection to expanding the boundary of racial justice, the Court makes clear that Congress may pass laws combatting racism in private.

Heart of Atlanta justifies this legal conclusion by treating private racism as a moral wrong.

> That Congress was legislating against moral wrongs in many of these areas rendered its enactments no less valid. In framing Title II of this

---

[106] *Heart of Atlanta* (1964) at 261.
[107] *Heart of Atlanta* (1964) at 259.
[108] *Heart of Atlanta* (1964) at 279, concurrence.

Act, Congress was also dealing with what it considered a moral problem. But that fact does not detract from the overwhelming evidence of the disruptive effect that racial discrimination has had on commercial intercourse. It was this burden which empowered Congress to enact appropriate legislation, and, given this basis for the exercise of its power, Congress was not restricted by the fact that the particular obstruction to interstate commerce with which it was dealing was also deemed a moral and social wrong.[109]

Heart of Atlanta points out that this kind of injustice is a moral wrong independent of its effect on commercial or economic intercourse. Private racism need not be commercial in nature. As noted above, it can also concern social opportunities such as the opportunity to find a mentor. According to Linda McClain, one of the legacies of *Heart of Atlanta* was the idea that Congress may legislate against moral wrongs.[110] This book takes that legacy seriously by considering the way in which these wrongs happen in our social lives.

Bruce Ackerman treats this boundary-enlarging principle as part of a constitutional moment that he calls "the civil rights revolution." According to him, statutes like the Civil Rights Act of 1964 and the Fair Housing Act of 1968

> self-consciously divide the world into different spheres of life: public accommodations, education, employment, housing, voting. They impose different regimes on different spheres – focusing on statistical patterns that suggest unequal treatment when it comes to voting, relying on an intent-based standard in regard to restaurants, and developing intermediate positions in other areas. They insist on a far more contextual understanding of the constitutional meaning of equality in different spheres of social and political life.[111]

In referencing the different spheres of social life, he also views the civil rights logic as one that ultimately expanded the boundary of racial justice. Ackerman goes on to say that this kind of boundary-enlarging event was part of a transformative moment that amended the Constitution without a formal amendment to the document.

[109] *Heart of Atlanta* (1964) at 257.
[110] McClain 2011: 107–108.
[111] Ackerman 2014: 12.

Even if we decide not to treat this revolution as a constitutional moment, we should at least treat this as an important set of laws that enlarged the boundary of racial justice in the United States. According to John O. McGinnis, classical liberalism defines racial injustice as treating people unequally on the basis of race. In his view, this also extends to racism in the private sphere.

> Whether classical liberalism should embrace laws that prevent *private* actors from treating people unequally on the basis of characteristics, like race and sex, is a more complicated question. But in my view, given the long history of Jim Crow in the United States, laws against discrimination on the basis of race or ethnicity were justified to break ingrained habits encouraged by government discrimination against African-Americans.[112]

He too sees the civil rights logic as addressing wrongs in our private lives. Robert C. Post and Reva B. Siegel also agree that this logic enlarged the boundary of racial justice:

> Before 1964, it was still commonplace for public figures like Robert Bork and Milton Friedman to decry the prospect of federal interference with the freedom of business owners to discriminate in their choice of customers or employees, and to equate it with McCarthyism, communism, fascism, socialism, involuntary servitude, or worse. [citations omitted] It is a measure of the fundamental changes wrought by the second Reconstruction that these public and prominent objections to federal enforcement of antidiscrimination norms now sound like voices from another world.[113]

Elizabeth Anderson also views civil rights law as endorsing an expansive view of racial justice that goes beyond the political sphere. She says:

> One of the important achievements of the civil rights movement was to vindicate an understanding of citizenship that includes the right to participate as an equal in civil society as well as in government affairs. A group that is excluded from or segregated within the institutions of civil society, or subject to discrimination on the basis of ascribed social identities by institutions in civil society, has been

---

[112] www.lawliberty.org/2016/12/08/renew-the-struggle-for-colorblindness/
[113] Post and Siegel 2000: 492–493; see also McClain 2011.

relegated to second-class citizenship, even if its members enjoy all of their political rights.[114]

Scholars agree that civil rights law enlarged the boundary of racial justice. This book endorses this scholarly consensus to motivate the arguments in the ensuing chapters. In doing so, this book will make arguments for enlarging this boundary that are consistent with our Constitution. In fact, in most cases I show that we do not need to alter the law to do something about private racism. We just need to enforce the laws we already have, or so I will argue.

[114] Anderson 1999: 317.

2 CASTING RACISM

Laws like Title VII of the Civil Rights Act of 1964 prohibit employers from discriminating on the basis of race. If Ford Motor Company, Starbucks, Amazon, or any number of other employers discriminated on the basis of race, it would be relatively straightforward to hold them accountable. Such discrimination is a form of private racism that civil rights law already prohibits. But what happens when the employer is a television network or a movie studio seeking to hire an actor for a particular role? What happens when a studio or network excludes actors for a role simply on the basis of race, what this chapter calls "casting racism"?

We know that casting racism happens. According to Russell Robinson, in a three-month period in 2006 he found that

> 45.2% of the listings specified a particular race, including 5.4% that used racial code words signifying to the average reader that the role was intended for a white actor. Examples included adjectives like "Waspy" and "pale skinned" that exclude many actors of color. Alternatively, some listings requested a "type" by aligning the role with an actor of a particular race. One breakdown omitted race for a few listings yet referred to "Gina Gerson," "Mickey Rourke," and "Chazz Palminteri" – all white actors – as "prototypes" for three different roles.[1]

And with regards to particular racial groups, Robinson found that a

> total of 22.5% of the listings identified the race as white; 8.1% identified the character as black; 5.2% as Latino; 4.3% as Asian

[1] Robinson 2007: 10–11.

American; and .5% as Native American. Another 8.5% of the listings were race conscious in a more inclusive way, stating that the
role was "open to all ethnicities."[2]

When the race was not specified, Robinson found that the industry
assumed that the role would go to someone white.[3] This explains why
the Hollywood Diversity report from the Ralph J. Bunche Center for
African American Studies at UCLA shows that as of 2016 whites constitute around 80 percent of all the leading roles in film and television:
86.1 percent of lead roles in film, 81.3 percent of lead roles in broadcast
scripted shows, and 79.8 percent of lead roles in cable scripted shows.[4]

 This chapter argues that casting racism is wrong and illegal under
federal law. First, according to the ideal society approach, I argue that
formal equality of opportunity is an essential feature of a liberal constitution. Private employers that discriminate on the basis of race
violate a just constitution where society treats race as a morally irrelevant characteristic. Second, according to the actual society approach,
I argue that by denying employment opportunities on the basis of race,
television and movie studios further the harm of cultural imperialism.
Third, I explain that racially discriminatory casting is illegal under
federal law. Employers may not discriminate simply to cater to their
customers' preferences. Fourth, I discuss whether television and movie
studios can avail themselves of an expressive right to discriminate
under the First Amendment in order to permit this kind of racial
discrimination. Fifth, in light of the argument of this chapter,
I analyze a federal case where two black men sued ABC for hiring
only white men for the network's reality show – *The Bachelor*.

FORMAL EQUALITY OF OPPORTUNITY AS
A CONSTITUTIONAL ESSENTIAL

Rawls's theory of justice represents an instance of the ideal society
approach. We can draw on his theory to show that formal equality of

[2] Robinson 2007: 11.
[3] Robinson 2007: 11.
[4] https://bunchecenter.ucla.edu/2018/02/28/new-hollywood-diversity-report-2018/

opportunity should be a constitutional essential that applies to private employers. This represents one way to enlarge the boundary of racial justice to cover employment in the private sphere.

Rawls's theory contemplates two principles of justice. The first principle includes a commitment to equal basic rights and liberties, and the second principle includes commitments to fair equality of opportunity and to the idea that inequalities should benefit the least advantage (what Rawls refers to as the "difference principle"). While fair equality of opportunity requires more than an "open social system" with "careers open to talents,"[5] formal equality of opportunity is the bare minimum of an "open" system.[6] If careers are open to talents, to qualified individuals, this means that employers are at least not engaging in "arbitrary discrimination"[7] like discrimination on the basis of a "morally irrelevant characteristic" such as race. Again, Rawls says that from "the standpoint of persons similarly situated in an initial situation which is fair, the principles of explicit racist doctrines are not only unjust. They are irrational. For this reason, we could say that they are not moral conceptions at all, but simply means of suppression."[8]

Rawls calls this a principle of "formal equality of opportunity."[9] I argue that this principle not only covers private employers but also represents an essential feature of a just constitution. I draw from Rawls's four-stage sequence to make this argument. This sequence suggests one way philosophical principles can translate into the design of a constitution. Rawls specifically contemplates that his theory ought to serve as the basis for a "just constitution"[10] in an ideal society. He envisions a theoretical constitutional convention where individuals adopt constitutional essentials in light of his principles of justice.[11] His "four-stage sequence" moves from the most abstract, the Original Position, to the most concrete, where judges decide cases. At each stage, the veil of ignorance is partially removed. Most scholars focus on the principles themselves, the substance or content of rights, rather than

---

[5] Rawls 2001: 47; Rawls 1999 rev. [1971]: Sec. 12, 57.
[6] See Taylor 2004.
[7] Taylor 2004: 334.
[8] Rawls 1999 rev. [1971]: 129.
[9] Rawls 1999 rev. [1971]: 64.
[10] Rawls 1999 rev. [1971]: Sec. 31: 172–176; Rawls 1996 [1993]: 397–398; Rawls 2001: 48.
[11] Rawls 1999 rev. [1971]: Sec. 31, 172–176; Rawls 1996 [1993]: Sec. 5, 227–230.

their inclusion in a written constitution. Most forgot that Rawls contemplates a four-stage process. The Original Position is just the first stage. The second and third stages are the constitutional and legislative stages, respectively. The fourth and final stage is the stage of interpretation where judges decide particular cases by applying the relevant constitutional essentials.

In drawing on this four-stage sequence, I show that a just constitution would affirm a principle of formal equality of opportunity that prohibits both private and public employers from discriminating on the basis of race. As a representative of the ideal society approach, this argument supports the conclusion that casting racism is not just wrong but also unconstitutional.

According to Rawls, the first stage or the Original Position is where "free and rational"[12] individuals arrive at the two familiar principles of justice, entailing equal moral rights and liberties along with fair equality of opportunity and the difference principle.[13] Scholarly work often ends here, discussing the nature of the Original Position and these two principles and the philosophical tension between liberty and social or economic equality. But the question of whether formal equality of opportunity is a constitutional essential is unanswerable by simply looking to this first stage. To bring Rawls to bear on this question and to see whether his argument includes private employers within this boundary of equality, we must examine the subsequent stages. Rawls describes these stages as follows.

> Limitations on knowledge available to the parties are progressively relaxed in the next three stages: the stage of the constitutional convention, the legislative stage in which laws are enacted as the constitution allows and as the principles of justice require and permit, and the final stage in which the rules are applied by administrators and followed by citizens generally and the constitution and

---

[12] Rawls 1999 rev. [1971]: 10.

[13] "First: each person is to have an equal right to the most extensive scheme of equal basic liberties compatible with a similar scheme of liberties for others. Second: social and economic inequalities are to be arranged so that they are both (a) reasonably expected to be to everyone's advantage, and (b) attached to positions and offices open to all" (Rawls 1999 rev. [1971]: Sec. 11, 53; see also Rawls 2001: Sec. 13, 42–50; Rawls 1996 [1993]: Sec. 1, 291–294).

laws are interpreted by members of the judiciary. At this last stage, everyone has complete access to all the facts.[14]

Rawls does not pretend that this sequence, and in particular the constitutional stage, will always lead to a certain kind of written constitution. Rather, he suggests that there may be a range of "feasible just constitutions," requiring hypothetical delegates to look "for the one that in the existing circumstances will most probably result in effective and just social arrangements."[15] In the second, constitutional stage, part of the veil is removed so delegates know their society's "natural circumstances and resources, its level of economic advance and political culture."[16] These delegates, in turn, will select various fundamental principles that specify the general structure of government along with basic rights and liberties (the first principle of justice). In the legislative, third stage the delegates become "representative legislator[s]" deciding the "application of the difference principle" in terms of laws and policies[17] (the second principle of justice).[18] The fourth stage of judicial interpretation asks judges to decide cases by appealing to the constitutional essentials.

Rawls makes clear that the first principle of justice is fulfilled in the constitutional stage and the second principle of justice is fulfilled in the legislative stage:

> The first principle of equal liberty is the primary standard for the constitutional convention. Its main requirements are that the fundamental liberties of the person and liberty of conscience and freedom of thought be protected and that the political process as a whole be a just procedure ... The second principle comes into play at the stage of the legislature. It dictates that social and economic policies be aimed at maximizing the long-term expectations of the least advantaged under conditions of fair equality of opportunity, subject to the equal liberties being maintained.[19]

---

[14] Rawls 2001: 48; Rawls 1999 rev. [1971]: Sec. 31, 171–176.
[15] Rawls 1999 rev. [1971: 174.
[16] Rawls 1999 rev. [1971]: 172–173.
[17] Rawls 1999 rev. [1971]: 174.
[18] See also Estlund 1996.
[19] Rawls 1999 rev. [1971]: 174–175.

This institutional separation, between constitutional essentials and legislative acts, informs Rawls's commitment to the priority of liberty, for the first principle of justice is lexically prior to the second.[20] This means that parties in the Original Position would not make "trade-off[s]" between "the basic rights and liberties covered by the first principle and social and economic advantages regulated by the difference principle."[21] This is Rawls's classic argument of the priority of liberty. While scholars have been critical of it,[22] I do not seek to defend it here. The idea that the first principle of justice is lexically prior to the second leads to the institutional separation of the constitutional stage representing a set of rights and the legislative stage representing laws and policies.

James Fleming captures this separation by suggesting that the second and third stage represent "dualist" constitutional democracy.[23] Fleming goes on to say that these stages distinguish

> the constituent power of We the People from the ordinary power of officers of government and, accordingly, distinguishes the higher law of We the People from the ordinary law of legislative bodies. At the judicial stage, courts may serve as one of the institutional devices to protect the higher law of the constitution against encroachments by the ordinary law of legislation.[24]

With regard to constitutional design, there is an important difference between those claims of justice arising under the first principle and those arising under the second. Rawls says:

> Although delegates have a notion of just and effective legislation, the second principle of justice, which is part of the content of this notion, is not incorporated into the constitution itself. Indeed, the history of successful constitutions suggests that principles to regulate economic and social inequalities, and other distributive principles, are generally not suitable as constitutional restrictions.[25]

---

[20] Rawls 1999 rev. [1971: Sec. 11, 54–55; Rawls 2001: 45–46.
[21] Rawls 2001: 47.
[22] See, e.g., Barry 1973; Hart 1989; Shue 1975.
[23] Fleming 1993: 287. See generally Ackerman 1991.
[24] Fleming 1993: 287.
[25] Rawls 1996 [1993]: 337.

This means that, as a matter of constitutional design, Rawls places certain claims of justice as embodying constitutional essentials, basic rights, and liberties such as the right to freedom of speech and other claims as embodying legislative acts that ensure economic and social equality.

Given this four-stage sequence, formal equality of opportunity is a constitutional essential and one that also covers private employers. This is because the issue of racial discrimination by private employers would occur in the second (constitutional) stage alongside other "fundamental liberties" rather than in the third (legislative) stage alongside other "social and economic policies." Even though *fair* equality of opportunity occurs at the legislative stage, Rawls states that "some principle of opportunity is a constitutional essential."[26] Formal equality of opportunity, the idea that jobs and opportunities should at least be open to all without regard to race, is a constitutional essential.

The structure of his four-stage sequence illuminates why delegates would not leave this commitment to nondiscrimination on the basis of race in matters of employment to the legislative stage. Central to deciding what issues are placed in the second versus the third stage is the relevant knowledge delegates need in order to decide constitutional essentials versus legislative ones. If social and economic inequalities under fair equality of opportunity must benefit the least advantaged, this requires that individuals know the "full range of general economic and social facts."[27] Precisely because societies differ with regard to economic and social development, we cannot specify in advance what the second principle of justice will look like in practice. There are a variety of ways that laws and policies could structure inequalities to benefit the least advantaged. Such judgments are best left to the legislative stage precisely because we cannot categorically say what will ensure the difference principle in every society. This is why Rawls leaves this to the legislative stage, where much of the veil of ignorance has been removed. Ensuring fair equality of opportunity requires empirical judgments that the veil prevents.

---

[26] Rawls 2001: 47.
[27] Rawls 1999 rev. [1971]: 175; Rawls 2001: Sec. 13.6, 48–49; Rawls 1996 [1993]: Sec. 5, 227–230).

The first principle of justice, however, does not require such judgments. It therefore encompasses constitutional essentials. The first
principle includes such rights as the rights to "political liberty,"
"speech and assembly," "liberty of conscience and freedom of
thought," the "right to hold personal property," and "freedom from
arbitrary arrest and seizure."[28] These rights do not require delegates to
make empirical assumptions.[29] Such rights can be specified in advance.
"[W]hether the constitutional essentials are assured is more or less
visible on the face of the constitution."[30] After all, the ideal society
approach is about formulating principles in the abstract.

Relevant to the argument of this chapter is that this list of constitutional essentials includes a principle of formal equality of opportunity.
This principle like the other rights just mentioned does not require that
the state provide any kind of benefit or redistribute any kind of
resource. It simply acts as a constraint on employers. They may not
discriminate on the basis of race. My analysis here hinges on the
distinction between formal equality of opportunity and fair equality
of opportunity. This means that while the latter includes the former, the
converse is not true. A system of "natural liberty"[31] will not seek to
mitigate the influence of social or natural contingencies, but it will
ensure that no individual is denied a job on the basis of race. Rawls's
egalitarianism assumes formal equality of opportunity. Scholarly work
often considers the two ideas together, leaving them as part of the
legislative, third stage.

For instance, fair equality of opportunity may very well require that
the state or even employers themselves provide educational assistance
to those who are economically disadvantaged.[32] If there are positive
rights – to food or shelter – that are part of fair equality of opportunity,
it may be that the state and even private individuals have
a responsibility to provide them. This would require a more activist
constitution, one that affirms certain economic or social rights.

---

[28] Rawls 1999 rev. [1971]: 53; Rawls 2001: Sec. 13.4, 45.
[29] See Michelman 2003: 401–402.
[30] Rawls 2001: 48.
[31] Rawls 1999 rev. [1971]: 57.
[32] See Nagel 2003: 79.

But we can see that formal equality of opportunity simply ensures that employers do not discriminate on the basis of race. Employers need not provide any kind of benefit or resource in complying with this constraint. No social or economic facts are needed to enforce it. Whereas there are various ways to implement the difference principle, there is only a single way to implement this principle of nondiscrimination: employers, both public and private, may not discriminate on the basis of race. Any employer, including television and movie studios, that denies applicants a job simply or only because of that person's race violates formal equality of opportunity. This means that the issue of racial discrimination by private employers would be undertaken at the constitutional stage.

Moreover, these delegates do not (yet) know their own status in society. This also explains why delegates would not leave this commitment to nondiscrimination in matters of employment to the legislative stage. This is the crucial implication of the veil of ignorance. Rawls suggests that at the second stage they may know such information as their society's "natural circumstances and resources, its level of economic advance and political culture."[33] But these delegates still do not know "their own social position, their place in the distribution of natural attributes, or their conception of the good."[34] Along with ignorance of these characteristics comes ignorance of factors that are "arbitrary from a moral perspective."[35] Rawls says that delegates do not know "their race and ethnic group, sex, or various endowments."[36] As Norman Daniels makes clear, when "careers are open to talents, we judge people for jobs and offices according to the actual talents and skills they display, not irrelevant traits such as their class background, race, gender, sexual orientation, or family connections."[37] Or, as the 2016 Republic Platform puts it, "[m]erit and hard work should determine advancement in our society."[38] Daniels goes on to say that this "idea is the core of antidiscrimination legislation."[39]

---

[33] Rawls 1999 rev. [1971]: 172–173.
[34] Rawls 1999 rev. [1971]: 172.
[35] Rawls 1999 rev. [1971]: 64.
[36] Rawls 2001: 15.
[37] Daniels 2003: 249.
[38] www.gop.com/the-2016-republican-party-platform/
[39] Daniels 2003: 249.

Daniels says this is a core principle of "legislation." I have argued that fully appreciating the four-stage sequence means that the matter of nondiscrimination in private employment would be taken up at the constitutional stage, not the legislative one. Employment is an important component of most conceptions of the good. With no knowledge of one's socioeconomic status or natural endowment/talents, these hypothetical constitutional delegates would ensure that "positions and offices [are] open to all."[40] If free and rational individuals seek more rather than fewer primary goods in order to, in part, "decide upon, revise, and rationally pursue a personal conception of the good,"[41] employment is the crucial mechanism by which they can procure resources, money, and even self-respect. This is not about a right to a job but a right to compete for one where "careers" are "open to talents." The nexus between primary goods and formal equality of opportunity necessitates that nondiscrimination in employment is a constitutional essential. Thus, Rawlsian delegates would ensure that the private employers abide by this constitutional constraint. If these individuals are to ensure (at a minimum) that positions are "open" to all, formal equality of opportunity must apply to all employers, both public and private.

The foregoing analysis suggests that formal equality of opportunity would be a constitutional essential for the ideal society approach. That means it is unconstitutional for the state to exclude individuals from an office or job simply based on their race. At the same time, and this is the crucial boundary argument, there is no moral difference between the state of New Hampshire denying an opportunity to those of a particular race and private employers refusing to do so. Rawlsian delegates would treat them the same given the four-stage sequence. Because of their rational self-interest, hypothetical delegates would ensure that jobs – both public and private – are indeed open to all independent of race. Employment is a crucial social primary good that self-interested agents would want to secure under the veil of ignorance. It would not matter whether this opportunity to procure resources, money, and even self-respect comes from the state or a private employer.

---

[40] Rawls 1999 rev. [1971]: 57.
[41] Rawls 1997: 277.

With regard to employment, delegates may not even know what percentage of jobs is public versus private. After all, Rawls argues that his theory is ultimately indifferent to capitalism or socialism.[42] It is indifferent to how much of the economy and, in particular, what percentage of employment opportunities is public and what percentage is private. It's worth noting that between 1955 and 2010 the vast majority of all jobs in the United States were private ones. In fact, in 2010, 87.2 percent of all jobs were in the private sphere.[43] Since delegates to this hypothetical convention may not know such facts, they will ensure that nondiscrimination applies to both public and private employment. The veil of ignorance would ensure formal equality of opportunity is indeed a constitutional essential and would extend this constitutional essential to private employers as well, thereby enlarging the boundary of racial justice.

That means that private employers, which include television networks and movie studios, are within the boundary of justice. And given that, this analysis suggests that it would be unconstitutional for these private employers to discriminate on the basis of race. In a just constitution, the scope or boundary of formal equality of opportunity would extend to private employers. Rawls's four-stage sequence supports that conclusion. Libertarians like Richard Epstein treat state or public employment as qualitatively different from its private counterpart.[44] But Rawls's framework rejects a distinction that would treat racial discrimination in public employment differently from racial discrimination in its private counterpart.

It is not simply that, given the nexus between employment and the rational desire for primary goods, Rawls's framework would reject a regime where racism by private employers may take place. More significantly, his four-stage sequence makes formal equality of opportunity a *constitutional* issue. A just constitution will ban racism in both public and private employment. As private employers, television networks and movie studios violate this ideal constitution by engaging in casting racism. By refusing to hire actors of a particular race, these employers deny individuals formal equality of opportunity. According

---

[42] Rawls 1999 rev. [1971]: 242, Sec. 42.
[43] Mayer 2011.
[44] Epstein (1992).

to the ideal society approach, this is not just wrong but also unconstitutional.

THE HARM OF CULTURAL IMPERIALISM

We can also look to the actual society approach to show that casting racism is wrong. Iris Marion Young's *Justice and the Politics of Difference* is a representative of the actual society approach to thinking about justice. Her account explicitly focuses on the "importance of social group differences in structuring social relations and oppression."[45] Rather than abstracting away from the "particular circumstances of social life"[46] as the ideal society approach does, Young's account begins with the "actual social context in which theorizing takes place."[47] Rather than deploy a veil of ignorance to abstract away from our social identities, Young argues that we should be attuned to these identities and how they mark out inequalities in our actual society.

One of Young's core claims is that too often our methodology of justice

> assumes a single model for all analyses of justice; all situations in which justice is at issue are analogous to the situation of persons dividing a stock of goods and comparing the size of the portions individuals have.[48]

This concept of distribution entails the idea that an individual has something less or more than another. It reduces an injustice to something that can be understood on the individual level. This is why the methodology of ideal theory does not require any kind of group- or identity-based analysis. Those in the Original Position abstract away from their race in order to demonstrate that formal equality of opportunity, like freedom of speech, is a constitutional essential, a crucial primary good that individuals would secure from the standpoint of persons in an initial fair situation.

---

[45] Young 1990: 3.
[46] Young 1990: 4.
[47] Young 1990: 4
[48] Young 1990: 18.

Young's critical theory, in contrast to the ideal society approach, "begin[s] from historically specific circumstances, because there is nothing but what is, the given, the situated interest in justice, from which to start."[49] According to Young:

> Reflecting from within a particular social context, good normative theorizing cannot avoid social and political description and explanation. Without social theory, normative reflection is abstract, empty, and unable to guide criticism with a practical interest in emancipation.[50]

This is why David Wiens argues that by focusing on the "actual injustices" we can see what institutions best address them in line with the actual society approach.[51]

I draw on Young's argument to explain the harm of cultural imperialism, a harm that implicates racism in the casting process. According to Young, it is our preoccupation with the public sphere that limits the range of actions that a theory of justice should address. As a clear indication that she adopts an expansive view of the boundary of racial justice, she says: "no social institutions or practices should be excluded a priori from being a proper subject for public discussion and expression."[52] This certainly means that private employment and, in particular, the entertainment industry ought to be subject to considerations of justice.

Adopting an expansive view of racial justice, Young's account recognizes the fact that ending state-sanctioned racial discrimination or oppression is not sufficient. Young's theory of justice explicitly goes beyond the realm of "public policy judgments," focusing on the way in which our "aversions, fears, and devaluations are at work" in the "mass entertainment media – movies, television, magazines and their advertisements."[53] Justice demands that we enlarge the boundary of racial justice and recognize that racial stereotyping happens outside the governmental or public sphere. For Young, justice must not "obscure the institutional context within which . . . distributions take place."[54] She goes on to make clear that

---

[49] Young 1990: 5.
[50] Young 1990: 5.
[51] Wiens 2012: 46.
[52] Young 1990: 120.
[53] Young 1990: 135.
[54] Young 1990: 20–21.

such contexts should be interpreted broadly to include the "language and symbols that mediate [our] social interactions."[55] These symbols and meanings can themselves be harmful.

One such harm, and the focus of this chapter, is the harm of "cultural imperialism." For Young, to "experience cultural imperialism means to experience how the dominant meanings of a society render the particular perspective of one's own group invisible at the same time as they stereotype one's group and mark it out as the Other."[56] And to understand the way in which such stereotypes and dominant cultural meanings oppress individuals requires that we begin with facts on the ground. That is the methodology of the actual society approach. Young explicitly looks to the casting process as a site of racial injustice. If race structures who gets what movie and television roles, this harms racial minorities.

This is why she focuses, in particular, on the role of stereotypes in the film and movie industry. She realizes that "mass entertainment media" often reinforce these tropes.

> Racist, sexist, homophobic, ageist, and ableist stereotypes prolifer-
> ate in these media, often in stark categories of the glamorously
> beautiful and the grotesquely ugly, the comforting good guy and
> the threatening evil one.[57]

Discrimination in the casting process can generate and sustain these stereotypes. For instance, it is precisely the lack of lead roles for minority actors that normalizes white faces but renders invisible their nonwhite counterparts. This kind of discriminatory casting reinforces racial hier-archy. If minority actors are primarily cast in stereotypical roles, this only validates such roles, creating a culture and set of meanings that do not treat individuals equally on the basis of race. This is why after the Oscar nominations in 2015 and 2016, the hashtag #OscarsSoWhite became a popular one, noting the few racial minorities who are nominated for these awards. Chris Rock, a famous black writer, director, and actor, wrote in 2014 that Hollywood is a "white industry."[58]

---

[55] Young 1990: 21.
[56] Young 1990: 58–59.
[57] Young 1990: 136.
[58] www.hollywoodreporter.com/news/top-five-filmmaker-chris-rock-753223

In fact, Young does not just recognize this kind of racial injustice but suggests ways society can address it. She argues that "removing oppressive stereotypes of Blacks, Latinos, Indians, Arabs, and Asians and portraying them in the same roles as whites will not eliminate racism from television programming."[59] In fact, according to Young, casting decisions must also provide "[p]ositive and interesting portrayals of people of color."[60] This chapter draws our attention to the idea that casting decisions should, at the least, not exclude actors based simply on their race.

This is because the "dominant meanings" that reinforce racial stereotypes and invisibility arise from the very discriminatory casting decisions that are the focus of this chapter. The employment decisions that Ford Motor Company or Starbucks make will not affect our cultural norms and meanings in the same ways as similar decisions about whom to cast in a movie or television show. It is not just that movie and television studios deny actors equality of opportunity by discriminating on the basis of race. Other private employers that also discriminate deny potential employees that opportunity. In so discriminating, television and movie studios also contribute to and further racial stereotypes. These studios are important gatekeepers that influence our culture. These casting roles structure our imagination and how we view the world and various racial groups. In so far as these employment casting decisions render racial minorities invisible, often placing them in stereotypical roles, this is unjust.

ENFORCING THE MORAL CONSENSUS

Both the ideal and actual society approaches place private employers, including television networks and movie studios, within the boundary of racial justice. According to the ideal society approach, private employers who discriminate on the basis of race deny individuals a fundamental opportunity, one that is an important part of a theory

[59] Young 1990: 174.
[60] Young 1990: 174.

of justice. Rawls's account, as a representative of the ideal society approach, does not distinguish among types of employers. For Rawls, it does not matter that the employer is a movie studio, an investment bank, or a coffee shop chain.

Young arrives at the same conclusion as Rawls about the injustice of discriminatory casting. In drawing our attention to cultural imperialism and in particular the entertainment industry, Young does single out casting as an important employment opportunity that affects the way we assign value and meaning to members of one racial group versus another. By discriminating against racial minorities in casting decisions, these employers do not simply violate formal equality of opportunity (as Rawls argues). They also reinforce the harms of cultural imperialism (as Young argues).

This means television and movie studios that exclude actors for a role simply on the basis of race act unjustly according to both the ideal society and actual society approaches. There is an overlapping moral consensus that casting racism is wrong.

The law enforces this moral consensus by banning employment discrimination on the basis of race. As outlined in Chapter 1, Section 1981 requires that "All persons within the jurisdiction of the United States shall have the same right in every State and Territory to make and enforce contracts . . . as is enjoyed by white citizens."[61] Television and movie studios violate this federal law by refusing to employ a black actor for a role simply because of their race. And we need not look just to Section 1981. Title VII of the Civil Rights Act of 1964 makes it unlawful for an employer

> (1) to fail or refuse to hire or to discharge any individual, or otherwise to discriminate against any individual with respect to his compensation, terms, conditions, or privileges of employment, because of such individual's race, color, religion, sex, or national origin; or
>
>   (2) to limit, segregate, or classify his employees or applicants for employment in any way which would deprive or tend to deprive any individual of employment opportunities or otherwise adversely affect his status as an employee, because of such individual's race, color, religion, sex, or national origin.[62]

[61] 42 U.S. Code § 1981.
[62] 42 U.S.C. § 2000e-2(a) (2000).

Casting racism is unlawful on both of these grounds. Refusing to hire on the basis of race is illegal, and classifying applicants in order to prefer actors of a particular race is also illegal. And Title VII covers any employer "engaged in an industry affecting commerce who has fifteen or more employees for each working day in each of twenty or more calendar weeks." This clearly applies to television networks and movie studios that hire many actors, generating billions of dollars of revenue.

Moreover, as I show, the law does not make any exception for employers to exclude in this way. Put simply, there are no legal or statutory grounds to permit casting racism.

No Bona Fide Occupational Qualification Based on Race

First, the law does not even entertain the idea that there could be a legitimate reason to exclude applicants for a job simply on the basis of race. Federal law does contain some exceptions to the ban on employment discrimination, which the law refers to as a "bona fide occupational qualification (BFOQ)." That exception reads in part:

> [I]t shall not be an unlawful employment practice for an employer to hire and employ employees . . . on the basis of his religion, sex, or national origin in those certain instances where religion, sex, or national origin is a bona fide occupational qualification reasonably necessary to the normal operation of that particular business or enterprise.[63]

The law allows an employer to discriminate on religion, sex, or national origin but only if that characteristic is a genuine qualification for the job. The Equal Employment Opportunity Commission (EEOC), a body that provides guidelines for applying federal law, specifically says that television and movie studios may avail themselves of this exception in cases of discrimination on the basis of sex: "Where it is necessary for the purpose of authenticity or genuineness, the Commission will consider sex to be a bona fide occupational qualification, e.g., an actor or actress."[64] This means that movie and television studios may discriminate on the basis of sex in deciding whom to cast for a particular role.

---

[63] § 2000e-2(e)(1).
[64] 29 C.F.R. § 1604.2.

Importantly, there is no BFOQ exception for race. The law makes
no exception that would permit studios to discriminate in this way. As if
that was not clear enough, the EEOC in its guidelines for considering
a BFOQ states:

> Title VII provides an exception to its prohibition of discrimination
> based on sex, religion, or national origin. That exception, called the
> bona fide occupational qualification (BFOQ), recognizes that in
> some extremely rare instances a person's sex, religion, or national
> origin may be reasonably necessary to carrying out a particular job
> function in the normal operation of an employer's business or
> enterprise. The protected class of race is not included in the statu-
> tory exception and clearly cannot, under any circumstances, be
> considered a BFOQ for any job.[65]

The EEOC says that race cannot "under any circumstances" be
considered a BFOQ for a job. And various courts of appeals have
affirmed this conclusion saying, for instance, that "Congress specifically excluded race from the list of permissible bona fide occupational
qualifications" (Second Circuit);[66] "The statutory BFOQ defense,
however, is pointedly restricted to religion, sex or national origin – it is
not permitted as a defense to race discrimination in employment"
(Fourth Circuit).[67] The law enforces the moral consensus above in
a categorical and unambiguous way. Television and movie studios
that exclude actors for roles on the basis of race are violating federal
law. The law makes clear that employers may not engage in private
racism under *any* circumstances.

No Catering to Customer Preferences

Second, and relatedly, the law does not permit employers to engage in
racism simply to cater to customer preferences. Title VII and Section
1981 make no exception for this kind of racial pandering. The EEOC
makes clear that employers may not discriminate on the basis of race,
refusing to hire individuals of a particular race, "under any

---

[65] E.E.O.C. 2006: 625.1.
[66] *Knight* v. *Nassau Cty. Civil Serv. Comm'n* (2nd Cir. 1981) at 162.
[67] *Burwell* v. *E. Air Lines, Inc.* (4th Cir. 1980) at 370.

circumstances." That is a powerful statement about the boundary of racial justice. Taking this seriously means that television and movie studios may not cast white actors simply because their audience is more likely to watch a movie with someone who is white. Racism in casting can be based on this rationale. The idea being that a predominantly white cast will make the movie or show more marketable even if the movie itself has nothing to do with race. Consider the movie *The Martian* where an astronaut is stranded on Mars and the movie is about the efforts to bring him back to Earth. Matt Damon played the lead role. Replacing Damon with an Asian actor, for instance John Cho, would have had no effect on the movie's narrative. The plot had nothing to do with race. Would filmgoers be less likely to see the movie with Cho? Of course, Damon has name recognition in the way that Cho does not. Part of that has to do with the fact that white actors are given more roles than nonwhite ones, making it easier for actors such as Matt Damon to become more famous than their nonwhite counterparts.

Allowing businesses to discriminate in order to maintain profits or to cater to the private prejudice of their audience would undo civil rights law. It would restrict the boundary of racial justice by now allowing individuals to discriminate on the basis of race. For instance, if employers may cater to their customers' preferences, an owner of a restaurant or other public accommodation may refuse to hire black servers simply because their customers are racist. Bork thought that this was permissible, simply because it occurs in private. Civil rights law rejects that argument. Again, the law does not permit any employer with fifteen or more employees to refuse to hire individuals simply based on their race. The fact that racial discrimination may be more profitable for an employer does not matter.

We need not look just to federal law to realize that catering to private racial bias is not a permissible justification for discriminating on the basis of race. We can also look to the Constitution to see that this kind of catering is not allowed. Clarence Palmore and Anthony Sidoti, both white, were divorced in 1981. At that time, a Florida court awarded custody to the child's mother, Palmore. Palmore then remarried a black man. Sidoti sued to alter the custody agreement, arguing that the child's best interests would not be served by living in a racially diverse family. The state court agreed, recognizing that a child raised by an interracial couple "may be subject to a variety of pressures and stresses not present if the child were living with parents of the same racial or ethnic origin."[68] The state court made clear that the best interests of the child ought to guide the state's decision. It concluded that because of the societal presence of racism, a child would suffer more in a racially diverse family than a racially homogenous one. On the basis of that, the state gave custody to the father.

In *Palmore* v. *Sidoti* (1984), the Court invalidated that custody decision. In a unanimous opinion, the Court held that the "Constitution cannot control such prejudices but neither can it tolerate them. Private biases may be outside the reach of the law, but the law cannot, directly or indirectly, give them effect."[69] Racial discrimination is wrong in decisions about custody. Even if the state seeks to protect the child from racism and private bias in crafting a custody decision, the Constitution does not permit a state to do so. If the state may not discriminate on the basis of race in deciding custody of a child, television networks and movie studios should not be able to discriminate on the basis of race just to cater to their customers' preferences.

If studios may cater to private racial bias in order to sell more movie tickets, these private employers may avoid the reach of laws like Title VII and Section 1981. Doing so would permit the very kind of racial discrimination in employment that is not just wrong but also illegal under federal law. Certainly, we would not permit a massage parlor or a barbershop to employ only white employees on the theory that their customers do not want to be touched by therapists or barbers who are not white.

In fact, even in those instances where the law permits employment discrimination on the basis of sex as a BFOQ, the law does not allow employers to cater to customer preferences. In *Diaz* v. *Pan American World Airways, Inc.* (Fifth Circuit 1971), an important case interpreting when sex may constitute a qualification under the law, the court held that an airline's decision only to hire female flight attendants was illegal. In that case, an airline refused to consider male flight attendants, because their customers preferred females. The court rejected that as a bona fide

[68] *Palmore* (1984) at 433.
[69] *Palmore* (1984) at 433.

occupational qualification. The court reasoned that the primary function of an airline was to transport passengers safely from one place to another, not to cater to their passengers' preferences. It reasoned:

> The primary function of an airline is to transport passengers safely from one point to another. While a pleasant environment, enhanced by the obvious cosmetic effect that female stewardesses provide as well as ... their apparent ability to perform the non-mechanical functions of the job in a more effective manner than most men, may all be important, they are tangential to the essence of the business involved. No one has suggested that having male stewards will so seriously affect the operation of an airline as to jeopardize or even minimize its ability to provide safe transportation from one place to another.[70]

So, even when the law contemplates sex as a qualification, the law does not permit employers to discriminate simply to cater to their customers' preferences. The law clearly and unambiguously enforces the moral consensus outlined above that casting racism is wrong.

PRIVATE RACISM AND THE FIRST AMENDMENT

Perhaps movie and television studios may draw on the First Amendment to engage in racially discriminatory casting. After all, there is a line of cases that interprets the First Amendment to permit voluntary, not-for-profit associations to discriminate on otherwise prohibited grounds, a principle of expressive association or what I have called a principle of "expressive exclusion."[71] This constitutional principle permits associations to exclude members on grounds that are inconsistent with the association's message even if such exclusion would otherwise be unlawful.[72] I argue that even if we extend this principle to television and movie studios (which are commercial, for-profit businesses), they may not easily invoke it.

Hurley v. *GLIB* (1995), *Boy Scouts of America* v. *Dale* (2000), and *Rumsfeld* v. *Forum for Academic and Institutional Rights* (2006) are three

---

[70] *Diaz* (5th Cir. 1971) at 388.
[71] Bedi 2010. See, e.g., Carpenter 2001, Koppelman 2004, Papcke 2018, Tushnet 2001.
[72] Tushnet 2001: 85.

important decisions that elaborate upon the principle of expression association. In *Hurley*, Massachusetts' public accommodation law required that the organizers of the St. Patrick's Day Parade in Boston permit the Irish American Gay, Lesbian, and Bisexual Group (GLIB) to march in the parade. There, the Court held that forcing the organization to include the gay group would violate their expressive message. *Hurley* reasoned that the "parade's organizers may not believe these facts about Irish sexuality to be so, or they may object to unqualified social acceptance of gays and lesbians or have some other reason for wishing to keep GLIB's message out of the parade."[73] Whatever the reason for seeking to exclude gays and lesbians from the parade, the Court held that the organizers have a First Amendment right to do so when doing so would be inconsistent with the group's message.

In *Dale*, the Boy Scouts had revoked the adult membership of James Dale when it learned that he was an out gay man. Dale sued under New Jersey's public accommodation law, a law that prohibits discrimination on the basis of, among other things, sexual orientation. The New Jersey Supreme Court ruled in favor of Dale, holding that the Boy Scouts counted as a public accommodation. The Boy Scouts appealed to the Supreme Court. The Boy Scouts argued that being gay is inconsistent with their values embodied in the Scout Oath and Law, particularly with the values represented by the terms "morally straight" and "clean."[74] The Court agreed, concluding that the Boy Scouts was a homophobic organization. By examining their oath, laws, and associative beliefs, the Court held that the Scouts' expressive message was one that was antigay. Forcing the organization to have a gay scoutmaster (as New Jersey's broad public accommodation law requires) violates its First Amendment right. The Court concluded that the Boy Scouts may discriminate against gays by refusing to have Dale as a scoutmaster. Openly gay scoutmasters are inconsistent with the organization's message. Complying with the public accommodations law, then, would frustrate the association's message. Thus, the First Amendment permits the Boy Scouts to discriminate in this way.

---

[73] *Hurley* (1995) at 574–575.
[74] *Boy Scouts* (2000) at 650.

The Court determined that homophobia was significant to the Scout's message. "[P]ublic or judicial disapproval of a tenet of an organization's expression does not justify the State's effort to compel the organization to accept members where such acceptance would derogate from the organization's expressive message."[75] Forced inclusion of openly gay individuals interferes with such expression. Because an antigay message is part of this group's expressive values, the First Amendment exempts the Scouts from complying with New Jersey's public accommodations law.

In supporting its decision that the Boy Scouts may discriminate on the basis of sexual orientation, the Court cited *Hurley*:

> Here, we have found that the Boy Scouts believes that homosexual conduct is inconsistent with the values it seeks to instill in its youth members; it will not "promote homosexual conduct as a legitimate form of behavior." [citations omitted] As the presence of GLIB in Boston's St. Patrick's Day parade would have interfered with the parade organizers' choice not to propound a particular point of view, the presence of Dale as an assistant scoutmaster would just as surely interfere with the Boy Scout's choice not to propound a point of view contrary to its beliefs.[76]

In both cases, the relevant association refused to comply with the public accommodation law based on its expressive message. And the Court found that complying with the law would interfere with the group's message.

In contrast, the Court held in *Rumsfeld* that law schools could not invoke this right to expressive association. In *Rumsfeld*, certain law schools had policies prohibiting on-campus employers from discriminating on the basis of sexual orientation. At that time, the military's "Don't Ask, Don't Tell" policy discriminated against gays and lesbians (Congress repealed the ban on gays serving openly in 2010).[77] Consequently, these schools excluded military recruiters from coming to campus to hire their students. In response, Congress passed the Solomon Amendment, a law that required schools to admit these

---

[75] *Boy Scouts* (2000) at 661.
[76] *Boy Scouts* (2000) at 654.
[77] Don't Ask, Don't Tell Repeal Act of 2010.

recruiters on campus. Under the law, those law schools that still refused to admit military recruiters would lose certain federal funds.

A group of law schools challenged the law, citing a right to expressive association. The Boy Scouts and the St. Patrick's Day parade organizers successfully argued that they had a constitutional right to exclude gays and therefore violate the relevant public accommodations law. These law schools argued that they too had a right to exclude military recruiters and therefore violate the Solomon Amendment. This was based on their expressive message that was pro-gay. Like the Boy Scouts and the parade organizers, law schools argued that complying with the relevant law (here the Solomon Amendment) also interfered with their message.

The Court unanimously rejected their expressive association claim. The Court held that forcing law schools to include military recruiters does not interfere with their pro-gay message. Whereas James Dale sought to be "part of" the Scouts, military recruiters merely sought to "associate" with law schools.[78] Unlike Dale, these recruiters were "outsiders."[79] Thus, complying with the Solomon Amendment does not interfere with the law school's message. In *Roberts* v. *Jaycees* (1984), the Court also rejected a similar expressive claim from the Jaycees, a nonprofit civic association "designed to inculcate ... a spirit of genuine Americanism and civic interest."[80] Here too the Court rejected the association's expressive claim. The Court held that the Jaycees may not exclude women members in violation of Minnesota's public accommodations law that prohibited discrimination on the basis of sex.[81] According to the Court, there was no central sexist message that would permit the Jaycees to exclude women in line with an expressive association claim.[82]

The cases discussed here are not about race but about sex and sexual orientation. I'm not aware of any case where the Court has held the First Amendment permits associations to discriminate on the basis of race and violate public accommodation or civil rights law. This reveals just how categorical and unambiguous the law's ban on racial

---

[78] *Rumsfeld* (2006) at 69.
[79] *Rumsfeld* (2006) at 69.
[80] *Jaycees* (1984) at 612.
[81] *Jaycees* (1984).
[82] *Jaycees* (1984).

discrimination is. In fact, in *Bob Jones University* v. *United States* (1983), the Court rejected the argument that the free exercise clause of the First Amendment protects private racism. In that case, Bob Jones University, a private university, had a policy of not permitting inter-racial relationships among its students. The university based that policy on its reading of the Bible. The Internal Revenue Service (IRS), in turn, revoked the university's not-for-profit status, reasoning that the law prohibits associations from discriminating on the basis of race. The university sued arguing that applying the IRS's policy violates its First Amendment right. It argued the "policy cannot constitutionally be applied to schools that engage in racial discrimination on the basis of sincerely held religious beliefs."[83] The Court summarily rejected the university's claim, reasoning, in part:

> Few social or political issues in our history have been more vigor-
> ously debated and more extensively ventilated than the issue of
> racial discrimination, particularly in education. Given the stress
> and anguish of the history of efforts to escape from the shackles of
> the "separate but equal" doctrine of *Plessy v. Ferguson* (1896), it
> cannot be said that educational institutions that, for whatever rea-
> sons, practice racial discrimination, are institutions exercising
> "beneficial and stabilizing influences in community life," [citations
> omitted], or should be encouraged by having all taxpayers share in
> their support by way of special tax status.[84]

We need not just look to *Bob Jones*. As outlined in the last chapter, the Court held in *Piggie Park* that a restaurant owner who has a religious objection to civil rights law does not have a First Amendment right to discriminate. Religious beliefs may not justify racial discrimination in the private sphere. In *Masterpiece Cakeshop* v. *Colorado Civil Rights Commission* (2018), the Court raised the issue of whether the First Amendment permits a wedding cake baker to discriminate against gays and lesbians in violation of public accommodation laws. (I consider this case in the concluding chapter.) Relevant here is that even those who have defended the baker's argument under the First Amendment have said that this argument fails in the case of racial discrimination. Both the baker's

---

[83] *Bob Jones* (1983) at 584.
[84] *Bob Jones* (1983) at 585.

lawyer and the US Solicitor General who also argued in favor of the baker said to the Court that "race is different."[85] This is why the counsel for the respondent remarked that "both Petitioner [the baker] and the United States recognize that these results [acts of discrimination] are unacceptable with respect to race."[86] Put simply, the First Amendment will not allow individuals to violate the law by discriminating on the basis of race.

This suggests that movie studios may not be suitable candidates to invoke the First Amendment to engage in private racism. For one, these are for-profit businesses, not voluntary associations like the Boy Scouts. This means we should be careful in extending the principle of expressive association to studios and other such corporations.[87] In fact, in her concurrence in *Jaycees*, Justice Sandra Day O'Connor is even explicit about the fact that commercial associations (which would include television and movie studios) get minimal constitutional protection to discriminate under this expressive association First Amendment claim:

> [T]here is only minimal constitutional protection of the freedom of commercial association ... the State is free to impose any rational regulation on the commercial transaction itself. The Constitution does not guarantee a right to choose employees, customers, suppliers, or those with whom one engages in simple commercial transactions, without restraint from the State. A shopkeeper has no constitutional right to deal only with persons of one sex.[88]

This suggests that television networks and movie studios may not easily invoke the First Amendment to justify racial discrimination in their casting decisions.

Moreover, even if we consider extending this principle of expressive association to networks and movie studios, it would permit racially discriminatory casting in only certain, limited cases. Russell Robinson considers the possibility of just such an extension, arguing that television and movie studios may be permitted under the First Amendment to discriminate when doing so furthers some expressive message. Robinson argues that only when the race of the actor is "integral to the narrative" of the film or show should the law permit racially

[85] www.supremecourt.gov/oral_arguments/audio/2017/16-111 (p. 22, 32).
[86] www.supremecourt.gov/oral_arguments/audio/2017/16-111 (p. 76).
[87] See Bedi 2017.
[88] *Jaycees* (1984) at 634.

motivated casting. According to him, courts should ask would "the script alterations necessary for a ... person of color to play the part originally scripted for a ... white actor impose a substantial burden on the narrative?"[89] If the answer is "yes," we should privilege freedom of speech and artistic freedom over nondiscrimination. "Drastically revising the storylines of films would impose a substantial burden in violation of the First Amendment."[90] If the answer is "no," we should apply laws like Title VII or Section 1981 to casting decisions. Again, replacing Matt Damon with John Cho in the *Martian* would not impact the movie's story line.

Robinson elaborates upon an outline "for a judicial test in casting discrimination suits."[91]

> Where race or gender plays an integral role in the storyline, the studio maintains a stronger argument that the actors need to possess certain traits to present the narrative accurately and clearly. Similarly, films set in a particular historical and social context deserve some leeway to convey an accurate image of that period.
>
> However, most films do not possess these special themes and needs, so studios should not be allowed to rely on an artistic defense unless they demonstrate some other legitimate justification for using discriminatory breakdowns.[92]

This suggests that in most cases television and movie studios engage in racial discrimination not because race is integral to the story line, possibly triggering the First Amendment. Rather, studios seek to cater to customer preference or to maintain their profits, reasons that are not about any expressive message.

CLAYBROOKS V. ABC, INC. (M.D. TENN. 2012)

In *Claybrooks* v. *ABC, Inc.* (M.D. Tenn. 2012), Nathaniel Claybrooks and Christopher Johnson, two African Americans, sued the American Broadcasting Company (ABC) for discriminating against them on the

[89] Robinson 2007: 4.
[90] Robinson 2007: 66.
[91] Robinson 2007: 66.
[92] Robinson 2007: 66–67.

basis of race in casting a reality television show, called *The Bachelor*. To
my knowledge, this is the first and only federal case to discuss private
racism in Hollywood and the entertainment industry. The court dismissed their lawsuit citing the First Amendment's principle of expressive association. I criticize that decision based on the argument of this
chapter.

The Bachelor is a reality show that depicts a group of women who
compete for the affections of a single man. The network also has
a spinoff show where a group of men compete for the affections of
a single woman – *The Bachelorette*. *The Bachelor* debuted in 2002 and
since then has only had one person who was not white, a Latino-
American bachelor in 2016.[93] *The Bachelorette* debuted in 2003 and
since then has also only had two people who were not white.[94] The
plaintiffs filed a class action on behalf of themselves and other minority
applicants against ABC for private racism, for engaging in racially
discriminatory casting. The plaintiffs specifically appealed to Section
1981, the federal law at issue in *Runyon*.

Those who ABC hires to play the Bachelor/Bachelorette receive
a stipend and enjoy "various other benefits of participating on either
show, including fully paid housing, food, and travel expenses, as well
the financial and professional benefits of celebrity status after his or her
participation ends."[95] The plaintiffs alleged that the show's "complete
lack of people of color is no accident."

> [As] a matter of internal policy, the defendants have intentionally
> cast only white Bachelors and Bachelorettes. According to a news
> article, the shows' producers have feared "potential controversy
> stemming from an interracial romance," [citations omitted] which
> they believe would alienate the Shows' predominantly white
> viewership.[96]

The plaintiffs argued that ABC discriminated on the basis of race
simply to cater to customer preference, something that, as outlined

[93] www.washingtonpost.com/news/wonk/wp/2015/02/04/the-bachelor-is-embarrassingly-white/?utm_term=.765fc258298a
[94] https://splinternews.com/a-history-of-black-contestants-on-the-bachelor-and-the-1793854495
[95] *Claybrooks* (M.D. Tenn. 2012) at 989.
[96] *Claybrooks* (M.D. Tenn. 2012) at 989.

above, the law does not permit. Referencing both the principle of formal equality of opportunity and the harm of cultural imperialism, the plaintiffs alleged that *The Bachelor* and *The Bachelorette* "are examples of purposeful segregation in the media that perpetuates racial stereotypes and denies persons of color of opportunities in the entertainment industry."[97] The language of "opportunity" references the ideal society approach. The language of "stereotypes" references the actual society approach. According to the plaintiffs:

> With such a massive viewership, [ABC has] the opportunity to help normalize minority and interracial relationships by showcasing them to mainstream America on *The Bachelor* and *The Bachelorette*. Instead, by discriminatorily refusing to cast people of color in the lead roles (as well as in the role of suitor), [ABC play] into the perceived racial fears of their audience and perpetuate outdated racial taboos.[98]

Invoking the expressive association principle outlined above, the court began its analysis by noting that the "First Amendment can trump the application of antidiscrimination laws to protected speech."[99] The central question in an expressive association claim is whether complying with the civil rights law (here Section 1981) frustrates an association's message. In *Boy Scouts* and *Hurley*, the Court concluded that complying with the relevant public accommodations law would frustrate the message of both groups. In *Claybrooks*, the question was whether complying with Section 1981 would frustrate or interfere with ABC's expressive message.

The district court dismissed the lawsuit reasoning that deciding this question would itself violate the First Amendment. It would involve scrutinizing ABC's casting process. The court specifically said:

> How would a court determine the point at which a television program, movie, or play is sufficiently "identity-themed", "specifically geared" to, or "about" a particular racial, religious, or gender group to construe the demographics of its cast as to constitute the show's "content"? How would one even define what the creative "content"

[97] *Claybrooks* (M.D. Tenn. 2012) at 990.
[98] *Claybrooks* (M.D. Tenn. 2012) at 990.
[99] *Claybrooks* (M.D. Tenn. 2012) at 993.

of a program is? These are intractable issues that, in light of the First Amendment, are plainly beyond the appropriate scope of a court to address.[100]

The court concluded that "whether enforcing Section 1981 here would frustrate, enhance, or be entirely consistent with the message that *The Bachelor* and *The Bachelorette* conveys, the First Amendment protects the producers' right unilaterally to control their own creative content."[101] That is, the court holds that the First Amendment prevents a court from even asking whether complying with Section 1981 frustrates ABC's expressive rights.

If we take the ideal and actual society approaches seriously, the court should not have dismissed the lawsuit. According to the ideal society approach, formal equality of opportunity should be a constitutional essential. That approach, as argued above, treats formal equality of opportunity as part of the first principle of justice alongside other more familiar constitutional principles such as freedom of speech. Rawls's argument suggests that formal equality of opportunity is just as important from a perspective of justice as the First Amendment. By dismissing the lawsuit, the court failed to treat equality in the private employment sphere as a constitutional essential on par with freedom of speech.

This is because formal equality of opportunity is not a constitutional essential under the US Constitution. Although Section 1981 prohibits employment discrimination, it is only a legislative principle, not a constitutional one. Samuel Freeman remarks that Rawls's four-stage sequence "is a way of discovering the degree to which our existing constitution and laws are compatible with the principles of justice, and provides a basis for justification, argument, and criticism in a democratic society."[102] As outlined here, our Constitution, then, does not live up to a just constitution envisioned by the ideal society approach, something I discuss in more detail elsewhere.[103]

Additionally, the actual society approach focuses on the way in which television and movie studios further the harm of cultural imperialism by discriminating on the basis of race. This is why the plaintiffs in

[100] *Claybrooks* (M.D. Tenn. 2012) at 998.
[101] *Claybrooks* (M.D. Tenn. 2012) at 1000.
[102] Samuel 2007: 203.
[103] See Bedi 2014.

the case argued that ABC's casting decisions perpetuate "racial stereotypes and [deny] persons of color of opportunities in the entertainment
industry."[104] According to Young, these racial stereotypes are
instances of injustice. By furthering such stereotypes by only casting
white bachelors, ABC harms society by reinforcing cultural norms that
stigmatize racial minorities. In dismissing the case, the court fails to
take seriously this kind of harm.

We need not look just to political theory to criticize the court's
dismissal. The court also failed to apply the constitutional principle
of expressive association properly. After all, lower courts are bound by
legal precedence. Even in seeking to follow this precedence, the court
erred in dismissing the lawsuit.

The principle of expressive association allows a court to engage in
the very determination that the district court claims the First
Amendment prohibits. By examining their oath, laws, and associative
beliefs, the Court held that the Boy Scouts did have an antigay message
and that discrimination against scoutmasters on the basis of sexual
orientation furthered that message. In making that determination, the
Court asked whether "homosexual conduct is inconsistent with the
values embodied in the Scout Oath and Law, particularly with
the values represented by the terms 'morally straight' and 'clean.'"[105]
The Court concluded that openly gay Scout masters would frustrate
these values and their attendant expressive message. This involved
a fact-based inquiry into the Boy Scouts' oath and values to determine
if the association really did profess this antigay message. A majority of
members of the Court agreed that it did. But in *Rumsfeld*, a unanimous
Court made the opposite determination, reasoning that complying with
the Solomon Amendment would not frustrate the expressive message
of law schools.

A court can conduct a similar kind of fact-based inquiry into ABC's
production of the *Bachelor*. A court can examine all the documents
associated with the production, including the script, the budget, advertising, emails, and other correspondence. With these documents,
a court is well placed to determine whether ABC sought to send some

---

[104] *Claybrooks* (M.D. Tenn. 2012) at 990.
[105] *Boy Scouts* (2000) at 650.

kind of expressive message related to race. In fact, given that the show is a commercial production, it may even be easier to conduct this kind of inquiry than an inquiry into the Boy Scouts' ethical values.

In fact, Robinson says that courts do engage in artistic judgment when deciding a range of intellectual property issues:

> [F]ederal judges are already required to make artistic judgments on a regular basis, primarily in cases involving federal intellectual property rights. In addition, they sometimes make such artistic determinations in right of publicity cases, contract disputes and even criminal cases. In numerous copyright decisions, courts have compared two musical or visual artistic works in order to determine whether they are substantially similar. In a leading intellectual property case, the Supreme Court passed artistic judgment in determining whether rap group 2 Live Crew's sexually explicit revision of the Roy Orbison song "Oh Pretty Woman" was a parody or a satire for the purposes of a fair use analysis. The courts regularly engage in qualitative judgments about art, which diminishes the critique that the type of inquiry casting discrimination lawsuits would require falls outside the realm of judicial competence or appropriate functioning.[106]

Just as courts engage in this kind of judgment in cases to protect an artist's intellectual property, they can engage in a similar analysis to protect equality of opportunity in the employment context. After all, it's relatively easy for a court to see that the race is irrelevant (let alone integral) to many movies, including, for instance, the following top domestic grossing movies of 2018: *Jurassic World: Fallen Kingdom, Mission Impossible: Fallout, Venom,* and *Bumblebee.*[107] The narratives here are not about race. Contrast this with *Black Panther,* another top-grossing movie in 2018, where the narrative is about race. Similarly, it's relatively easy to see that race is integral to the story lines of *Twelve Years a Slave* or *Gandhi.* Both are historical narratives about individuals who were not white, so the race of the actor does seem integral to the narrative. Or consider Amazon's television show *The Man in the High Castle,* a dystopic future where the Nazis beat the Allies. Casting white

---

[106] Robinson 2007: 54–55.
[107] www.salon.com/2018/12/31/top-10-blockbuster-movies-of-2018-ranking-the-years-major-action-films-and-franchise-behemoths/

actors in this case may also be central to the show's narrative or story line.

The court states that "casting decisions are part and parcel of the creative process behind a television program – including the Shows at issue here."[108] The question here is whether casting for *The Bachelor* and *The Bachelorette* was indeed about some expressive message. Perhaps ABC has an expressive reason for casting only white individuals in these lead roles; in the same way, Amazon may have an expressive reason for casting white actors in its show *The Man in the High Castle*.

In order for ABC to avail itself of the First Amendment's expressive claim, it must proffer a reason for why at the time of the lawsuit it cast only white bachelors for its reality show. Is it because ABC disapproves of interracial romance? Is it because ABC rejects racial diversity? Is it because ABC seeks to express a message that only same-race romance is valuable or legitimate?

We do not need to speculate about how ABC would answer these questions, because the network went out of its way to say that its casting had nothing to do with race. In fact, ABC said it values racial diversity.

> [ABC] share[s] the Plaintiffs' goals of reducing racial bias and prejudice and fostering diversity, tolerance and inclusion," and "have never discriminated based on race in connection with the casting process" for the Shows.[109]

That is, ABC made clear that they are not like the Boy Scouts or the parade organizers, two associations that argued that complying with the relevant civil rights law interfered with their message. The court explicitly cites *Hurley* to support its decision to dismiss the employment discrimination lawsuit against ABC. Again, in that case the parade organizers sought to exclude the gay and lesbian marchers in their parade. Here, ABC went out of its way to say that it does *not* discriminate on the basis of race. The network went out of its way to say that it did not seek to exclude anyone on the basis of race. ABC believes in diversity, tolerance, and inclusion. The court did not need to speculate about what racial message ABC was seeking to send. ABC made clear

---

[108] *Claybrooks* (M.D. Tenn. 2012) at 993.
[109] *Claybrooks* (M.D. Tenn. 2012) at 996.

that there was no such racial message. The network told the court that "race is not a factor in casting the Shows."[110] They denied engaging in any kind of racial discrimination. This means that there is no expressive message that ABC seeks to send about race. The fact that white actors ended up playing the bachelor had nothing to do with race. That is what ABC told the court.

Now the plaintiffs alleged that ABC did engage in racial discrimination and did so simply to cater to their audience's prejudices. According to Claybrooks and Johnson, ABC cast white actors simply for ratings. That, as outlined above, is illegal. The law does not allow employers to discriminate simply to cater to customer preferences. On the one hand, ABC claims that there is no expressive message related to race. The studio argued that it did not discriminate on the basis of race. This is because, as the network itself said, ABC cares about racial diversity and inclusion. On the other hand, the plaintiffs allege that ABC did discriminate and did so precisely for those reasons that the law forbids. Rather than allowing the case to proceed – to determine whether ABC did, in fact, violate civil rights law – the court dismissed the case by citing *Hurley* and the First Amendment principle of expressive association.

The expressive association claim allows associations such as the Boy Scouts or the parade organizers to discriminate when doing so advances their expressive message. These two associations admitted that they discriminated against gays and lesbians. And they did so in order to further their antigay message. Imagine if the Boy Scouts said that they are pro-gay and do not discriminate against gay scoutmasters. In that case, which would have been more similar to the case against ABC, the only question would be whether the association discriminated against Dale on the basis of his sexual orientation. Dale says "yes," the Boy Scouts say "no." That would have been a run-of-the-mill discrimination lawsuit, having nothing to do with the First Amendment. There would likely have been a trial to determine whether the Boy Scouts violated New Jersey's civil rights law, which bans discrimination on the basis of sexual orientation.

---

[110] *Claybrooks* (M.D. Tenn. 2012) at 997.

ABC admitted that this was not about a First Amendment principle of expressive discrimination. The network denied discriminating against Claybrooks and Johnson on the basis of race. The network said it did not seek to send any sort of racist message through its casting decisions. The court should have listened to the network, treating this case as a run-of-the-mill case of employment discrimination. A trial would have allowed the court to determine whether ABC did in fact discriminate or not. According to the court, "no federal court has addressed the relationship between anti-discrimination laws and the First Amendment."[111] This was a case of first impression; the court admitted as much. The argument of this chapter suggests that the court erred. I hope the next time this kind of discriminatory suit comes before the court, it will not be dismissed. Otherwise, we allow television and movie studios to engage in casting racism. In particular, we allow them to continue to exclude nonwhite actors from roles with impunity. This is all the more striking, because the law is categorical and unambiguous in not making any exceptions for this kind of racial discrimination in private employment.

---

[111] *Claybrooks* (M.D. Tenn. 2012) at 995.

3 DIGITAL RACISM

This chapter shows that discrimination and steering also happen in our digital lives. Digital racism is racial injustice that happens in the digital world. This chapter expands the boundary of racial justice by focusing on racism that happens in our private, online lives. According to a 2018 Pew Research poll, one quarter of adults in the United States say they are "almost constantly" online.[1] This means that many of us conduct much of our private lives online or digitally. And as websites and platforms such as Facebook, Amazon, Twitter, Netflix, Uber, and Airbnb become even more ubiquitous, more of our private life will happen digitally. This is why it's imperative that we expand the boundary of racial justice by recognizing and addressing digital racism.

This chapter considers two kinds of injustice that happen online: digital discrimination and digital steering. Digital discrimination occurs when users discriminate on the basis of race. Numerous studies have documented the existence of such discrimination on various platforms and websites.[2] For instance, studies using Ebay transactions show that buyers preferred buying products from white rather than black sellers.[3] The studies found that items that were in black hands received 13 percent fewer responses and 17 percent fewer offers than those same items in white hands.[4] The studies also found that online purchasers trust

---

[1] www.pewresearch.org/fact-tank/2018/03/14/about-a-quarter-of-americans-report-going-online-almost-constantly/

[2] See generally Ayres, Banaji, and Jolls 2015; Doleac and Stein 2017; Bartlett and Gulati 2016.

[3] Ayres, Banaji, and Jolls. 2015; Doleac and Stein 2017; Nardinelli and Simon 1990.

[4] Doleac and Stein 2017.

black sellers less than white sellers. Purchasers "are 17% less likely to include their name in e-mails, 44% less likely to accept delivery by mail, and 56% more likely to express concern about making a long-distance payment" with black sellers than with white sellers.[5]

We can also look to the sharing economy as another place where digital discrimination occurs. Airbnb is a popular commercial platform and website that pairs those looking for housing (users who are "guests") with those seeking to rent out their rooms, apartments, condos, or houses (users who are "hosts"). Recent studies show digital discrimination occurs here too. One study in the *American Economic Journal* used guest accounts with white- and black-sounding names to try to book 6,400 available listings. The study found that guests with white-sounding names were 16 percent more likely to be accepted compared to those with names suggesting that the guest is black.[6] In another paper, titled "Digital Discrimination: The Case of Airbnb.com," the authors show that black hosts have to charge 12 percent less for the same rental property than their nonblack counterparts, holding location, quality, and rental characteristics constant.[7] The study also reveals that black hosts receive a larger price penalty on the website for rentals in a poor location relative to nonblacks. A version of that study concludes that black hosts earned 15 percent less than white hosts in renting out properties on the website.[8] In light of this kind of digital racism, #AirbnbWhileBlack became a trending hashtag on Twitter, where individual users on the website shared their experience of digital discrimination.[9]

The motivating question of this chapter is how to combat this kind of discrimination. Even though digital discrimination is wrong, the law makes it difficult to hold websites responsible for it. This is because Section 230 of the Communications Decency Act of 1996 (CDA) specifically says that websites and platforms may not be liable for discrimination that occurs on their sites. After all, the platform itself is not engaging in the discrimination, only its users. This poses a difficulty in holding the platform or website responsible for simply hosting the discrimination.

---

[5] Doleac and Stein 2017.
[6] Edelman, Luca, and Svirsky 2017.
[7] Edelman and Luca 2014.
[8] Edelman and Luca 2014.
[9] www.npr.org/2016/04/26/475623339/-airbnbwhileblack-how-hidden-bias-shapes-the-sharing-economy

However, this chapter argues that we can hold websites responsible for facilitating discrimination, what I call "digital steering." We can hold websites responsible for encouraging or directing their users to discriminate on the basis of race. These platforms structure how we interact online. They make decisions, for instance, about website design, user interface, profile creation, and filtering and searching mechanisms. If these websites make it easy for us to discriminate on the basis of race, they engage in digital steering. Movoto.com did exactly that by disclosing the racial demographics of particular communities or areas. The website chose to structure how users interact and search for housing by making it easy for their users to discriminate. If a user did not want to live near individuals of a particular race, the website facilitated that discriminatory choice through their decision to disclose the racial composition of the neighborhood. This is why the Fair Housing Alliance called this a form of steering. Movoto.com promptly stopped. This chapter argues that holding websites such as Movoto.com responsible for steering is consistent with the CDA. After all, the website or platform is the one doing the steering. In short, this chapter distinguishes steering from discrimination as an important way to combat racism in our digital lives.

The chapter is in five sections. First, I explain why these platforms should be thought of as digital public accommodations within the boundary of justice. Second, I discuss why it is difficult to hold them responsible for simply hosting the discrimination. Third, I argue that holding these platforms responsible for steering avoids these difficulties. Fourth, I apply this distinction between discrimination and steering to a lawsuit brought by the Fair Housing Council of San Fernando Valley against Roommates.com, a website that allowed users to discriminate on the basis of sex, sexual orientation, and family status. Fifth, I explain that Congress has the power under the commerce clause of the Constitution to prohibit steering on websites.

DIGITAL PUBLIC ACCOMMODATIONS

Platforms and commercial websites structure how we live our private lives. Amazon tells us how to shop, browse, and find a range of private goods and services. Like Netflix, it also tells us what we can watch and how to find it. Facebook, Twitter, and Instagram tell us how to interact and meet others. Airbnb tells how to go about finding housing. Uber tells us how to get somewhere. Rather than use physical spaces to meet and interact with others and to find housing, employment, entertainment, and other private goods and services, we can now use the digital world to do so. Much of our private life (including mine) happens digitally.

Both the ideal and actual society approaches would view digital platforms as sites of justice that structure our private lives. According to the ideal society approach, our major social institutions, including the principal and economic social arrangements, should distribute private opportunities without regard to race. These platforms and websites are major social institutions. Because many of us are interacting in our private life online or digitally, these sites may be the most important social institutions of today. They structure the terms of social cooperation. That means it matters how these websites distribute private opportunities. If they do so in a way that limits racial equality of opportunity, this is wrong. These sites are therefore within the boundary of justice.

According to the actual society approach, these platforms and websites can further racial inequality. If the digital world makes it easy for us to discriminate on the basis of race, this stands to make our actual society more unjust. Essential to the methodology of the actual society approach is to realize that racism does not exist simply or only in our public or political lives. It is also evident in our private lives. The actual society approach takes seriously how our private lives have now changed, where platforms such as Facebook, Airbnb, and Uber now structure how we find various private goods and services. Although her focus is not on digital spaces but residential ones, Clarissa Hayward instructively argues that society ought to be attuned to the way in which social spaces can further and reinforce racial inequality.[10] Here, the social space is the digital world, where racial discrimination occurs on websites and platforms.

---

[10] See generally Hayward 2013.

Both these approaches suggest that in so far as websites and platforms structure our digital lives, they are within the boundary of justice.
Accordingly, I agree with Nancy Leong and Aaron Belzer that these
platforms and websites "should be considered public accommodations." This is because:

> Like the public accommodations traditionally covered by Title II of
> the Civil Rights Act, [platform economy businesses] are held out as
> open to the public, so ensuring that such entities do not engage in
> race discrimination comports with the purpose that legislation.
> Moreover, if the traditional economy business that a [platform
> economy business] is replacing is a public accommodation, then it
> makes sense to categorize the two in the same way. To act differ-
> ently would move an increasingly large number of businesses out-
> side the scope of our civil rights enforcement mechanism.[11]

In effect, Leong and Belzer contend that these websites should be
treated as digital public accommodations. Treating them as public
accommodations is one way to operationalize the idea that these platforms are within the boundary of justice. Norrinda Brown Hayat also
sees the importance of treating these platforms as public accommodations. She writes that

> it was clear that Airbnb had become the canonical modern public
> accommodation. Airbnb began partnering with airlines and credit
> card companies to be part of their points and rewards programs.
> And tellingly, after coming under some pressure in some of its
> largest markets, such as San Francisco and New York, Airbnb
> agreed to require its hosts to comply with some regulation by
> collecting hotel taxes. Its attempt to strike a deal with the largest
> union of hotel housekeepers is another sign that Airbnb operates
> more like a hotel than a home. Each of these moves has helped to
> solidify Airbnb's position as a legitimate public accommodation
> whether the company intended that result or not.[12]

Title II of the Civil Rights Act of 1964 defines "public accommodations" to cover "inns, hotels, restaurants, cafeterias, any motion picture
house, theater, concert hall, sports arena," along with any premises

[11] Leong and Belzer 2017: 1301.
[12] Hayat 2017: 637.

which are "physically located" within a covered establishment.[13] Treating websites and platforms as public accommodations under federal law may be difficult, because of the limiting language of "physical location." In 1964 none of our private life was online. This has now changed. Our laws should reflect this changed reality, where many of us conduct our private lives digitally.

State public accommodations, in contrast, are sometimes written and interpreted by courts in a way that would include platforms and websites. Consider in this respect California and New Jersey's public accommodation laws. California's Unruh Civil Rights Act, for instance, says:

> All persons within the jurisdiction of this state are free and equal, and no matter what their sex, race, color, religion, ancestry, national origin, disability, medical condition, genetic information, marital status, sexual orientation, citizenship, primary language, or immigration status are entitled to the full and equal accommodations, advantages, facilities, privileges, or services in all business establishments of every kind whatsoever.[14]

And the California Supreme Court has made clear that the term "business establishments" must be interpreted "in the broadest sense reasonably possible."[15] And subsequent cases have applied the Unruh Act to for-profit commercial business and nonprofit organizations with an underlying business or economic purpose.[16] New Jersey's public accommodation law is similarly broad. In *Clover Hill Swimming Club v. Goldsboro* (N.J. 1966), the New Jersey Supreme Court held that a swimming club could not discriminate on the basis of race in excluding a black applicant who sought to be a member. The Clover Hill Swimming Club argued that they were not a public accommodation under New Jersey's public accommodation law. In defining a public accommodation, the court reasoned that Clover Hill is not only "a commercial venture operated to return a profit to its owner"[17] but

---

[13] 42 U.S.C. §2000a(b) (2012).
[14] Civ. Code, Section 51b (2015).
[15] *Curran* v. *Boy Scouts* (Cal. 1998) at 236.
[16] See, e.g., *Stevens* v. *Optimum Health Inst.* (S.D. Cal. 2011) at 1088–89; *O'Connor* v. *Village Green Owners* Ass'n (Cal. 1983) at 431; *Rotary Club of Duarte* v. *Bd. of Dirs.* (Cal. Ct. App. 1986) at 221–226.
[17] *Clover Hill* (N.J. 1966) at 34.

also an "establishment [that] extends an invitation to the public" to join.[18] The platforms and commercial websites discussed here are also commercial ventures and also extend an invitation to the public to join. We should, in line with this more expansive interpretation of public accommodations, consider these sites such as Amazon, Facebook, Uber, and Airbnb as digital public accommodations. They structure our private lives and hence are within the boundary of justice.

DIGITAL DISCRIMINATION

In 2016 Gregory Selden sued Airbnb for discrimination.[19] His complaint argued that the platform violated public accommodations law. Selden had used the website as a guest to secure vacation housing, creating a profile that included his picture, name, education, sex, age, and residential location. After a host had rejected his request for accommodation on the site, Selden soon realized that the listing was still available online. With the belief that Selden had been discriminated for being black, Selden created fictitious profiles with similar demographics but with pictures of someone who was white. The same host that had rejected Shelden's request accepted the requests from these fictitious profiles. This in turn generated the hashtag #AirbnbWhileBlack, spotlighting the discrimination faced by racial minorities on the website.[20]

Suing on behalf of other black travelers who reported similar treatment on Airbnb, Selden likened "Airbnb to a hotel and its hosts to rental agents or hotel employees."[21] The lawsuit sought "to hold the company responsible under federal civil rights laws for the discriminatory conduct of those who offer accommodations on its website."[22] Although the lawsuit was dismissed on procedural grounds (Airbnb required its users to agree to arbitration rather than litigation), the

[18] *Clover Hill* (N.J. 1966) at 33.
[19] *Selden* v. *Airbnb, Inc.* (D.C. 2016).
[20] www.theguardian.com/technology/2016/may/05/airbnbwhileblack-hashtag-highlights-potential-racial-bias-rental-app
[21] *Selden* (D.C. 2016) at 2.
[22] *Selden* (D.C. 2016) at 2.

complaint contended that the business discriminated against hosts such as Selden on the basis of race. The complaint alleges that this discrimination violates Title II of the Civil Rights Act of 1964, Section 1981, and the Fair Housing Act.[23]

Holding Airbnb responsible for the discrimination is difficult to do for at least three reasons.

The Website May Not Be Discriminating

First, the website or platform may not be discriminating against anyone on the basis of race. The website treats Selden and all its other users the same. Of course, if Airbnb did not allow black users to post certain kinds of properties on its site or treated users in some way differently because of their race, it would be relatively straightforward to hold Airbnb responsible for that. But Selden did not allege that the platform engaged in that kind of racial discrimination. This is because (to my knowledge) Airbnb provides access to its platform economy and services without regard to race, as do the other digital public accommodations mentioned in this book.

In fact, Airbnb's community guidelines make clear that users should not engage in private racism. The website has an explicit nondiscrimination policy that states: "Airbnb employees, hosts and guests alike, agree to read and act in accordance with."[24] Part of that policy even says:

Airbnb hosts *may not*

- Decline a guest based on race, color, ethnicity, national origin, religion, sexual orientation, gender identity, or marital status.
- Impose any different terms or conditions based on race, color, ethnicity, national origin, religion, sexual orientation, gender identity, or marital status.
- Post any listing or make any statement that discourages or indicates a preference for or against any guest on account of race, color, ethnicity, national origin, religion, sexual orientation, gender identity, or marital status.[25]

[23] *Selden* (D.C. 2016) at 7–10.
[24] www.airbnb.com/help/article/1405/airbnb-s-nondiscrimination-policy–our-commit ment-to-inclusion-and-respect
[25] www.airbnb.com/help/article/1405/airbnb-s-nondiscrimination-policy–our-commit ment-to-inclusion-and-respect

Airbnb explicitly repudiates racial discrimination. The platform makes clear that its users should not discriminate on the basis of race. Users should provide everyone equality of private opportunity. Users should not treat Selden differently simply because of his race. Doing so, in fact, violates Airbnb's stated policy.

Websites Are Not Responsible for Discrimination under Federal Law

Second, Section 230 of the CDA says that these platforms and websites are not responsible for digital discrimination and courts have interpreted the law in just this way. That section of the CDA states:

> No provider or user of any interactive computer service shall be treated as the publisher or speaker of any information provided by another information content provider.[26]

This section was essential in dismissing a case against Craiglist.com for discrimination by its users. In 2006, the Chicago Lawyers' Committee for Civil Rights under Law (CLC), a nonprofit consortium of forty-five law firms dedicated to promoting and protecting civil rights and in particular the civil rights of the poor, ethnic minorities, and the disadvantaged, sued Craiglist.com under the Fair Housing Act for housing discrimination.[27] The CLC argued that Craiglist.com was responsible for various discriminatory housing advertisements on its site, including the following:

– African Americans and Arabians tend to clash with me so that won't work out
– NO MINORITES
– Non-Women of Color NEED NOT APPLY
– looking for gay latino
– Requirements: Clean Godly Christian Male
– Only Muslims apply[28]

Craigslist sought to dismiss the lawsuit arguing that Section 230 provides "broad immunity from liability for unlawful third-party

---

[26] 47 U.S.C. Section 230 (c).
[27] *Chicago Lawyers' Committee for Civil Rights* v. *Craigslist* (N.D. Illinois 2006).
[28] *Craigslist* (N.D. Illinois 2006) at 686–686.

content."[29] The court agreed. It reasoned that the website "is not the author of the ads and could not be treated as the 'speaker' of the posters' words" under Section 230.[30] The court stated:

> Nothing in the service craigslist offers induces anyone to post any particular listing or express a preference for discrimination; for example, craigslist does not offer a lower price to people who include discriminatory statements in their postings. If craigslist "causes" the discriminatory notices, then so do phone companies and courier services (and, for that matter, the firms that make the computers and software that owner use to post their notices online), yet no one could think that Microsoft and Dell are liable for "causing" discriminatory advertisement.[31]

Courts continue to interpret the CDA in this way. In 2016, victims of sexual trafficking sued Backpage.com for violating laws against trafficking.[32] Backpage.com maintained an Adult Escorts section. The lawsuit involved advertisements posted on that section for three young women – all minors at that time – who were victims of sex trafficking. The lawsuit sought to hold Backpage.com responsible for these advertisements even though the website did not create or post them. Its users did. The content in that section often advertised for illegal sex with minors. The three women sued Backpage.com. They alleged that the website, "with an eye to maximizing its profits, engaged in a course of conduct designed to facilitate sex traffickers' efforts to advertise their victims on the website. This strategy, [they argued], led to their victimization."[33]

A unanimous three-judge panel of the federal court of appeals for the first circuit dismissed the lawsuit on the basis of the immunity in Section 230. The court made clear that under the CDA, a website is not responsible for what its users do. The court reasoned that there "has been near-universal agreement that [this section] should not be construed grudgingly."[34] Rather, it should be construed broadly to

---

[29] *Chicago Lawyers' Committee for Civil Rights* v. *Craigslist* (7th Cir. 2008) at 669.
[30] *Craigslist* (7th Cir. 2008) at 671.
[31] *Craigslist* (7th Cir. 2008) at 671–672.
[32] *Jane Doe* v. *Backpage.com* (1st Cir. 2016).
[33] *Backpage.com* (1st Cir. 2016) at 16.
[34] *Backpage.com* (1st Cir. 2016) at 18.

ensure that websites and platforms are not held responsible for what their users do, even when their users engage in sex trafficking.

> This preference for broad construction recognizes that websites that display third-party content may have an infinite number of users generating an enormous amount of potentially harmful content, and holding website operators liable for that content "would have an obvious chilling effect" in light of the difficulty of screening posts for potential issues.[35]

Websites and platforms cannot monitor everything their users do. Section 230 informs that reality by making it nearly impossible to hold websites responsible for what their users do, even if this is human trafficking.

In response to this decision in favor of Backpage.com, Congress amended Section 230 in April 2018. In that amendment, Congress made clear that the law "was never intended to provide legal protection to websites that unlawfully promote and facilitate prostitution and websites that facilitate traffickers in advertising the sale of unlawful sex acts with sex trafficking victims."[36] The amendment carved out an exception under Section 230 that allowed victims to hold websites and platforms such as Backpage.com responsible for hosting sex trafficking. Certainly, Congress could amend the CDA to say that these sites are also responsible for racial discrimination that occurs on their platforms. The National Fair Housing Alliance suggests in its 2018 report that "Congress must amend the CDA by expressly stating that the CDA itself, and specifically § 230, does not give immunity from the Fair Housing Act to any platform that allows for the publishing of discriminatory third-party content."[37] Such an amendment would make it easier to hold websites such as Airbnb and Craigslist responsible for digital discrimination. Without such an amendment, however, Section 230 remains a central legal impediment to holding sites responsible in this way.

---

[35] *Backpage.com* (1st Cir. 2016) at 18–19.
[36] 47 U.S.C.A. § 230.
[37] 2018 Fair Housing Trends Report: 79.

Websites Cannot Stop Every Instance of Discrimination

Third, websites cannot monitor and prevent every instance of discrimination that happens on their platforms. In the case against Craigslist.com, the court concedes that unlike common carriers such as "FedEx and UPS, which do not read the documents inside packages," online sites and platforms may lawfully screen the content posted by their users. (In contrast, FedEx and UPS cannot generally open the package unless the carrier is suspicious about what's inside.)[38] But this process of screening is "hard."[39]

> Simple filters along the lines of "postings may not contain the words 'white' " can't work. Statements such as "red brick house with white trim" do not violate any law, and prospective buyers and renters would be worse off if craigslist blocked descriptive statements.[40]

The court goes on to say:

> An online service could hire a staff to vet the postings, but that would be expensive and may well be futile: if postings had to be reviewed before being put online, long delay could make the service much less useful, and if the vetting came only after the material was online the buyers and sellers might already have made their deals. Every month more than 30 million notices are posted to the craigslist system. Fewer than 30 people, all based in California, operate the system, which offers classifieds and forums for 450 cities. It would be necessary to increase that staff (and the expense that users must bear) substantially to conduct the sort of editorial review that the Lawyers' Committee demands – and even then errors would be frequent.[41]

This kind of vetting may also make it more likely that the website will remove content, even when it's not discriminatory. If individuals could sue websites or platforms for what their users do or post, this could easily put the platform out of business. For instance, if Craigslist.com is responsible for the content posted on its website which may include information that is discriminatory, someone harmed by that information

---

[38] *Craigslist* (7th Cir. 2008) at 668.
[39] *Craigslist* (7th Cir. 2008) at 668.
[40] *Craigslist* (7th Cir. 2008) at 668.
[41] *Craigslist* (7th Cir. 2008) at 668–669.

could sue Craigslist. And if there are many such lawsuits, the platform
may likely shut down its business rather than risk being sued. And if there
are fewer such sites, there are fewer spaces for individuals to find
employment, housing, accommodation, and a range of other private
goods and services.

This is why an earlier federal appeals case justifies Section 230 as
a way to ensure that the digital world remains a robust space for the
exchange of information:

> Consistent with these provisions, courts construing § 230 have
> recognized as critical in applying the statute the concern that law-
> suits could threaten the "freedom of speech in the new and bur-
> geoning Internet medium." [citations omitted] "Section 230 was
> enacted, in part, to maintain the robust nature of Internet commu-
> nication, and accordingly, to keep government interference in the
> medium to a minimum." [citations omitted] Making interactive
> computer services and their users liable for the speech of third
> parties would severely restrict the information available on the
> Internet. Section 230 therefore sought to prevent lawsuits from
> shutting down websites and other services on the Internet.[42]

Certainly, the users that posted the advertisements and engaged in
the trafficking are legally responsible for it. In the same way those users
that engage in housing discrimination whether on Craiglist.com or
Airbnb are also responsible for doing so. As Michael Todisco points
out, we can go after individual users. According to him, holding users
responsible in this way operates "within the current paradigm and
bring[s] enforcement actions against individual ... users." It could
deter at least some "future acts of discrimination."[43]

However, as Todisco goes on to say:

> [T]his method seems inefficient, labor intensive, and costly. The
> National Fair Housing Alliance (NFHA), a consortium of 220
> nonprofits dedicated to ending housing discrimination, pursued
> this route, reporting in May 2009 that it had filed over 1000
> complaints against discriminatory online postings in the past year
> alone. Given the persistence of online discrimination in the face of
> this deluge of suits, the NFHA concluded "that pursuing

---

[42] *Batzel* v. *Smith* (9th Cir. 2003) at 1027–1028.
[43] Todisco 2015: 127.

complaints against the thousands of discriminatory advertisers who use the internet" was not feasible.[44]

Moreover, as Ronald J. Mann and Seth R. Belzley argue:

> [T]he relative anonymity the Internet fosters makes remedies against primary malfeasors less effective than in the brick-and-mortar context. For example, obtaining a relatively anonymous e-mail account from a provider such as Google for use in illicit conduct is easier than obtaining a post office box in the offline world. This is not to say that anonymity is impossible in the offline world or perfect in the online world; engaging in relatively anonymous conduct online is simply easier than it ever has been offline.[45]

Just as the website cannot stop every instance of discrimination on its platforms, it's also impractical for users on these sites to bring lawsuits or complaints against other users. That too would prove costly and inefficient.

DIGITAL STEERING

The foregoing analysis means that we cannot combat digital discrimination by holding websites responsible for it. There is an additional way to proceed. Instead of holding websites responsible for hosting the discrimination, I argue we can hold them responsible for steering. A focus on digital steering avoids the three difficulties noted above.

The Website May Be Steering

First, digital steering occurs when websites and platforms encourage or direct their users to discriminate on the basis of race. Movoto.com did just that by disclosing race on its website. The platform steered its users to discriminate on the basis of race. It structured the decision-making process on its website to make it easier for them to do so.

---

[44] Todisco 2015: 127.
[45] Mann and Belzley 2005: 268.

This is why the Fair Housing Alliance called them out for racial steering. The Alliance did not have to impose a new responsibility on the website. After all, Movoto.com made the decision to allow its users to access information about race. Websites like Movoto.com create the platform and relevant search engines and in doing so may decide to cater to user demand and preferences. By setting up their website in ways that allow users to discriminate on the basis of race, these businesses engage in an obvious and open form of racial steering. Civil rights law already prohibits individuals such as real estate agents from steering, from making it easy for buyers to discriminate on the basis of race. Once the Alliance made its objection known, Movoto.com stopped steering. The website stopped encouraging its users from discriminating on the basis of race by ending its practice of disclosing the racial demographics of areas or communities. We can and should hold these public accommodations responsible for steering their users to discriminate.

In the case of Movoto.com, this steering was blatant. The website explicitly disclosed racial information about areas or communities. Without that disclosure, it would be a lot more difficult for users to discriminate digitally. In other cases, the steering may be less blatant but still facilitative of digital discrimination. For instance, Airbnb asks users both to provide their name and post pictures. Users can use these photos and names to discriminate on the basis of race. Users can draw inferences about the race of guests or hosts by looking at their photo or name. A well-known experiment by economists, for instance, shows not just that racism exists in private employment decisions but that employers can use an applicant's name as a proxy in order to discriminate on the basis of race.[46] In the experiment, résumés were sent to various help-wanted ads in Boston and Chicago. The study randomly assigned to each résumé a name suggesting that the applicant was white (e.g., Emily, Greg) or black (e.g., Lakisha, Jamal). If employers were unable to discern the race of the prospective applicants, the callbacks should have been roughly equal for both groups. But, as it turns out, the résumés with white-sounding names received 50 percent more callbacks than their black counterparts. In fact, the study found that this

[46] Bertrand and Mullainathan 2004: 991–1013.

disparity was "uniform across occupation, industry, and employer size."[47] This means that private racism can occur when users have access to someone's name.

Airbnb engages in steering, then, by disclosing its users' names and photographs. This kind of digital steering may not be as brazen as disclosing racial demographics, but it may still permit or facilitate racial discrimination. In a 2018 article titled "Discriminatory Designs on User Data," Olivier Sylvain also argues that we should hold websites and platforms responsible for the way they design their digital interface:

> Airbnb still facilitates discrimination through its main service to the extent that it continues to rely on names and pictures. The "instant bookings" feature, paired with the main service, create a "two-tiered reservation system": In one system (instant bookings), guests lose a sense of conviviality with hosts but obtain some peace of mind in knowing that they will not be discriminated against on the basis of race, while in the other system (the main service), discrimination is inevitable but also exploited to promote "authentic" connections.[48]

If the website design makes it easy for users to discriminate on the basis of race, it engages in digital steering. Without names or pictures, for instance, Airbnb users would have a much harder time discriminating against Selden and others on the basis of race. After all, he had created a profile with a picture of a white person and was then able to book his accommodation successfully. That means that the picture was a proxy for signaling a prospective guest's race. In addition to removing pictures and names, Airbnb has an instant booking feature that guests can use to book instantly through the website. If that feature were available for all listings, this would make it difficult for hosts to discriminate on the basis of race, because they could not review any request before accepting it. For once the guest instantly books an accommodation, the host cannot now deny their request digitally. That feature can structure our digital life on Airbnb in a way that makes discrimination more difficult. But it also means that hosts do not have the discretion to

---

[47] Bertrand and Mullainathan 2004: 991.
[48] Sylvain 2018: 15.

review requests and deny them for reasons unrelated to race. Airbnb therefore allows instant bookings for only some listings.

Moreover, even if guests could not share their names or photographs, hosts may very well want to do so. According to the paper on digital discrimination and Airbnb referenced above, this may be a way to signal trustworthiness. "Hosts who provide LinkedIn, Facebook, and Twitter accounts as well as phone numbers demonstrate a stable occupation, social life, and identity, all of which increase the likelihood that the host is trustworthy."[49] The authors of that paper also found that

> pictures are an important part of Airbnb's design: from discussions with Airbnb guests, we understand that pictures help guests accept the Airbnb model, including staying in a property with, or offered by, a stranger. Foregoing host pictures would likely reduce some guests' willingness to use Airbnb.[50]

This suggests that perhaps use of names, photographs, or other such biographical information may in certain cases further Airbnb's business model and profitability. The authors suggest that "if Airbnb were to take action to reduce the extent of discrimination, the decision would be driven by ethics, rather than profit."[51] The argument of this chapter is about precisely the website or platform's moral commitment not to steer. As mentioned in Chapter 1 real estate agents have also steered in order to make a quick profit or sale.

Websites Are Responsible for Steering under Federal Law

Second, Section 230 holds that a website may not be held responsible for the content its users post. The website shall not be treated "as the publisher or speaker of any information provided by" one of its users. But this legal principle does not apply to steering. After all, the users are not the ones doing the steering. Steering is about what the website or platform does. It is about the deliberate decisions the platform makes to structure our digital lives. Airbnb decides how hosts and guests will interact on its site. It decides whether this interaction will

---

[49] Edelman and Luca 2014: 8.
[50] Edelman and Luca 2014: 7.
[51] Edelman and Luca 2014: 7.

be mediated by names or photographs. Airbnb decides what kind of information to disclose to its users. These are all decisions made not by the users but by the digital public accommodation itself. Just as Airbnb is responsible for how much it charges for its service or how much it spends on advertising on the site, it is also responsible for how it structures interactions that take place on its platform.

So, the ban on digital steering is not about imputing what users do to the website itself. It is precisely that kind of liability or attribution that Section 230 rules out. In holding websites responsible for digital steering, we are not imputing what the users say or do to the website. Rather, we are holding the website responsible for its own decision to structure its digital space in a way that facilitates digital discrimination.

Websites Can Stop Steering

Third, just as civil rights law already prohibits racial steering, most notably by real estate agents, we can prohibit websites and platforms from steering its users to discriminate. Whether it creates platforms that facilitate racial discrimination or not is entirely in the website's control. The website is unable to monitor, let alone control everything its users do on its site. But we should hold these sites responsible for what they do in structuring our digital lives. For instance, when Movoto .com permitted its users to access the racial demographics of particular neighborhoods or communities, the platform made it easy for its users to discriminate on the basis of race. Digital steering is entirely within the control of the platform or website.

Real estate agents cannot stop their customers from discriminating on the basis of race. If buyers refuse to purchase housing from those of a particular race or if sellers refuse to sell on the basis of race, the real estate agent may not be able to stop that. But agents can ensure that they do not racially steer (again, the Realtor Code of Ethics makes clear it is unethical for them to do so). The examples cited in Chapter 1 show how real estate agents refuse to answer questions from their clients that would steer them to decide based on race. Even if buyers or sellers want the racial information, the agent is not allowed to disclose it. Movoto.com violated the ban on racial steering by doing just that. Even if its users wanted the racial demographics of particular communities or neighborhoods, the website should not disclose it. Doing so is a form of digital steering. We can and should hold websites and platforms responsible for providing this information. This is not about imputing discriminatory acts of users to the site. The ban on steering is about what the site decides to do.

Websites are public accommodations, structuring how we interact in our private, digital lives. These sites are intermediaries connecting one set of users (e.g., hosts) to another (e.g., guests). In the same way, real estate agents are also intermediaries connecting buyers to sellers and vice versa. In fact, websites are far more consequential in our private lives than real estate agents in performing this kind of intermediary role. These sites structure how we access a range of private opportunities and goods, including, most notably, housing. Brick and mortar public accommodations do not structure our interactions in this way. Websites are major social institutions that are structuring more and more of our private lives. This means that it is even more important from a perspective of justice to ban these sites from steering.

This kind of prohibition will not have a chilling effect on what users say or do online. It only prohibits sites from creating a digital platform that encourages users to discriminate on the basis of race. When Movoto.com stopped steering, this did not interfere with its users' liberty to find housing. It merely stopped a practice of making it easy for users to discriminate.

Websites cannot so easily shirk their responsibility for steering. This is why in 2016 Airbnb agreed "to reduce the prominence of user photographs, which indicate race and gender, and that it would accelerate the use of instant bookings, which lets renters book places immediately without host approval."[52] Still, it's important to point out that these are voluntary measures undertaken by the website. Once we view steering as a civil rights violation, this provides a legal way to hold websites such as Airbnb responsible for facilitating digital discrimination. Selden's complaint did not highlight steering as a relevant cause of action. This chapter suggests that future lawsuits should. Doing so provides us a more straightforward way to hold these digital public accommodations responsible for racism in our digital lives, thereby avoiding the difficulties outlined above.

[52] www.nytimes.com/2016/09/09/technology/airbnb-anti-discrimination-rules.html

Banning steering on these websites and platforms will not end
discrimination on them. In the same way, prohibiting real estate agents
from steering has not ended racial discrimination in housing.
Nevertheless, before the ban on steering, these agents would routinely
engage in "racial blockbusting." They would encourage individuals to
sell by stoking racial fears and prejudice. Banning steering has made
these practices less prominent. As digital public accommodations,
websites and platforms should be subject to the same ban.

ROOMATES.COM: A CASE STUDY

I apply the foregoing analysis to a lawsuit filed against Roommates.com
by the Fair Housing Council of San Fernando Valley. Roommates.com
is a website that matches individuals with potential roommates.
Subscribers or users of the website must create a profile in order to
access the service. In creating the profile and providing basic information such as name, location, and email address, the website also requires
each subscriber to disclose their sex, sexual orientation, and whether
they would bring a child to the household. And because the platform
matches individuals with potential roommates, it also asks each subscriber to describe their preferences with regard to sex, sexual orientation, and family status. Simultaneously, the site also encourages
subscribers to use an Additional Comments section where they can
describe their desired roommate in a more open-ended essay.

The Fair Housing Council of San Fernando Valley sued the website
in 2004 for violating the Fair Housing Act and California housing
law.[53] The council argued that Roomates.com engaged in steering.
The website required "subscribers to disclose their sex, family status
and sexual orientation."[54] This encourages users to make decisions
based on these characteristics. The website even goes so far as to match

---

[53] The Fair Housing Act prohibits discrimination on the basis of "race, color, religion, sex,
familial status, or national origin." 42 U.S.C. Section 3604 (c). (1994). The California fair
housing law prohibits discrimination on the basis of "sexual orientation, marital status, ...
ancestry, ... source of income, or disability," in addition to the federally protected
characteristics. Cal. Gov. Code Section 12955 (2011).
[54] *Fair Housing I* (9th Cir. 2008) at 1164.

individuals on these discriminatory characteristics.[55] It encourages and facilitates discrimination that according to the Council is illegal under federal and California law.

The platform first sought to dismiss the case by invoking Section 230. Roommate.com argued that the lawsuit should be dismissed because the website is not responsible for what its users do. The district court agreed. But in *Fair Housing Council* v. *Roommates.com* (Ninth Circuit 2008) ("Fair Housing I") the court of appeals reversed, recognizing that this was not a case of digital discrimination but a case of digital steering. The court recognized that the website does not just host discrimination but actually facilitates it.

> [In] addition to requesting basic information – such as name, location and email address – Roommate requires each subscriber to disclose his sex, sexual orientation and whether he would bring children to a household. Each subscriber must also describe his preferences in roommates with respect to the same three criteria: sex, sexual orientation and whether they will bring children to the household.[56]

By specifically operating this kind of filtering system, Roomates.com is "'responsible' at least 'in part' for each subscriber's profile page, because every such page is a collaborative effort between Roommate and the subscriber."[57]

Because this system "steer[s] users based on the preferences and personal characteristics that Roommate itself forces subscribers to disclose,"[58] Roommates.com is not entitled to immunity under Section 230:

> Roommate is not entitled to CDA immunity for the operation of its search system, which filters listings, or of its email notification system, which directs emails to subscribers according to discriminatory criteria. Roommate designed its search system so it would steer users based on the preferences and personal characteristics that Roommate itself forces subscribers to disclose.[59]

---

[55] *Fair Housing I* (9th Cir. 2008) at 1165.
[56] *Fair Housing I* (9th Cir. 2008) at 1161.
[57] *Fair Housing I* (9th Cir. 2008) at 1167.
[58] *Fair Housing I* (9th Cir. 2008) at 1167.
[59] *Fair Housing I* (9th Cir. 2008) at 1167.

Roommates.com was not just an Internet service provider, passively displaying information that others (e.g., those seeking a roommate) had posted or created. In designing the very discriminatory categories at issue here, Roommates.com was providing its own content on the webpage, acting as "both a service provider and a content provider."[60] And in doing so, Roomates.com was digitally steering, facilitating the underlying discrimination. Hence, it could not claim immunity under Section 230, which only applies to websites that do not "create" any content themselves.

Roommates.com's search system

> differs materially from generic search engines such as Google, Yahoo! and MSN Live Search, in that Roommate designed its system to use allegedly unlawful criteria so as to limit the results of each search, and to force users to participate in its discriminatory process. In other words, Councils allege that Roommate's search is designed to make it more difficult or impossible for individuals with certain protected characteristics to find housing – something the law prohibits. By contrast, ordinary search engines do not use unlawful criteria to limit the scope of searches conducted on them, nor are they designed to achieve illegal ends – as Roommate's search function is alleged to do here. Therefore, such search engines play no part in the "development" of any unlawful searches.[61]

There is a difference between hosting discrimination and steering it. The court correctly realizes that this is not just about digital discrimination (which is difficult to hold a website responsible for) but digital steering. The very creation of the categories and their subsequent use by Roommates.com's users constitute the charge of steering. The website facilitates the underlying discrimination. *Fair Housing I* states that the website's platform is not just or only about content posted by its users or subscribers. Roommates.com designs the very discriminatory categories on its website. In doing so, the website makes it easy for its users or subscribers to discriminate. This is an instance of digital steering.

---

[60] *Fair Housing I* (9th Cir. 2008) at 1162.
[61] *Fair Housing I* (9th Cir. 2008) at 1167.

The court of appeals sent the case back to the district court. The district court held that Roommates.com must stop steering. Roommates.com refused to stop and appealed the decision. This time the website argued that it would violate the Constitution if the city could ban steering on their site. Why? The website simply turned the case from one about steering to one about discrimination. The website argued that what the city was seeking to do was ban discrimination on the site. Roommate.com argued that this would interfere with a private opportunity to select the roommate of one's choice. The site argued that the Constitution prevented the state from enlarging the boundary of justice to include the opportunity to find a roommate.

This strategy of turning a case about steering into one about discrimination worked. The court of appeals in *Fair Housing Council* v. *Roommates.com* (Ninth Circuit 2012) ("Fair Housing II") agreed with the website. The court said that the "Supreme Court has recognized that 'the freedom to enter into and carry on certain intimate and private relationships is a fundamental element of liberty protected by the Bill of Rights.'"[62] The court reasoned that the "roommate relationship easily qualifies" as an "intimate association."[63] The court goes on to say, "it's hard to imagine a relationship more intimate than that between roommates, who share living rooms, dining rooms, kitchens, bathrooms, even bedrooms."[64] In elaborating upon this conclusion, the case cites possible instances where a woman "will often look for female roommates because of modesty or security concerns."[65] Or "an orthodox Jew may want a roommate with similar beliefs and dietary restrictions."[66] According to the court, prohibiting Roommates.com from steering would interfere with this private opportunity that is protected by the Constitution.

The court's conclusion is faulty for the simple reason that it failed to distinguish steering from discrimination, the distinction that is at the center of this chapter. After all, if the Fair Housing Council had been seeking to prohibit users from discriminating on the website, it could

---

[62] *Fair Housing II* (9th Cir. 2012) at 1220.
[63] *Fair Housing II* (9th Cir. 2012) at 1221.
[64] *Fair Housing II* (9th Cir. 2012) at 1221.
[65] *Fair Housing II* (9th Cir. 2012) at 1221.
[66] *Fair Housing II* (9th Cir. 2012) at 1221.

have gone after those individuals, filing lawsuits against them indivi-
dually. Those cases may raise the constitutional concerns put forth by
the court with regard to modesty and privacy in light of a roommate's
sex. But the Council's concern was about steering, not discrimination.
The Council was targeting the website and its involvement in facilitating discrimination by its users.

The Council was not proceeding against any of the individuals in
this case. They did not sue a Roommates.com user. The Council sued
the website for steering, for structuring the digital space in such a way
so as to facilitate discrimination on the basis of sex, sexual orientation,
and family status. By failing to distinguish steering from discrimination, *Fair Housing II* failed to see how this was about the website and not
its users. The language of "intimate association" applies to the users on
the platform, not the commercial platform that hosts them. This case
was only about getting the website to stop steering, to stop providing its
users discriminatory criteria to make it easy for them to discriminate.
And by failing to distinguish steering from discrimination, the court
effectively treated a digital public accommodation, in this case
Roommates.com, as an intimate association worthy of constitutional
protection. Roommates.com still discloses sex, sexual orientation, and
family status in matching users to prospective roommates.

In reading cases like *Fair Housing II* and the secondary literature,
I'm struck that much of the language is about "discrimination."
Although litigants and scholars will focus on the website and how it
structures the platform or digital space, the tendency is still to view this
as a case of digital discrimination. That is, the language often references
"discrimination" rather than "steering." I suspect this may be because
civil rights law is often associated with a ban on racial discrimination
rather than a ban on steering. One purpose of this book is to draw our
attention to steering as a distinct and important legal basis for combatting private racism.

Discrimination may certainly be the most obvious and in certain
cases the more visible form of racism in our private lives, so I'm not
surprised that we generally focus on it. But in doing so, we neglect
a legal principle that captures the type of injustice that websites and
platforms such as Roommates.com engage in when they facilitate
discrimination. Obviously, the ban on steering was historically aimed

at real estate agents, because they were the primary intermediaries that structured the way we find housing. If we view this ban as applicable only to real estate agents, we are likely to miss the way in which websites also steer.

With the advent of digital space, websites and platforms now serve the function of real estate agents for a range of private goods and services, including but not limited to housing. We use websites as intermediaries to find these goods and services. These sites connect one set of users to another just as real estate agents connect buyers to sellers. Once we see clearly the fundamental role platforms play in our private lives, digital steering becomes an injustice that society should prohibit.

For purposes of the argument of this book, it is also worth noting that the discriminatory criteria at issue in *Fair Housing II* do not include race. Roommates.com did not go so far as to steer users to discriminate on the basis of race in choosing a roommate. Movoto.com did just with regard to housing more generally and then promptly stopped that practice once the Fair Housing Alliance objected to it. Steering on the basis of sex, sexual orientation, and family status may raise different normative issues. There may not be an overlapping moral consensus that private sexism or private homophobia is wrong, something I consider in the concluding chapter. So, we may disagree about whether sex, sexual orientation, or family status should limit private opportunities such as the opportunity to find a roommate. However, as the book's consensus shows, we do agree that this kind of opportunity should not be limited on the basis of race.

This is why there is a moral consensus that racism in private is wrong, or so this book has argued. This may be one reason that Roommates.com provides its subscribers with information about sex, sexual orientation, and family status but not about race. The website also recognizes the consensus that steering on the basis of race is wrong. In fact, had Roommates.com included race as one of the discriminatory criteria, I believe the court would not have protected the website by drawing on the Constitution. Perhaps in that case the court would have been more careful not to confuse steering for discrimination. If the website engaged in racial steering, I believe the court would have made the website stop. And in doing so, I suspect the court would have held, in line with the cases discussed in Chapter 1, that private opportunities, including the opportunity to find a roommate, are within the boundary of racial justice. The law may indeed reach them as it already reaches other kinds of private opportunities.

In fact, one of the judges in *Fair Housing II* pointed out that California law makes clear that the opportunity to find a roommate is within the boundary of *racial* justice. The judge noted that racial discrimination would have dictated a different outcome. The judge pointed to a 1998 case under California law where "two roommates . . . decided not to rent to a potential third roommate because she was black."[67] The commission charged with enforcing the state's housing law held that the California civil rights statute applied to the roommate relationship. The commission decided, as quoted by the court, that state law prohibited roommates "from rejecting an applicant on the basis of race and color" and that there were no exceptions in this case.[68] Although the commission held that sex-specific advertisements were allowed for "single dwellings with shared living areas" (finding a roommate), race-specific advertisements were not.[69] In the same way, as outlined in the last chapter, federal law is clear that while there may be a bona fide qualification for sex (even if rare), there is none for race. In that 1998 California housing commission decision, there was no constitutional argument about protecting the roommate relationship from a ban on racial discrimination due to its intimate nature.

As digital public accommodations, these websites and platforms structure the way we interact with others. This structuring is not some natural or pre-political state of affairs. Websites determine how we interact with others in our digital lives. They determine what information we can and must disclose. They determine how and under what circumstances this personal information will be used by others. And, of course, websites determine how easy it will be for us to discriminate in our digital lives. Roommates.com made it easy for its users to discriminate on the basis of sex, sexual orientation, and family status. Banning steering attempts to ensure that our digital world is not

---

[67] *Fair Housing II* (9th Cir. 2012) at 1228, concurring and dissenting.
[68] *Fair Housing II* (9th Cir. 2012) at 1228, concurring and dissenting.
[69] *Fair Housing II* (9th Cir. 2012) at 1228, concurring and dissenting.

structured in a way that facilitates discrimination. It attempts to ensure a more just digital space.

DIGITAL STEERING AS COMMERCE

In focusing on steering, it is also clear that Congress has the power to ban this practice. After all, the Fair Housing Act already prohibits steering in the context of housing. That ban on steering should apply not just to real estate agents but to any business, including websites or platforms, that steers users to discriminate on the basis of race. This is why the Fair Housing Alliance warned that Movoto's practice of racial disclosure on its platform was a form of steering, prohibited by federal law.

Congress has the power to ban digital steering on any website, because this is a form of commerce under the commerce clause. That clause says that Congress has the power to regulate "commerce among the states." In the *Civil Rights Cases* (1883), the Court invalidated Congress's first attempt at passing a civil rights act. Radical Republicans passed the 1875 Civil Rights Act. That Act, which was very similar to Title II of the 1964 Act, also prohibited a range of individuals and business from discriminating on the basis of race. These included "accommodations, advantages, facilities, and privileges of inns, public conveyances on land or water, theatres, and other places of public amusement."[70] The Court held that the power granted to Congress under the Fourteenth Amendment to enforce the Equal Protection Clause reached only actions by the state, not actions by individuals or businesses.

Congress tried again almost one hundred years later by passing the Civil Rights Act of 1964. And in *Heart of Atlanta*, Justice Thomas Clark, writing for the Court, upheld the Act, reasoning that Congress had the power to do so under the commerce clause. According to the Court,

> Congress was legislating against moral wrongs in many of these
> areas rendered its enactments no less valid. In framing Title II of

[70] *Civil Rights Cases* (1883) at 9.

this Act, Congress was also dealing with what it considered a moral problem. But that fact does not detract from the overwhelming evidence of the disruptive effect that racial discrimination has had on commercial intercourse.[71]

In basing its decision on the commerce clause power, the Court refused to consider whether Congress had this power under the Reconstruction Amendments, leaving the holding of the *Civil Rights Cases* intact. That road not taken has been a lament of many scholars (including me) who see civil rights legislation as way for Congress to assert its power under the Fourteenth Amendment to ensure racial equality. I leave the larger issue of state action to one side, in part because I have addressed it elsewhere.[72]

Relevant here is that the commerce clause power is also an important tool Congress can use in order to combat private racism and enforce the moral consensus at the center of this book. The clause is not simply a convenient constitutional hook on which to hang Congress's power to pass civil rights legislation. There is a logic to the idea that those engaged in commerce are subject to regulation by Congress.

The fact that Justice Clark associates the moral wrongs here with "commercial intercourse" provides Congress the power to reach a range of individuals and businesses. The New Deal had inaugurated an expansive interpretation of commerce that informed the reach of Title II's ban on discrimination. This is why Title II could reach not just a motel but also a remote restaurant such as Ollie's Barbeque where most of the patrons are "local people, rather than transients."[73] Racial discrimination could not be confined to some local area or state. Any individual engaged in commerce who discriminates on the basis of race falls within the purview of Congress. According to Justice Clark, this means that Congress has the power to prohibit them from discriminating in this way. "One need only examine the evidence which we have discussed above to see that Congress may – as it has – prohibit racial discrimination by motels serving travelers, however 'local' their operations may appear."[74]

[71] *Heart of Atlanta* (1964) at 257.
[72] See Bedi 2014.
[73] *Heart of Atlanta* (1964) at 274, concurring.
[74] *Heart of Atlanta* (1964) at 258.

In drawing on the commerce clause power, Justice Clark concludes that at the time of the *Civil Rights Cases*, commerce was more local and, as a result, Congress's power under the commerce clause could not so easily reach racial discrimination by individuals and businesses. But, according to Clark, "the fact that certain kinds of businesses may not in 1875 have been sufficiently involved in interstate commerce to warrant bringing them within the ambit of the commerce power is not necessarily dispositive of the same question today."[75] Clark goes on to say that "[o]ur populace had not reached its present mobility, nor were facilities, goods and services circulating as readily in interstate commerce as they are today."[76] This suggests a synergy between the power to regulate commerce on the one hand and the power to eradicate discrimination on the other. *Heart of Atlanta*, decided in 1964, argued that society had become more mobile and individuals and goods traveled more easily across the United States. As commerce becomes more expansive, touching more individuals and businesses, Congress has the power to eradicate more racial discrimination. After all, when individuals and businesses engaged in commerce among the states discriminate on the basis of race, this triggers Congressional power under the commerce clause.

Just as the economy has become more interconnected from 1875 to 1964, Justice Clark's opinion has even more resonance today. Individuals and goods now travel across the United States in ways that no one in 1964, let alone 1875, could have imagined. In particular, the digital world allows individuals and businesses to engage in commerce from their homes. Many of our decisions about where to eat, where to stay, and what to buy are now done on websites and platforms. These transactions routinely occur between individuals and businesses across state lines, triggering Congress's commerce clause power. Economic activity taking place over the Internet (e-commerce) is activity that is paradigmatically commerce among the states. Although the framers obviously did not anticipate the sharing economy or the digital world, it is obvious that this counts as commerce for purposes of the commerce clause.

---

[75] *Heart of Atlanta* (1964) at 251.
[76] *Heart of Atlanta* (1964) at 251.

In *South Dakota* v. *Wayfair* (2018), the Court considered whether states have the power to tax interstate commerce. The Court, with the conservative justices in the majority, held that states may tax online businesses that have no physical presence in the state as long as the business sells products to individuals in that state. In effect, states have the power to tax e-commerce. Central to the Court's reasoning was the recognition that the Internet has created an "interstate marketplace," something that did not really exist in 1992 when the Court considered a similar issue about taxing out-of-state sellers.[77] As the Court reasons:

> In 1992, less than 2 percent of Americans had Internet access. [citations omitted] Today that number is about 89 percent ... The Internet's prevalence and power have changed the dynamics of the national economy. In 1992, mail-order sales in the United States totaled $180 billion. [citations omitted] Last year, e-commerce retail sales alone were estimated at $453.5 billion. Dept. of Commerce, U.S. Census Bureau News, Quarterly Retail E–Commerce Sales: 4th Quarter 2017 ... And it is likely that this percentage will increase. Last year, e-commerce grew at four times the rate of traditional retail, and it shows no sign of any slower pace.[78]

According to the Court, states have the power to tax online commercial transactions, because of this interstate marketplace. Even if one disagrees with the Court's decision that states have the power to tax these transactions, it is relatively clear that Congress has the power to regulate this marketplace. If the marketplace is an interstate one – as the Court says – Congress has the power to regulate it under the commerce clause.

If the digital or "internet marketplace" is within the scope of Congress's power to regulate, how websites and platforms structure this marketplace is also within the scope of this power. These websites are businesses that draw in users from not just across the United States but across the globe. One way these websites structure the marketplace is by engaging in steering. As outlined in this chapter, websites decide how their users will interact with each other. These decisions affect the profitability of the business. Websites and platforms want to host more

---

[77] *Wayfair* (2018) at 2097.
[78] *Wayfair* (2018) at 2097.

users and more activity on their sites. Steering can be one way these platforms can seek to expand their presence in the digital marketplace.

By disclosing the racial demographics of various communities, for instance, Movoto.com engaged in digital steering. The website may have thought that making it easy for their users to discriminate on the basis of race would generate more traffic on their platform and therefore greater profits. Historically, real estate agents sometimes steered in order to be more profitable, an unlawful practice called "racial block-busting." Real estate agents are forbidden from doing so even if this turns out to be more profitable for them. The argument of this chapter suggests that digital public accommodations such as Airbnb and Roommates.com should also not steer. The fact that this steering is not confined to a local geographical area but part of the larger digital marketplace easily places this activity within the scope of Congress's commerce clause power. Digital steering is a form of commerce among the states. As such, Congress can and should prohibit it.

As the digital world structures even more of our private lives, even more commerce will take place on this interstate marketplace. This makes it more likely that sites will attempt to steer. After all, if these sites seek more rather than fewer users, they will be inclined, like any business, to cater to their users' preferences. In so far as these preferences are about race, this will raise the specter of digital steering.

4 SEXUAL RACISM

The last chapter sought to enlarge the boundary of racial justice by including our digital decisions within it. Sexual racism is another form of private racism. Here too racial discrimination affects our private lives. This kind of discrimination concerns perhaps the most private of opportunities. It too is wrong, or so this chapter argues. I show that racism makes it more difficult for those who are not white to find intimacy, where intimacy is the opportunity to be in a romantic or sexual relationship. This chapter shows that racial discrimination, stereotypes, and intersectionality occur in our intimate lives, what I call "sexual racism." Websites and platforms that steer their users to discriminate on the basis of race facilitate sexual racism. Because they are public accommodations, we should prohibit them from doing so. This is one way to address sexual racism.

This chapter crafts this argument in three sections. First, taking seriously the idea that the the personal is the political, I show that racial minorities are often discriminated against when they seek out intimacy. Racial discrimination, stereotypes, and intersectionality underwrite this charge. Second, I argue that sexual racism denies individuals equality of intimacy. I draw on John Rawls and Martha Nussbaum to support this conclusion. I argue that intimacy is a social primary good (according to Rawls) and a capability central to human dignity (according to Nussbaum). As such, both theories would support the idea of equality of intimacy, suggesting that we should expand the boundary of racial justice to treat racial discrimination in our intimate lives as an issue of justice. Third, I discuss how we can address this kind of inequality. I suggest that we can combat sexual racism by openly condemning it and, in doing so, prohibiting commercial dating websites and platforms from steering us to discriminate on the basis of race in finding intimacy.

RACISM IN OUR INTIMATE LIVES

In her book *Inequalities of Love*, Averil Y. Clarke uses the personal narratives of college-educated black women to show that in the realm of love, romance, and family they are "disadvantage[d] relative to other women at [their] age and station in life."[1] In fact, she concludes that "degreed black women's experience of deprivation in romantic partnership and marriage develops and intensifies over time."[2] Christian Rudder, the creator of OkCupid, a popular online dating site founded in 2004, published statistical results that inform this disparity. Rudder stated that "[W]hen you're looking at how two American strangers behave in a romantic context, race is the ultimate confounding factor."[3] His results show that white users are more likely to be messaged or responded to than their nonwhite counterparts. They show, in particular, that black women and Asian men are the least likely to be messaged or responded to.[4]

Sexual racism involves racial discrimination, stereotypes, and intersectionality in our intimate lives. First, racial minorities are often discriminated against because they are not white. They have fewer opportunities to find intimacy than their white counterparts. Second, racial stereotypes make it more difficult for racial minorities to enjoy intimacy, because they must navigate these stereotypes. Third, racial discrimination in intimacy also has an intersectional dimension, where racial minorities often experience double discrimination, based on their race along with other markers of social hierarchy. This shows that sexual racism is about individuals and structure. I show that in our

[1] Clarke 2011: 15.
[2] Clarke 2011: 117.
[3] Rudder 2014: 99.
[4] Rudder 2014: 102–113.

intimate lives, individuals discriminate directly (and often explicitly) but also in ways that further existing inequality and stereotypes.

Racial Discrimination

First, racial minorities are often discriminated against simply for not being white. Consider research data from OkCupid, which, as of April 2014, had ten million users.[5] In 2009, Christian Rudder published results titled "How Race Affects the Messages You Get."[6] OkCupid has a distinctive percentage matching system. The user answers a list of questions (the more questions answered, the more "accurate" the match percentage) and then can search for compatible matches. The OkCupid match/compatibility algorithm does not consider appearance, including the user's racial identification. It is self-described as considering the users' "inner selves."[7] Consequently, the match scores of individuals across different racial groups were roughly even, in the same way that the match scores of individuals across different zodiac signs were roughly even.[8]

But although the data found that reply rates did not vary among those with different zodiac signs, such rates vary significantly based on whether the user is white.[9] For instance, OkCupid concluded that among those who identify as straight, white men get a greater percentage of responses than any other racial group. "White women prefer white men to the exclusion of everyone else – and Asian and Hispanic women prefer them even more exclusively."[10] So women of all racial groups prefer men who are white, findings that persisted in a more recent analysis of the data from OkCupid.[11] In fact, this disparity in racial matching was similar for gay users as well.[12] This discrimination makes it harder for

[5] Rudder 2014.

[6] http://blog.okcupid.com/index.php/your-race-affects-whether-people-write-you-back/ (October 5, 2009)

[7] Rudder 2014: 101.

[8] Rudder 2014: 101.

[9] http://blog.okcupid.com/index.php/your-race-affects-whether-people-write-you-back/ (October 5, 2009)

[10] http://blog.okcupid.com/index.php/your-race-affects-whether-people-write-you-back/ (October 5, 2009)

[11] Rudder 2014: 102–109.

[12] Rudder 2014: 243; see also Robinson and Frost 2018.

those who are not white to find intimacy. Racial minorities have fewer opportunities to find intimacy than similarly situated whites.

We need not look just to OkCupid. Recent empirical work also reveals that individuals discriminate against racial minorities, often preferring intimacy with whites. This work primarily uses online dating profiles and response rates as well as more conventional survey data to reveal the relationship between race and dating preferences. With regard to heterosexuals these studies conclude that females prefer whites over nonwhites;[13] white men and women are more likely to seek out potential dates with whites rather than with blacks;[14] white women are less willing to date nonwhites than white men;[15] college students are more likely to exclude blacks as potential dates;[16] whites are least likely to date outside of their race and Asians and Latinos are least likely to date blacks;[17] blacks were ten times more likely to contact whites than whites were to contact blacks;[18] and controlling for appearance, Arabs suffered an ethnic penalty in one of Sweden's largest online dating sites.[19]

With regard to gay men these studies (of which there are generally fewer) also reveal that gay men discriminate against racial minorities: Asian men are the least desired in a sample of online profiles of urban males seeking sex with men;[20] interviews reveal sexual marginalization of Asian men in the gay community;[21] an ethnic hierarchy exists with whites and Latinos as the most desirable racial groups in the online gay male community;[22] and gay men of all races prefer to date whites over nonwhites.[23]

These data show that just as racial minorities have difficulty in finding employment,[24] housing,[25] and credit,[26] they also have

[13] Tsunokai, McGrath, and Kavanagh 2013.
[14] Herman and Campbell 2012; Lin and Lundquist 2013.
[15] Hwang 2013.
[16] Bany, Robnett, and Feliciano 2014; MClintock 2010.
[17] Robnett and Feliciano 2011.
[18] Mendelsohn, Taylor, Fiore, and Cheshire 2014.
[19] Jakobsson and Lindholm 2014.
[20] White, Reisner, Dunham, and Mimiaga 2014.
[21] Han 2008a; see also Han and Choi 2018
[22] Brown 2003; Robinson 2007a.
[23] Tsunokai, McGrath, and Kavanagh 2013.
[24] See, e.g., Bertrand and Mullainathan 2004.
[25] See, e.g., Hanson and Hawley 2011; Ewens and Wang 2014.
[26] See, e.g., Kau, Keenan, and Munneke 2012; Ladd 1998.

difficulty in finding intimacy, because they are not white. This discrimination is not simply a proxy for other factors such as socioeconomic status or ideology. If that were the case, individuals would be discriminating not on the basis of race but on the basis of these other characteristics. These data and studies reject that conclusion, showing that racial minorities are often discriminated against simply and only on the basis of their race. Again, OkCupid's data on race preferences controlled for match percentage. That is, it considered the response rate for pairs of individuals that had a similar match score – the only difference being their race. The match score considers a wide variety of compatibility questions relating to education, income, expectations, and likes/dislikes. Even when compatibility is the same across racial groups, individuals still discriminate against those who are not white.

Or consider that the studies above conclude, in part, that white women prefer to date Latinos and blacks over Asians and East Indians, even though the former have lower-than-average economic statuses;[27] college students exclude blacks as potential dates based just on physical attractiveness;[28] randomizing occupation on one of the largest Swedish online dating sites still generates an ethnic penalty for Arabs;[29] and education does not mediate the observed racial preference among white Internet daters.[30] This suggests that race is not simply a proxy for compatibility in terms of socioeconomic status or education. These data suggest that sexual racism is exactly what is going on.

We can easily see this, and this is where I first encountered it, on gay dating sites. Consider racism on Grindr, perhaps the most popular platform for gay men to find intimacy. It is not surprising to see profiles on Grindr that read: "No Asians" or "Whites only."[31] These monikers express unambiguous instances of intentional racial discrimination in our private, intimate lives. These are not isolated instances of discrimination. Studies show that among gay men, racial minorities have a more difficult time finding intimacy as compared to those who are

[27] Feliciano, Robnett, and Komaie 2009.
[28] Bany, Robnett, and Feliciano 2014.
[29] Jakobsson and Lindholm 2014.
[30] Lin and Lundquist 2013.
[31] www.advocate.com/commentary/2018/7/19/no-asians-not-preference-its-racism

white.[32] In fact, in some of these studies researchers discovered that racial discrimination persists even using the same photo, where the study altered only the name to suggest a different race or explicitly stated that the individual was of another race.[33] This suggests that individuals discriminate against a potential romantic or intimate partner because of, not in spite of, their race. In the same way, the state or government has also discriminated because of, not simply in spite of, an individual's race.

Racial Stereotypes

Second, it is difficult for racial minorities to find intimacy not simply because of the presence of racial discrimination but also because of racial stereotypes. Here, individuals may prefer those who are not white but only on the condition that the person fulfills a certain sexual or romantic stereotype. Robin Zheng describes this as a racial fetish. She defines a fetish as a "person's exclusive or near-exclusive preference for sexual intimacy with others belonging to a specific racial *out-group*."[34] Zheng's article titled "Why Yellow Fever Isn't Flattering: A Case Against Racial Fetishes" focuses on the stereotype that Asian and Asian-American women are often seen as the "docile, domestic 'Lotus Blossom' or the seductive, treacherous 'Dragon Lady.'"[35] Or what Sheridan Prasso calls the "Asian Mystique."[36] These racial stereotypes of Asian women often view them as submissive and sexual. According to Zheng, individuals may prefer Asian women over women of other races as long as they fulfill this kind of stereotype.

Zheng argues that this kind of fetish limits the opportunity of individuals to enjoy intimacy. She draws on testimony from Asian and Asian-American women, whose voices are often at the "margins of contemporary academic philosophy but whose unique racial vantage point complicates a racial discourse overwhelmingly centered on the

---

[32] See Brown 2003; Robinson 2007; Robinson and Frost 2018; White, Reisner, Dunham, and Mimiaga 2014.
[33] See, e.g., Jakobsson and Lindholm 2014; Robinson 2007.
[34] Zheng 2016: 401.
[35] Zheng 2016: 405.
[36] Prasso 2005.

Black/White binary."[37] Zheng argues that this kind of stereotype poses a "psychological burden" on these women, constituting a "form of racial disadvantage."[38] Zheng argues that even

> those Asian/American women who ultimately resolve doubts about yellow fever by being unbothered by it or by embracing it or by undergoing the relational work required to establish definitively that their partners are not homogenizing and otherizing them were still saddled, in the first place, with a problem that others are not forced to deal with; very few Asian/American women, if any, can be wholly oblivious to or untouched by it. And it is worth noting that women reporting more positive experiences of yellow fever are often quickly disillusioned, conflicted, or accept the stereotypes themselves.[39]

This poses a disadvantage on Asian women, a difficulty that does not exist for white women. This can make it harder for these women to find intimacy that is not subject to this kind of caricature or stereotype. This is why according to Zheng some Asian-American women will simply "embrace" the stereotype. Whatever they decide to do, this burden arises only because of their race. Zheng argues that the "racial depersonalization inherent in yellow fever threatens Asian/American women with doubts as to whether they are or can be loved as individuals rather than as objects in a category."[40] This makes it more difficult for Asian women to access intimacy fully, because they must now navigate this racial stereotype in their intimate lives.

This kind of racial stereotype also affects Asian males.[41] This kind of stereotype views Asian men as effeminate and asexual (what David Eng calls a kind of "racial castration"[42]), furthering discrimination against them simply on the basis of their race. According to Chongsuk Han, this is why gay Asian men must sometimes also assume this "submissive" intimate role.[43] Doing so may be the only way to find

---

[37] Zheng 2016: 401.
[38] Zheng 2016: 407.
[39] Zheng 2016: 409.
[40] Zheng 2016: 408.
[41] Robnett and Feliciano 2011.
[42] Eng 2001.
[43] Han 2008.

intimacy given the powerful force of this kind of racial stereotype about Asians.

Asians are not the only racial group that face racial stereotypes. Black men also face difficulties in finding romantic or sexual relationships. Here too racial stereotypes can impose obstacles to intimacy. Black men and, in particular, black gay men must contend with the stereotype that they are aggressive, sexually dominant, and physically well-endowed.[44] Drawing our attention to this kind of stereotyping, Nathaniel Coleman argues:

> "The African American male who isn't sexually well endowed or isn't as sexually aggressive as both homosexual and heterosexual society say he must be, may feel inferior."[45] Such a black MSM [men who have sex with men] is likely to consider himself to have lessened bartering power in the market-place for sex with MSM. He is likely to have lessened confidence in his ability to attract sexual approbation from, and to achieve sexual activity with other MSM. He is likely to have low sexual self-confidence. Young black MSM, fraught with the insecurities of adolescence and of "coming out of the closet," are especially likely to find themselves with low self-confidence.[46]

Gay black men, especially those who are just "coming out," will face this burden in finding intimacy – burdens that white gay men will not experience. In fact, Coleman suggests that because of sexual racism, black men are often forced to take on the sexually aggressive role. So, like some Asian men and women, they too may have to "embrace" the racial stereotype in order to find intimacy.

Given these difficulties in finding intimacy, some racial minorities may decide not to date outside their race. An Asian woman may, for instance, seek to date only other Asian men. A black gay man may decide only to date others who are black. It may be easier for racial minorities to find intimacy with others who are not white. This may be one way to avoid racial discrimination or stereotypes.

In an article titled "Do Black Men Have a Moral Duty to Marry Black Women?" Charles Mills even asks whether there is a requirement

---

[44] See, e.g., Coleman 2011; Smith 2014.
[45] Coleman 2011: 13, quoting Brown 2003: 24.
[46] Coleman 2011: 13.

that those who are black seek out intimacy with others who are black. I do not consider this question here, but in raising it, Mills takes seriously the relationship between intimacy and justice. Mills says, in passing, that the idea that "'whites should only marry whites' *will* in general be based on philosophically uninteresting racist reasons."[47] These reasons may not be that interesting once we enlarge the boundary of racial justice and recognize that racial injustice occurs in our intimate lives as well. But we must first enlarge this boundary, as this chapter seeks to do.

Intersectionality

Third, racial minorities often experience racism along with other forms of discrimination. Kimberlé Crenshaw defines intersectionality to include the experience of double discrimination, where racial minorities experience racial discrimination in the context of other kinds of social disadvantage. She draws on the way in which black women can experience this kind of double discrimination in finding employment. As Crenshaw points out, they often experience racism and sexism.

> Black women can experience discrimination in ways that are both similar to and different from those experienced by white women and Black men. Black women sometimes experience discrimination in ways similar to white women's experiences; sometimes they share very similar experiences with Black men. Yet often they experience double-discrimination – the combined effects of practices which discriminate on the basis of race, and on the basis of sex. And sometimes, they experience discrimination as Black women – not the sum of race and sex discrimination, but as Black women.[48]

This happens in our private, intimate lives as well. As the examples above make clear, in addition to discrimination based on a race, racial minorities experience discrimination based on their gender as well as their sexual orientation. Asian women experience discrimination on the basis of their race and their gender. Gay black men do so on the basis of

---

[47] Mills 1994: 131.
[48] Crenshaw 1989: 149.

their race, gender, and sexual orientation. These are instances of intersectionality.

Sexual racism also means that racial minorities often experience racial bias along with a bias against their height or body shape, professional status, educational pedigree, or family history. These too are instances of intersectionality, showing the way in which race can intersect with any number of social categories or hierarchies. This reveals how racism intersects with class-ism and look-ism where racial minorities face "double-discrimination" in their intimate lives based on their race and, at the same time, how they look or what they do for work.

Generally, whites do not face "double-discrimination" in finding intimacy, because they do not generally experience racial discrimination in their private, intimate lives. As Iris Marion Young notes: "White males . . . in so far as they escape group marking, can be individuals."[49] Whites are often seen as individuals in the intimate sphere, escaping the racial discrimination and stereotypes that face racial minorities in finding intimacy. Whites also are likely to escape discrimination and stereotypes in finding other private goods, including housing and employment. Zheng informs this intersectional approach. She says:

> Nor does hair or eye color track categorical differences across all social, economic, and political dimensions of life, including opportunities for health, education, jobs, relationships, legal protections, and more. But race does – in ways that Asian/American women and other people of color experience on a daily basis. Thus while some doubts about fungibility might be an inescapable part of all sexual and romantic relationships, whether grounded in physical appearance, personality, or other bases of attraction, racial fetish raises additional and uniquely racialized doubts that require emotionally taxing work to set to rest.[50]

These disadvantages based on physical appearance or personality make it difficult for all of us to find intimacy, regardless of race. But it means that racial minorities often experience this disadvantage as an additional obstacle in finding intimacy along with the disadvantage they

---

[49] Young 1990: 59.
[50] Zheng 2016: 409–410.

face on the basis of race, a form of double discrimination or intersectionality.

EQUALITY OF INTIMACY

The foregoing analysis shows that sexual racism denies individuals equality of intimacy just like racism can deny individuals equality of opportunity in finding other private goods and services. I argue that this is unjust because intimacy is a primary good and a capability central to human dignity. Equality of opportunity is an important principle of justice. Often, we discuss this principle in the context of finding other private goods such as housing and employment. I apply this principle of equality of opportunity to intimacy. I argue that equality of intimacy is a matter of justice.

I draw on John Rawls's account of social primary goods and Martha Nussbaum's capabilities approach to support this claim. In doing so, I once again treat Rawls's account as a representative of the ideal society approach. I also treat Nussbaum's approach as representative of the actual society approach. Both support the conclusion that equality of intimacy is an issue of justice.

According to Rawls, in an ideal society, social primary goods would be distributed without regard to race. This is because society should treat race as "arbitrary from a moral perspective."[51] According to Nussbaum, a just society is one where capabilities central to human dignity are not limited on the basis of race. Nussbaum ties principles of "self-respect" and "non-humiliation" to the idea that we should not discriminate on the basis of race.[52] Race should not affect one's life chances to exercise these capabilities in our actual society. Although these are two distinct accounts of justice,[53] both support the idea that equality of intimacy matters. This is because intimacy is a social primary good and a capability central to human dignity.

[51] Rawls 1999 [1971]: 64.
[52] Nussbaum 2001: 79.
[53] See generally Brighouse and Robeyns 2010.

124   **Sexual Racism**

Primary Social Good

According to John Rawls, justice is about the distribution of social primary goods. He defines these goods as those things that "it is supposed a rational man wants whatever else he wants."[54] Rawls contends that all of us are characterized by two capacities: "capacity for a sense of right and justice" and our "capacity to decide upon, revise, and rationally pursue a conception of the good."[55] Primary social goods are central to exercising these capacities. Rawls's list of primary goods include: "rights, liberties and opportunities, income and wealth."[56] Rawls also includes on this list the "social bases of self-respect."[57] For instance, the right to religious freedom is a primary social good, and hence a concern for justice, because it is crucial in pursuing certain life plans and projects. Since I do not know what my life plans and projects will be in the Original Position, I will ensure that there is equality of religious freedom.

Similarly, the opportunity for employment is also a primary social good. If free and rational individuals seek more rather than fewer primary goods in order to, in part, "pursue a personal conception of the good," employment is the crucial mechanism by which they can procure resources, money, and even self-respect. This is why Rawls contends that, at a minimum, there ought to be formal equality of opportunity where offices and positions are open to all.[58] This means that in addition to governmental jobs justice demands equality of private opportunity, as outlined in Chapter 2.

I argue that Rawls's theory would also include the opportunity to find intimacy as a social primary good and therefore subject to the principle of equality. Intimacy is a distinct primary social good, not reducible to other such goods. First, intimacy is something that most (if not all) of us pursue in some fashion. Most individuals seek some kind of sexual closeness coupled with love or romantic affection. Even if individuals decide not to pursue a long-term, monogamous

---

[54] Rawls 1999 [1971]): 79, 92.
[55] Rawls 1997: 277.
[56] Rawls 1999 [1971]: 79.
[57] Rawls 1999 [1971]: 54 Rawls 1999 [1971]: 54.
[58] Rawls 1999 [1971]: 47, 64.

relationship, the desire to be sexually and romantically intimate with another and to have that affection or love returned is ubiquitous.

Elizabeth Brake argues that the opportunity to form caretaking relationships is also a social primary good. She argues that such "relationships are 'all-purpose means normally needed' in the pursuit of widely different conceptions of the good."[59] This argument holds even more force in the case of intimacy. For Brake, caring relationships "are normally an ongoing site of development" pointing to their status as long-term associations.[60] Intimacy, as I have defined it here, may include such long-term relationships, but also those short-lived romances where affection and love may exist for a brief time. This points to intimacy's obvious "all purpose" character. Intimacy is an opportunity that an individual will tailor to his or her own idiosyncratic conception of the good.

Second, intimacy often contributes to self-respect, which Rawls cryptically refers to as perhaps "the most important primary good."[61] Being desired by someone else informs our own self-worth and sense of confidence. Brake goes on to say that the "clear connections between close interpersonal relationships and mental (as well as physical) health suggest that caring relationships are comparable to self-respect in psychologically supporting individuals in their plans of life."[62] This support is even more compelling in the case of intimacy. Caring relationships may not have an element of romantic interest. They may provide individuals with the psychological (and material) support, a sibling caring for his father or his sister, but not the kind of romantic relationship that comes with intimacy.

Third, mere resources are not sufficient for intimacy. The adage that money can't buy love points to the idea that intimacy is a distinct primary social good. Although money may have the potential to secure affection and desire from someone, this is not always the case. Intimacy often rests on precisely that kind of deeply emotional and physical connection that mere money or resources cannot easily create. From the standpoint of those persons in the Original Position, individuals

---

[59] Brake 2010: 329.
[60] Brake 2010: 329.
[61] Rawls 1999 [1971]: 386.
[62] Brake 2010: 329.

would rationally seek to secure more of this opportunity rather than less, independently of securing anything else.

Although extant scholarly work suggests that Rawls does not go far enough in applying his principles of justice to the intimate sphere,[63] this chapter has argued otherwise. Taking seriously the idea that social primary goods should be distributed equally in an ideal society means that intimacy should also be distributed equally. As a representative of the ideal society approach, Rawls's argument provides moral support for the conclusion that sexual racism as a form of inequality of intimacy is wrong.

Capability

Martha Nussbaum's capability approach offers another framework from which to consider intimacy a matter of justice. Nussbaum's account of justice proffers the idea of a "basic social minimum" that "focuses on human capabilities, that is, what people are actually able to do and to be – in a way informed by an intuitive idea of a life that is worthy of the dignity of the human being."[64] By focusing on what people are actually able to do and be, I consider her account as representative of the actual society approach.

Central to her understanding of justice is a commitment to human dignity, a commitment, according to Nussbaum, that has "broad cross-cultural resonance and intuitive power."[65] This kind of dignity means that human beings "have worth as an end, a kind of awe-inspiring something that makes it horrible to see this person beaten down by the currents of chance – and wonderful, at the same time, to witness the way in which chance has not completely eclipsed the humanity of the person."[66] She contends that individuals from various cultural and religious backgrounds can affirm such dignity, and in turn, a core set of capabilities. She identities ten such capabilities, including: "life, bodily health, bodily integrity, sense, imagination, and thought,

[63] See, e.g., Nussbaum 2003a, Okin 1989a, 1989.
[64] Nussbaum 2001: 5, see also Nussbaum 2003.
[65] Nussbaum 2001: 72.
[66] Nussbaum 2001: 97.

emotions, practical reason, affiliation, other species, play and control over one's environment."[67]

In elucidating the capability of emotions, Nussbaum affirms the importance of intimacy:

> Being able to have attachments to things and people outside our-
> selves; to love those who love and care for us, to grieve at their
> absence; in general, to love, to grieve, to experience longing, grati-
> tude, and justified anger. Not having one's emotional development
> blighted by fear and anxiety or by traumatic events of abuse or
> neglect. (Supporting this capability means supporting forms of
> human association that can be shown to be crucial in their
> development.)[68]

The capability of emotions validates the significance not just of intimacy but also of other opportunities such as the chance to grieve and experience gratitude. These are all types of human associations that involve attachment to others. Nussbaum talks about human dignity where Rawls speaks in the language of self-respect. Both concepts point to the importance of intimate attachments. A life without it, a life without loving and being loved in return, is one that would lack dignity. It's obvious that mutual romantic affection is the kind of affiliation that is a nearly universal capability, one that can be endorsed by all cultures. Nussbaum even argues that love can be central to maintaining a society's sense of justice. By loving another we engage in "a vigorous imaginative engagement with another persons' particularity."[69] This, in turn, informs a sense of compassion and empathy that has the potential to counter and reduce inequality.

By appealing to the language of capabilities versus rights, Nussbaum challenges the idea that the intimate sphere is beyond the purview of justice. She suggests that "the sphere of rights was typically imagined as the public sphere, and the family was typically imagined as a private sphere to which the discourse of rights had no applicability."[70] But, as she goes on to say, the "concept of capabilities has no such baggage to jettison, and the idea of being able to do or be something is

[67] Nussbaum 2001: 79–80.
[68] Nussbaum 2001: 79.
[69] Nussbaum 2013: 165.
[70] Nussbaum 2005: 176.

obviously applicable inside the family, as well as outside of it."[71] Fully appreciating intimacy as important to a capability central to human dignity suggests that justice is "applicable" even to those decisions that stand to create the very bounds or parameters of the intimate or familial sphere. As a representative of the actual society approach, Nussbaum's argument provides moral support for the conclusion that sexual racism as a form of inequality of intimacy is wrong.

Expanding the Boundary of Racial Justice

Taking seriously the idea that equality of intimacy matters means that sexual racism is wrong. Sexual racism denies individuals equality. The arguments of Rawls and Nussbaum support the idea that racial inequality in finding intimacy is unjust. According to the ideal society approach, race limits a social primary good. According to the actual society approach, race limits an actual capability central to human dignity.

This suggests that we should take an expansive view of the boundary of racial justice and include intimacy within it. These intimate or romantic decisions are deeply personal ones. Given the argument of this chapter, racial minorities often experience these personal decisions as political ones, especially when racial discrimination, stereotypes, and intersectionality make it hard to find intimacy. This informs Catharine MacKinnon's famous claim:

> The private is the public for those for whom the personal is the political. In this sense, there is no private, either normatively or empirically.[72]

MacKinnon may not have had sexual racism in mind. But if we enlarge the boundary of racial justice, we realize that racial injustice happens in both public and private. This means that those who experience racial discrimination and stereotypes will be hard pressed to find a "private" space where racism does not occur. If racial injustice happens even in the private, intimate sphere, as this chapter shows, the private sphere is also a political one. This challenges the idea that we can distinguish the

---

[71] Nussbaum 2005: 176.
[72] MacKinnon 1987: 100.

public from the private in some categorical or definitive way to limit the boundary of racial justice.

This is why liberal democratic theorists argue the boundary between the public and the private must be open to democratic contestation, debate, or justification.[73] According to this approach, this boundary is not rigid and pre-political but contingent and open-ended. Corey Brettschneider argues for what he calls a commitment to "strong political reconstruction."[74] He describes this in the following way:

> Although the phrase "public reason" seems to suggest an inherent divide between public and private life, on the strong public reconstruction there is no such clear or prior divide. Rather, to the degree that privacy exists at all, its boundaries must be determined by and normatively argued for through public reason. This has a major implication for traditional understandings of privacy: domestic life is not immune from political examination.[75]

The reclassification approach invites a dialogue that is framed by a theory of public reason, grounded in the idea that the boundary between the private, "domestic life" and its public counterpart is not rigid or set but itself open to political renegotiation. This dialogue permits democracies to reclassify private matters as issues of public concern.

Once we recognize that intimacy is a matter of justice, the very decisions that stand to create the intimate sphere now become a site for racial injustice. This means we should, in line with this democratic classification approach, consider and now classify the intimate sphere as within the boundary of racial justice. Opportunities to find intimacy, as outlined above, are often limited on precisely those racial terms that have limited individuals historically and socially.

The personal nature of our intimate decisions does not mean, then, that they are outside the boundary of racial justice. Insofar as intimacy is important to a capability central to human dignity and a social primary good, it is a matter of justice. Racial discrimination, stereotypes, and intersectionality occur not just in our public or political life

---

[73] See, e.g., Benhabib 1992, 2004; Brettschneider 2007; Cohen 2002; Habermas 2001: 116; Zivi 2011. See generally Bedi 2009: 24–38; Kelly 2003: 42–46.
[74] Brettschneider 2007.
[75] Brettschneider 2007: 24–25.

but also in our private, intimate one. This begs for an expansive view of the boundary of racial justice.

ENFORCING EQUALITY OF INTIMACY

How should the law go about addressing sexual racism? I have argued that racial inequality in our intimate lives is wrong. It represents a form of injustice. Nevertheless, I argue that it is difficult to enforce this kind of equality coercively. This is because we do not simply wake up one day and proclaim that we are attracted to those of a particular race (or not attracted to those of another race). We cannot switch our desires on or off. That's not how desire operates. Our romantic desires seem ineffable and often beyond our conscious control. This is why Rachel Moran, who analyzes the historical and social impact of anti-miscegenation laws in light of issues of race and intimacy, recognizes that sexual desire entails an elusive "X factor" where "intimacy [is] an affirmation of personal uniqueness." Relationships, she goes on to say, are "unmediated, unquantifiable, and indescribable." "Love and identity are beyond the reach of rational judgment."[76]

These considerations suggest that sexual racism may be a kind of "unconscious racism."[77] Sometimes this is defined by research in political science as an "implicit bias."[78] Charles Lawrence explains that we

> inevitably share many ideas, attitudes, and beliefs that attach significance to an individual's race and induce negative feelings and opinions about nonwhites. To the extent that this cultural belief system has influenced all of us, we are all racists. At the same time, most of us are unaware of our racism. We do not recognize the ways in which our cultural experience has influenced our beliefs about race or the occasions on which those beliefs affect our actions.[79]

Our sexual desires are influenced by such beliefs, attitudes, and culture. Considering that these norms can be racist, they obviously influence

[76] Moran 2003: 14.
[77] Lawrence 1987.
[78] See generally Ksiazkiewicz and Hedrick 2013.
[79] Lawrence 1987: 322.

whom we find attractive. If whiteness or being white is prioritized in finding intimacy, it stands as a reflection of the larger culture and its "negative feelings" about those who are not white. This means that we cannot simply decide to be attracted to those of a particular race. Sexual racism may not be a conscious deliberate choice we make. Although we may be aware that we are not attracted to people on the basis of race, this may not be an intentional decision we make one morning while contemplating possible romantic partners. Thus, we can view those who discriminate on the basis of race in their personal or intimate lives as operating on a kind of unconscious racism.

G.A. Cohen also seeks to enlarge the boundary of racial justice. His focus is not on racial injustice but economic injustice (something I make clearer in the conclusion). Cohen focuses on what he calls "high-flying marketeers."[80] These are individuals who are particularly talented in society and can therefore command high salaries. Cohen argues that the difference principle, the idea that economic inequalities should benefit the least advantaged, should apply to these individuals. He too believes that principles of justice apply to individuals in their private lives.

We may disagree about whether the difference principle applies to individuals. Nevertheless, I follow Cohen here in thinking that individuals who act unjustly in private should not be condemned in some categorical way. Although Cohen's focus is not on private racism, what he says here is instructive:

> So, for example, a properly sensitive appreciation of these matters allows one to hold that an acquisitive ethos is profoundly unjust in its effects, without holding that those who are gripped by it are commensurately unjust. It is essential to apply principles of justice to dominant patterns in social behavior that, as it were, is where the action is – but it doesn't follow that we should have a persecuting attitude to the people who emit that behavior. We might have good reason to exonerate the perpetrators of injustice, but we should not deny, or apologize for, the injustice itself.[81]

[80] Cohen 1997: 5.
[81] Cohen 1997: 26.

For Cohen, this does not mean that the relevant private injustice is any less a form of injustice. In the same way, sexual racism is not any less wrong. Condemning individuals in some categorical or persecuting way for sexual racism may not be a productive way to respond to this kind of racial injustice. And, in line with Cohen's approach, I do not seek to do so here.

That's why it may not make sense to treat intimacy exactly like employment. Whereas we force employers to work with individuals of a different race, that form of coercion may not work in the intimacy context. Employment decisions are not beyond the reach of rational judgment, for we can define the extent and scope of what it means to be an employee in a particular workplace. But we cannot force someone to be attracted to someone they simply are not attracted to. After all, we cannot define the extent and scope of what it means to be a romantic, intimate partner. This means that it makes more sense to prohibit racial discrimination in the employment sphere than to prohibit it in the intimate sphere. The delicate, unpredictable, and irrational nature of intimacy suggests that we need an alternative to prohibiting such discrimination.

Digital Steering on Dating Websites and Platforms

One alternative is to prohibit steering on websites and platforms that structure our intimate lives. Most major dating websites and apps permit users to both identify their race and screen potential dates on the basis of it. Consider in this regard Okcupid.com and Match.com, two of the most popular online sites.[82] These sites do not just ask users for their name or to upload a photograph. They also ask users to disclose their race. I'm not aware of any dating website or platform where users create profiles that does not ask for this racial information.

---

[82] www.match.com; www.okcupid.com. Match.com lists the following racial groups (allowing users to select more than one): Asian, Black/African descent, East Indian, Latino/ Hispanic, Middle Eastern, Native American, Pacific Islander, White/Caucasian, Other. Okcupid.com lists the following groups (also allowing users to select more than one): Asian, Black, Hispanic/Latin, Indian, Middle Eastern, Native American, Pacific Islander, White, Other.

eHarmony, for instance, asks, "What ethnicities would you be willing to accept as matches?" and "How important is your match's ethnicity?"[83] You must answer these questions before you will be matched by the platform. Elizabeth Emens, who highlights the way in which racial discrimination intersects with our intimate decisions, makes clear that "all these sites allow you to indicate your racial preferences or search by race. All ask for your race, and some require you to state it."[84]

So, it is not just that these platforms ask for and then disclose a user's race. They also allow us to search for and therefore exclude potential romantic and sexual partners of a particular race. Similarly, by disclosing the race of the area or neighborhood, Movoto.com made it easy for users to discriminate on the basis of race in their housing decisions. It made it easy for them to avoid areas that were racially diverse. In doing so, the website facilitated racism in our housing decisions. The website made it easy for users to avoid living next to those of a particular race. That is why the Fair Housing Alliance said that this kind of racial steering must stop. Steering facilitates racism by making it easy to discriminate on the basis of race.

Whereas Movoto.com structured how we found housing in a way that facilitated racial discrimination, dating sites structure our intimate, digital lives in a way that does the same. They make it easy for us to discriminate on the basis of race. The ease with which users can racially discriminate is noteworthy on these sites.

The argument of this chapter suggests that we should prohibit these sites from steering us to discriminate on the basis of race in our intimate, digital lives. Although he does not frame the issue as one involving racial steering, Russell Robinson suggests that "[l]awmakers might consider regulating web site design decisions that produce, exacerbate, or facilitate racial preferences."[85] Such regulations could include prohibiting users from searching on the basis of race.[86] I argue, in turn, that these sites are digital public accommodations and therefore subject to the ban on steering.

---

[83] Emens 2009: 1322, fn. 59.
[84] Emens 2009: 1322.
[85] Robinson 2007: 2794.
[86] Robinson 2007: 2794.

Dating Websites and Platforms as Digital Public Accommodations

Once we recognize sexual racism, the very decisions that stand to create the intimate sphere now become sites of justice: in this case, the way websites permit race-based searches. Taking seriously the democratic reclassification approach referenced above means that we should include online dating websites and smart phone applications as within the boundary of justice. They facilitate the terms of social cooperation. Consider that a Pew research survey finds that 38 percent of all American singles use either the Internet or cell phone apps to meet others.[87] And 5 percent of those who are currently married or in long-term relationships met their partners online.[88] Of those who have been together for ten years or less, the percentage that met online is even higher at 11 percent.[89] As more individuals conduct their intimate lives digitally, these websites will become even more ubiquitous platforms for social cooperation. Romantic pairings are more likely to occur via the digital world. Our social interactions are constantly being mediated by these sites.

Because intimacy is a capability central to human dignity and a social primary good, dating websites act unjustly by structuring this opportunity in a way that facilitates racism. Making it easy for us to discriminate on the basis of race in our intimate decisions is wrong. Websites should stop steering. If websites could not steer users to discriminate, users may still end up doing so. In the same way, the fact that Movoto.com stopped disclosing racial demographics did not mean that all users suddenly stopped discriminating. But, at the very least, the website stopped encouraging and facilitating housing discrimination. Dating websites such as OkCupid and Match.com should do the same. Prohibiting this kind of steering may be one possible way society can address sexual racism.

In fact, there is also a legal basis for treating these websites as digital public accommodations and thereby subject to a ban on steering. As outlined in the last chapter, some state public accommodations laws

---

[87] www.pewinternet.org/2013/10/21/online-dating-relationships/
[88] www.pewinternet.org/2013/10/21/online-dating-relationships/
[89] www.pewinternet.org/2013/10/21/online-dating-relationships/

cover any kind of business that extends an invitation to the public to join. Under these laws that enforce an expansive view of justice, Eric McKinley, a gay man, and Linda Carlson, a lesbian woman, filed suit against eHarmony.com under the New Jersey and California public accommodations law, respectively.[90]

eHarmony.com, one of the most popular commercial online dating websites, distinguishes itself from other sites by providing an algorithm that proclaims to match individuals on twenty-nine dimensions.[91] The website boasts that it is responsible for nearly 4 percent of US marriages.[92] eHarmony only provided its matching services for oppo-site-sex couples. The site did not allow individuals such as McKinley and Carlson to sign up for its services, because they were seeking a same-sex partner. These lawsuits alleged that the platform discrimi-nated on the basis of sexual orientation. Drawing on the relevant public accommodation laws, McKinley and Carlson sued the website for discriminating against gays and lesbians. Both the New Jersey and California cases were ultimately settled without eHarmony.com admit-ting fault or liability. As part of the settlement, eHarmony.com agreed to operate a companion website, called Compatible Partners.com, that would be available to gays and lesbians seeking to find a match with someone of the same sex.[93]

Although the courts did not reach a decision on the merits, these complaints make out a claim that eHarmony.com and by implication other dating sites and platforms are public accommodations under state civil rights law. eHarmony, Match.com, OkCupid.com, Airbnb, and Uber are all digital public accommodations. As such, they are within the boundary of justice and should therefore be subject to the ban on digital steering. The lawsuit against eHarmony makes clear that these sites are already within the boundary of the law. The fact that they structure how we find intimacy rather than employment (LinkedIn) or housing (Airbnb) should not make a difference. If websites that

---

[90] www.cnn.com/2008/LIVING/11/19/eharmony.same.sex.matches/index.html; www
.sfgate.com/bayarea/article/CALIFORNIA-EHarmony-accused-of-discrimination
-2557745.php
[91] www.eharmony.com
[92] www.eharmony.com
[93] www.cnn.com/2008/LIVING/11/19/eharmony.same.sex.matches/index.html

structure the latter are subject to regulation, so too are websites that
structure the former. This book builds on the way civil rights law and,
in particular, laws from California and New Jersey thereby enlarge the
boundary of racial justice.

Racial Advertising as a Form of Steering

We can support the ban on steering by considering that the law already
bans racial advertising. It treats racial advertising as another kind of
steering. The FHA makes it unlawful under section 3604 (c):

> To make, print, or publish, or cause to be made, printed, or pub-
> lished any notice, statement, or advertisement, with respect to the
> sale or rental of a dwelling that indicates any preference, limitation,
> or discrimination based on race, color, religion, sex, handicap,
> familial status, or national origin, or an intention to make any
> such preference, limitation, or discrimination.

In *U.S.* v. *Hunter* (Fourth Circuit 1972), the Fourth Circuit held that
the FHA may prohibit a newspaper from running a racially discriminatory advertisement. In *Hunter*, the Attorney General instituted an
action under the provision above against Bill R. Hunter, editor and
publisher of *The Courier*, a weekly newspaper with a circulation of
29,000 in Prince George County in Maryland. A single family homeowner wanted to rent out his furnished basement. He took out two
similar advertisements in the newspaper, both of which specified that
there was a furnished basement apartment and that this was a "white
home."[94] The district court noted that the homeowner included the
language of a "white home" in the advertisement, because he had no
intention of renting his basement home to someone nonwhite. He
figured there was "no use making them spend money to call here or
come here when I'm not going to rent to them."[95]

The appeals court noted that although the FHA prohibits landlords
from discriminating on the basis of race, the law contains an exemption
for homeowners who seek to rent out rooms or living quarters in which

[94] *Hunter* (4th Cir. 1972) at 209.
[95] *Hunter* (D. Md. 1971) at 532.

they also live.[96] This is called the "Mrs. Murphy exemption," so named for a hypothetical elderly woman who has converted a portion of her home into a rental apartment. The Fair Housing Act of 1968 exempts dwellings "occupied or intended to be occupied by no more than four families living independently of each other, if the owner actually maintains and occupies one of such living quarters as his residence."[97]

Given that kind of exemption, the appeals court acknowledged that the homeowner in this case "is free to indulge his discriminatory preferences in selling or renting that dwelling."[98] The homeowner is free to turn away all applicants who are not white and who happen to come to his door seeking to rent his furnished basement apartment. The FHA exempts only this particular kind of homeowner from the ban on racism in finding housing.

Even still, the court makes clear that the FHA does not "give [the homeowner] a right to publicize his intent to so discriminate."[99] This means that even when the law may permit individuals to engage in racial discrimination, it prohibits newspapers from facilitating that decision. Whereas the FHA exempts the homeowner from the ban on discrimination, the ban on racial advertising applies to everyone, all landlords and homeowners.

> The Act specifically states that [the ban on racial advertising] shall apply to sellers or lessors of dwellings even though they are otherwise exempted by [the FHA]. The draftsmen of the Act could not have made more explicit their purpose to bar all discriminatory advertisements, even those printed or caused to be printed by persons who are permitted ... to discriminate in selling or renting.[100]

This ban on racial advertising applies to everyone in the housing market, ensuring that individuals may not use a newspaper to facilitate their racial preferences. This ban, in turn, restricts what newspapers may do. Bill R. Hunter may very well abhor racial discrimination. The ad in question did not make any kind of false claim. It expressed

[96] *Hunter* (4th Cir. 1972) at 213–214.
[97] Fair Housing Act (1968), Section 3603 (b)(2).
[98] *Hunter* (4th Cir. 1972) at 213.
[99] *Hunter* (4th Cir. 1972) at 213.
[100] *Hunter* (4th Cir. 1972) at 213–214.

the genuine racial preference of the homeowner, a preference that the Mrs. Murphy legal exemption even allows him to act upon. Still, the prohibition on racial advertising restricts what newspapers and individuals like Bill R. Hunter may do.

So, even if the law may allow us to indulge our discriminatory preference in finding intimacy, this does not mean that the law should allow us to advertise and facilitate this preference. But that is exactly what dating sites and platforms do. They make it easy for us to discriminate on the basis of race in finding intimacy. Just as a newspaper is not allowed to facilitate the homeowner's decision to discriminate (the FHA bans racial advertising), sites such as OkCupid and Match.com should also not facilitate our decisions to discriminate on the basis of race. Allowing users to search and filter on the basis of race is a blatant way these sites encourage racial discrimination, stereotyping, and intersectionality. Banning that practice is akin to the law's existing ban on racial advertising.[101]

Perhaps in *Hunter* the newspaper editor should have known better. After all, the racially discriminatory advertisement used the words "white home." But in *Ragin* v. *New York Times* (Second Circuit 1991), the court held that a newspaper could not publish advertisements that contained actors or models that were predominantly white. Here, black prospective home buyers sued the *New York Times* for running housing advertisements that featured

> thousands of human models of whom virtually none were black . . . [W]hile many of the white human models depict representative or potential home owners or renters, the few blacks represented are usually depicted as building maintenance employees, doormen, entertainers, sports figures, small children or cartoon characters.[102]

The *New York Times* argued that these advertisements did not express a racial preference as defined under the FHA. Unlike *Hunter*, there was no unambiguous preference for individuals of a particular race – "white home." The *Times* argued that these advertisements were not "facially discriminatory" and they had "no other evidence of a discriminatory intent" by those who paid for the advertisements in the paper.[103]

---

[101] See also Note 1994.
[102] *Ragin* (2nd Cir. 1991) at 999–1000.
[103] *Ragin* (2nd Cir. 1991) at 999.

Still, the court held that the FHA restricts the *Times* from publishing this advertisement. Just because the *Times* does not see a racial preference does not mean one does not exist. The court reasoned:

> Ordinary readers may reasonably infer a racial message from advertisements that are more subtle than the hypothetical swastika or burning cross, and we read the word "preference" to describe any ad that would discourage an ordinary reader of a particular race from answering it.[104]

According to the court, an "ordinary reader" is one who realizes that racial preferences need not be explicit; they may very well be implicit but equally unlawful. The court does not say that recognizing this kind of racial bias is something that is an extraordinary task. Rather, it is an ordinary one.

Steering may also be implicit. If dating websites and platforms use mainly white models to promote their matchmaking services or require users to disclose their name, this may have the effect of steering us to discriminate on the basis of race. Once we are attuned to the way in which websites facilitate sexual racism, cases like *Ragin* suggest that this method of facilitation need not be explicit.

Moreover, both cases also make clear that the ban on racial advertising does not violate the First Amendment. In *Pittsburgh Press Co. v. Human Relations Comm'n*, (1973), the Court upheld a city ordinance that prohibited any advertisement indicating that an employer intends to discriminate on the basis of sex. *Ragin*, quoting *Pittsburg Press*, held that

> [a]ny First Amendment interest which might be served by advertising an ordinary commercial proposal and which might arguably outweigh the governmental interest supporting the regulation is altogether absent when the commercial activity itself is illegal and the restriction on advertising is incidental to a valid limitation on economic activity.[105]

And *Hunter* upheld the constitutionality of this ban on racial advertising even though the FHA permits the landlord who took out the advertisement in the newspaper to discriminate. According to *Hunter*:

---

[104] *Ragin* (2nd Cir. 1991) at 999–1000.
[105] *Ragin* (2nd Cir. 1991), quoting *Pittsburg Press* (1973) at 389.

> [An] unbroken line of authority from the Supreme Court down . . .
> distinguishes between the expression of ideas protected by the First
> Amendment and commercial advertising in a business context.
> [citations omitted] It is now well settled that, while "freedom of
> communicating information and disseminating opinion" enjoys the
> fullest protection of the First Amendment, "the Constitution
> imposes no such restraint on government as respects purely com-
> mercial advertising."[106]

We can understand this ban on racial advertising as another way the law
prohibits racial steering. Just as a newspaper may not facilitate racial
discrimination by allowing a landlord to advertise his discriminatory
preference, as digital public accommodations, online dating sites should
not be allowed to facilitate racial discrimination by their users. That
facilitation or steering is part of the website's business or commercial
model. Like the commercial advertising in *Hunter* or *Ragin*, it too occurs
in a business context. Websites should not serve as intermediaries that
allow us to facilitate racial discrimination, stereotyping, and intersectionality. The law should prohibit these websites from facilitating racial
discrimination in finding intimacy just as the law prohibits newspapers
from facilitating discrimination in finding housing.

Facilitating Sexual Racism

Permitting users to search on the basis of race on these online dating
websites facilitates sexual racism. It makes it easy for users to discriminate on the basis of race and therefore exclude potential romantic or
intimate partners in ways that further racial inequality and stereotypes.
As noted in Chapter 1, Elizabeth Anderson adopts an actual society
approach that considers racial integration a requirement of justice.
According to her, there is a moral imperative for us to ensure that
"members of different races form friendships, date, marry, bear children or adopt different race children."[107] Anderson argues that an
"ideal of integration" challenges segregation. She defines "segregation" as embodying the "structures and norms of spatial and social
separation" and dictating the terms of racial interaction based on

---

[106] *Hunter* (4th Cir. 1972) at 211.
[107] Anderson 2013 [2010]: 116.

"domination and subordination."[108] Again, the argument of this book assumes a less demanding claim, one where we, at the very least, do not further racial inequality and stereotypes. That is, even if society does not go so far as to require integration, there is at least a requirement not to further or facilitate segregation.

But that is exactly what the websites referenced in this chapter do by steering us to discriminate on the basis of race. Making it easy for users to discriminate, these websites and platforms reinforce the two pillars of segregation as outlined by Anderson. Such searches make it easy to ensure a norm of "separation" and permit interaction in ways that affirm racial stereotypes. These search engines allow us to avoid those of a different race. We can ensure that we do not even see (let alone respond to) profiles of those whose race we disfavor. These search engines also allow us to focus on those racial groups we do fetishize. This kind of steering facilitates segregation by reinforcing social separation and subordination.

The argument of this chapter suggests that we should treat Match.com or OkCupid in the same way as we would Airbnb, Uber, or Movoto.com. Just as the latter sites should not steer their users to discriminate on the basis of race, the former should not as well. Steering in all these cases structures our private, digital world to make it easy to discriminate on the basis of race and thereby further racial inequality.

Title II of the Civil Rights Act of 1964, which prohibits racial discrimination in public accommodation, states that the "provisions of this title shall not apply to a private club or other establishment not in fact open to the public."[109] This law excludes as public accommodations those establishments that are not in fact open to the public. I'm not sure how to define "not in fact open to the public" in some clear way. But at the least, websites and platforms do not fit this definition. Websites like Amazon, Uber, and Movoto are not private clubs but large, powerful, and profitable businesses that structure how we interact with others. So too are dating websites. Consider that Match Group, Inc. is the corporation that owns not only OkCupid and Match.com but also other dating platforms like Tinder. In fact, they have a portfolio of forty-five brands,

[108] Anderson 2013 [2010]: 112.
[109] 42 U.S.C. § 2000a(e).

all designed to manage their users' "likelihood of a romantic connection."[110] The Match Group offers dating products in 42 languages and across more than 190 countries. It had a revenue of 457 million dollars in December 2018.[111] These are for-profit businesses that seek to increase the number of people that use their services. The fact that some of these sites concern our intimate lives does not change their status as public accommodations under the law, providing their services to the public.

Moreover, as outlined in the last chapter, Congress has the power to ban racial steering on websites and platforms. Congress has the power to combat digital racism, because the digital marketplace is a form of commerce that is not just interstate but global. Banning steering may not end sexual racism, but it will end the way in which websites allow their users to filter and search on the basis of race, thereby furthering racial discrimination, stereotypes, and intersectionality. If all of Match Group's forty-five platforms stopped steering, this would structure our private, digital world in a way that would be more just. By enlarging the boundary of racial justice to include intimacy, this chapter argues that justice demands at least that.

---

[110] www.reuters.com/finance/stocks/financial-highlights/MTCH.O
[111] www.reuters.com/finance/stocks/financial-highlights/MTCH.O

5 REPRODUCTIVE MARKET RACISM

This chapter shows that racism occurs in the reproductive market. In particular, it shows that reproductive banks provide buyers the option to segregate on the basis of race. I define "segregation" here as exclusion on the basis of race in order to avoid racial diversity or integration. The school in *Runyon*, for instance, engaged in segregation. It excluded black applicants in order to avoid creating a racially diverse or integrated study body. The school made clear to the parents that "only members of the Caucasian race were accepted."[1] The school excluded on the basis of race in order to ensure that its student body would remain racially homogenous.

In selling sperm and ova, this chapter shows that reproductive banks also provide buyers the option to exclude donors on the basis of race. Reproductive banks provide this option by discriminating against potential donors on the basis of race and steering buyers to do the same. Most notably, these banks engage in racial steering by disclosing the race of the donor. In doing so, they provide buyers the option to form a biological family that is racially homogenous. This allows buyers the option to avoid racially integrating their families. This is how banks sell segregation, or so this chapter argues. I argue that this practice of selling segregation is wrong and unlawful.

Most scholarly work on race and the family is about the state's decision to match children with parents willing to adopt.[2] This work is about whether the government should discriminate on the basis of race

---

[1] *Runyon* at 165.
[2] See, e.g., Bartholet 1999: 134–137, Bowen 1988, Howe 1997, Kennedy 2003: ch. 10.

in matching children with prospective parents. This book discusses racial discrimination outside the governmental or public sphere. It is not about what the government should do. It is about what the reproductive market should do. And this chapter will argue that the reproductive market should not sell segregation. This does not mean that the arguments made in the adoption context are not useful here (I revisit one of these arguments below). The issue here is not about adoption. It is about expanding the boundary of racial justice to include our decisions about forming our biological family.

This chapter, in turn, is in six sections. First, I explain the importance of the liberty to form a biological family, something that the market for gametes in the United States currently provides. The liberty to buy sperm and eggs assists many of us to create a family who may find it difficult to do so without a reproductive market. Second, I show that racism happens in this market. In particular, the combination of discrimination and steering underwrites the claim that reproductive banks are in the business of selling segregation. Third, I draw on both the ideal society and actual society approaches to argue that selling segregation is wrong. Fourth, I argue that selling segregation is unlawful. Fifth, I argue that the Constitution forbids enforcing this kind of sale. Finally, I consider the family as an important site of desegregation given the argument of this chapter.

THE LIBERTY TO FORM A BIOLOGICAL FAMILY THROUGH THE MARKET

Some argue that the very existence of a market in reproductive materials or gametes – like a market in organs or surrogacy – is wrong.[3] Michael Sandel, for instance, argues that there is a problem if individuals may purchase gametes based on various characteristics. This, as he suggests, raises the troubling case of "designer babies."[4] He has even suggested that a market for sperm may corrupt our notions of

---

[3] See, e.g., Anderson 1990, 2000; Radin 2000; Sandel 2009, 2012; *see also* Walzer 1983: 100–108.
[4] Sandel 2009: 127.

fatherhood by commodifying male reproduction.[5] And it is worth noting that only in 1973 did the Commissioners on Uniform State Laws, the body that provides model legislation for states, promulgate the Uniform Parentage Act. That Act importantly affirmed donor insemination as a legally recognizable way to establish parentage.[6] Before then, the only acceptable way to become a legal parent was through natural insemination.

Although these objections to a market in gametes may be note-worthy, I do not engage them here. This is for two main reasons. First, the liberty to form a biological family by purchasing gametes already exists in the United States. The main individuals in the repro-ductive market are reproductive banks and buyers. Banks sell the reproductive material and buyers purchase them. Selling gametes (or eggs and sperm) is a profitable business. The market for gametes is almost a 180-million-dollar industry and part of a larger multibillion-dollar infertility industry in the United States. In addition to the buying and selling of gametes, this industry includes fertility drugs, clinics, reproductive banks, and surrogacy programs.[7] As technology gets better and more sophisticated – reducing the cost of accessing this market, the infertility industry is sure to become even larger and more profitable.

In fact, the United States may have one of the most laissez-faire markets in gametes.[8] There are no federal or state laws banning the anonymous donation of sperm or the purchase of egg donations. In contrast, the United Kingdom and Canada have regulations on the sale of gametes.[9] This is why many individuals from other countries come to the United States to access this market for gametes and assisted reproductive technologies.[10] One scholar even refers to the market for gametes as the "Wild West" of fertility.[11]

Second, and more importantly, I assume that the liberty to form a biological family by being able to buy gametes is important. The

[5] Sandel 2000: 103.
[6] www.uniformlaws.org/Act.aspx?title=Parentage%20Act%20(1973)
[7] Marketdata Enterprises 2013: Press Release.
[8] See generally Mutcherson 2012.
[9] Mutcherson 2012: 352–364.
[10] Mutcherson 2012: 352–364.
[11] See, e.g., Coeytaux et al. 2011, Dresser 2000, Leigh 2006.

majority of births in the United States still occur within families that are
heterosexual and married. Even though most individuals may not use
this market, it is important to many who may otherwise find it difficult
to start a biological family naturally. The market for gametes provides
individuals an opportunity to do so. As Martha Ertman argues, this
market

> provide[s] unique opportunities for law and culture to recognize
> that people form families in different ways. If state or federal law;
> rather than the laws of supply and demand, determines who can
> have children using reproductive technologies, then many single
> and gay people likely will be excluded from this important life
> experience ... Gamete markets allow some minorities – those who
> by virtue of their numbers are unlikely to obtain legal rights and
> protection through the legislative process – to skirt the majoritarian
> morality that would otherwise prevent them from forming
> families.[12]

Those individuals include "many single and gay people" (including
myself) who are unable to form a family without access to a market for
gametes. John Harris defends this as a right to reproductive liberty,
recognizing that the

> freedom to pass on one's genes is widely perceived to be an import-
> ant value; it is natural to see this freedom as a plausible dimension of
> reproductive liberty, not least because so many people and agencies
> have been attracted by the idea of the special nature of genes and
> have linked the procreative imperative to the genetic imperative.[13]

Some individuals in forming a family may not be able pass down their
genetic information or they may decline to do so. Perhaps they seek to
pass down their partner's genetic or biological information. I assume
for purposes of this chapter that the reproductive market is valuable,
because it enables many of us to exercise an "important life experience" of passing down our genetic information in forming a family.
The liberty to buy gametes provides a range of individuals the liberty to
do so and to start a family.

---

[12] Ertman 2010: 23.
[13] Harris 2007: 2.

Unfortunately, according to the Ethics Committee of the American Society for Reproductive Medicine, individuals in the market for gametes sometimes discriminate on the basis of sexual orientation or marital status. For instance, banks sometimes refuse to assist or to sell gametes to those who are single or who are gay and lesbian.[14] The Committee Report concludes:

> Although professional autonomy in deciding who to treat is also an important value, we believe that there is an ethical obligation, and in some states there is a legal duty, to treat all persons equally, regardless of their marital status or sexual orientation.[15]

The Report makes clear that limiting the liberty to form a biological family on the basis of sexual orientation or marital status is wrong. Reproductive banks should treat all buyers equally. That informs the significance of the liberty to form a biological family through the reproductive market.

RACIAL DISCRIMINATION AND STEERING IN THE GAMETE MARKET

Dov Fox instructively points out that the market in gametes is like any other:

> Prospective parents and sperm donors transact at arm's length through a corporate broker who does not ordinarily permit either party even to learn the name of the other, let alone to have interpersonal contact. The market in donor insemination mediates reproduction to eliminate the intimacy that both typifies the relationship between consensual procreative partners, and also grounds the associational autonomy interests at stake in the act of procreation.[16]

This market allows individuals to form a biological family who may find it difficult to do so without such a market. And just as racism occurs in the market for employment, housing, and other goods and services, it

[14] ASRM 2013: 1525.
[15] ASRM 2013: 1524.
[16] Fox 2009: 1883.

also occurs in the market for gametes. Other scholars mentioned in this chapter also raise concerns with the role of race in the reproductive market.[17] Although these arguments also take aim at the practice of disclosing a donor's race, they do not focus on the way in which reproductive banks sell segregation by discriminating and steering on the basis of race.

Reproductive Banks Discriminate

Reproductive banks discriminate on the basis of race in buying gametes from donors and often advertise this fact openly. These banks act as brokers or intermediaries, buying gametes from donors and then selling them to interested buyers. In soliciting gametes, and in particular eggs, these banks specify a range of donor characteristics, which often include race. For instance, Craigslist advertisements in major cities solicit donors from particular racial groups. Physician Surrogacy, a reproductive bank, says that egg donors may earn $7,000 to $25,000 per cycle of donation and up to $100,000 per year. The advertisement states that the "criteria" are "19 to 29 years old," "Healthy Lifestyle," and a "Non-Smoker." The bottom of the advertisement states that "Chinese, Japanese, and Caucasian egg donors are in high demand!"[18] Another reproductive bank, A Jewish Blessing, LLC, makes clear that a qualifying donor must in addition to other characteristics have "Jewish ethnic heritage on Mother and/or Fathers side of their family."[19] In another advertisement, a self-described "global medical service company" says they are seeking "Healthy Asian or Caucasian women" for their egg donation program.[20] According to a study of almost 200 clinic and agency websites, only about half actively recruited donors online. Of those that do recruit online, about 34 percent mentioned ethnicity.[21] This kind of racial

[17] See, e.g., Fox 2009, Quiroga 2007, Russell 2015.
[18] https://boston.craigslist.org/gbs/hea/d/san-diego-egg-donor-needed-earn-7k-25k/6819565187.html (accessed on March 9, 2019) (screen shot on file with author).
[19] https://boston.craigslist.org/gbs/etc/d/boston-jewish-egg-donors-needed-apply/6824146148.html (accessed on March 9, 2019) (screen shot on file with author).
[20] https://newyork.craigslist.org/fct/tlg/d/stamford-egg-donor-and-surrogate-wanted/6818661265.html (accessed on March 9, 2019) (screen shot on file with author).
[21] Keehn, Holwell, Abdul-Karim, Chin, Leu, Sauer, and Klitzman 2012.

advertising, which the law prohibits in the housing market, is so common in the reproductive market that one advertisement on Craigslist for egg donors says in the subject line "All Ethnicities," making clear that this bank does not discriminate.[22]

In soliciting donors of one race, these banks can refuse to contract with prospective donors of another. This is most salient in the case of egg donation where the process of removing eggs is often costly and invasive. As a result, banks offer prospective egg donors more money than their prospective sperm counterparts. Egg donors can receive upwards of thousands of dollars per cycle.[23] In her book *Sex Cells: The Medical Market for Eggs and Sperm*, Rene Almeling concludes that for "the vast majority of egg and sperm donors" she interviewed "their initial interest in donation was sparked by the prospect of financial compensation, which is understandable given their life circumstances."[24] A prospective donor may meet every other physical, educational, and professional requirement but the reproductive bank could still decide refuse to contract with them simply based on their race.

Reproductive Banks Steer

Reproductive banks do not just discriminate on the basis of race. They also steer, making it easy for buyers to discriminate on the basis of race. Even if some banks do not advertise or even discriminate in contracting with donors, these banks still steer. Sometimes, this steering is outright explicit. For instance, the Sperm Bank of California has a section on its website titled "Choosing a Donor."[25] Directed at the prospective buyer, that section states:

> Our goal is to help contribute to your future child's and family's long-term well-being. In this spirit we present reasons to consider selecting a donor who looks like you, your partner, and the people who will surround your child as they grow up.[26]

[22] https://seattle.craigslist.org/see/etc/d/become-an-egg-donor-all-ethnicities/6827809415.html (accessed on March 9, 2019) (screen shot on file with author).
[23] Almeling 2011: 119.
[24] Almeling 2011: 112.
[25] www.thespermbankofca.org/choosing-donor-0 (webpage on file with author).
[26] www.thespermbankofca.org/tsbcfile/choosing-ethnicity-my-donor (webpage on file with author).

The website encourages segregation by steering buyers who already live in racially homogenous communities and families to avoid racially integrating their families. The reproductive bank encourages buyers to select a donor who matches their race, thereby ensuring that their biological family will remain racially homogenous.

> Having an ethnically different child means that the child will experience the world in ways in which the parent(s) cannot always prepare for or adequately understand. For these reasons, while looks or color should not matter, they matter.[27]

The website points out that some adults who grew up as a result of the donor insemination process through the sperm bank resembled

> no one in their family – their ethnicity matched only their donor. All described strong attachment to their family, but also uncomfortable instances of difference. Some felt outed as being donor-conceived when they wanted privacy; all were questioned repeatedly about their family.[28]

The website steers buyers to pick a donor who will ensure that the buyer's family remains racially homogenous. According to the website, this can be important to "your future child's and family's long-term well-being." The website does not require that buyers choose gametes that match their race. Toward the end of the page, the website provides resources regarding transracial adoption:

> We acknowledge that the donor experience is not the same as adoption and at the same time there are enough parallels that we wanted to provide some transracial adoption resources to help families considering an ethnically different donor and for those families reading this who may have already made that choice.[29]

This kind of steering encourages, but not does not require, buyers to discriminate on the basis of race in selecting a donor.

---

[27] www.thespermbankofca.org/tsbcfile/choosing-ethnicity-my-donor (webpage on file with author).

[28] www.thespermbankofca.org/tsbcfile/choosing-ethnicity-my-donor#Why%20Ethnicity (webpage on file with author).

[29] www.thespermbankofca.org/tsbcfile/choosing-ethnicity-my-donor#Why%20Ethnicity

Even if a bank does not engage in this kind of steering, banks routinely disclose the race of the donor to buyers. By so disclosing the race of the donor, reproductive banks also make it easy for us to discriminate on the basis of race. This is a form of racial steering. That is, these banks take it upon themselves to classify the gametes on the basis of race. These banks create search engines on their websites that permit buyers to search, filter, and ultimately exclude donors on the basis of race. Although he does not frame the issue in terms of racial steering, Fox also suggests that by disclosing the donor's race, reproductive banks convey the "troubling notion that same-race families should be preferred to mixed-race ones."[30]

For instance, the California Cryobank, one of the world's leading sperm banks, allows customers seeking to purchase sperm to search and filter by a range of ten or so characteristics, including height, educational level, area of study, and ethnic origin.[31] Under "ethnic origin," they list the following categories: American Indian or Alaska Native, Asian, Black or African American, Caucasian, East Indian, Hispanic or Latino, Middle Eastern or Arabic, Mixed or Multi-Ethnic, Native Hawaiian or Other Pacific Island, and South American Indian. It is worth noting that on its homepage, Cryobank prioritizes hair color, eye color, and ethnicity as the three main searchable criteria. Another seller of sperm and ova, Fairfax Cryobank[32] and Eggbank,[33] also permits customers to screen on a range of characteristics, including height, education, and race. And under "race," Fairfax lists only five choices: Caucasian, Asian, Latino, Black, or Multi.

These kinds of racial search engines are common in the gamete market. In fact, I'm not aware of any such bank that does not allow buyers to search and exclude on the basis of race in this way. Banks actively classify gametes on the basis of race in order to create these searchable categories.

---

[30] Fox 2009: 1891.
[31] https://cryobank.com/
[32] https://fairfaxcryobank.com/
[33] www.fairfaxeggbank.com/

Selling Segregation

This combined practice of discrimination and steering means that reproductive banks are selling buyers the option to segregate. Again, I define segregation as exclusion on the basis of race in order to avoid racial diversity or integration. As intermediaries, these banks are like real estate agents, connecting prospective buyers with donors. These banks discriminate against donors on the basis of race and then classify the reproductive materials in light of this racial discrimination. In selling gametes to buyers, these banks disclose this classification to buyers. With this information, buyers can decide not to purchase a particular sperm or egg, simply based on the donor's race. In doing so, buyers can ensure that their biological family remains racially homogenous. Buyers can avoid racially integrating their families, because reproductive banks provide them the option to exclude racially diverse donors. This is how these banks sell segregation.

In considering the argument here, it is worth pointing out that buyers in this market are predominantly white. Middle- to upper-class whites are more than twice as likely as their black and Hispanic counterparts to access fertility services.[34] Another study of infertility services in Massachusetts, a state that mandates comprehensive insurance coverage for such services, found similar racial disparities. The authors conclude that the "majority of individuals accessing those services" are "Caucasian, highly educated, and wealthy."[35]

Another study by Cynthia R. Daniels and Erin Heidt-Forsythe surveyed 1,156 sperm donors from the top twelve sperm banks in the United States. That survey found that 80 percent of this sperm donor population was white, 3.5 percent black, 2.8 percent Latino, 8.6 percent Asian, and 4.7 percent other.[36] A study surveying 359 egg donors from eight fertility clinics revealed similar kinds of demographics: 76 percent of this egg donor population was white, 6.1 percent black, 5.29 percent Latina, 6.1 percent Asian, and 6.4 percent other.[37] Daniels and Heidt-Forsythe suggest that sperm banks may be "less inclined to provide

---

[34] Chandra et al. 2005: 29–30.
[35] Jain and Hornstein 2005.
[36] Daniels and Heidt-Forsythe 2012: 724.
[37] Daniels and Heidt-Forsythe 2012: 730.

semen from nonwhite donors based on lack of consumer demand."[38] And Daniels and Heidt-Forsythe also note that the "egg donation industry is increasingly targeting consumers of color," to meet the demands of a "more diverse customer base."[39] By providing buyers an option to segregate, the industry will then be able to provide even more buyers the option to do so.

SELLING SEGREGATION IS WRONG

According to the ideal and actual society approaches, I argue that this practice of selling segregation is wrong. It is also based on a discredited biological view of race. Before considering this practice in light of those two methodologies of justice, I explain why the practice of providing voters a political option to segregate is unjust, something that the Court struck down as unconstitutional in *Anderson* v. *Martin* (1964).

Anderson v. *Martin* (1964)

In *Anderson*, the state of Louisiana sought to provide voters a political option to segregate. The Court invalidated the law, reasoning that by providing this kind of option to segregate, the state violates the Equal Protection Clause of the Fourteenth Amendment. Louisiana passed a law that required election ballots to disclose the race of the candidate. It required all candidates to identify their race on the ballot. In effect, the state provided voters an option to segregate. This kind of blatant steering made it easy for voters to discriminate on the basis of race and select officials who were of the same race. In doing so, the state of Louisiana provided voters the option to ensure that their public officials remain racially homogenous.

In striking the law down as unconstitutional, the Court concedes:

At the outset, it is well that we point out what this case does not involve. It has nothing whatever to do with the right of a citizen to cast his vote for whomever he chooses and for whatever reason he

---

[38] Daniels and Heidt-Forsythe 2012: 724.
[39] Daniels and Heidt-Forsythe 2012: 724.

pleases, or to receive all information concerning a candidate which is necessary to a proper exercise of his franchise.[40]

The law did not interfere with anyone's liberty to run for office or to vote. The law did not discriminate against anyone on the basis of race. Nevertheless, the Court strikes down the law as unconstitutional, reasoning that "by placing a racial label on a candidate at the most crucial stage in the electoral process – the instant before the vote is cast – the State furnishes a vehicle by which racial prejudice may be so aroused as to operate against one group because of race and for another."[41] The state of Louisiana violated the Constitution by providing voters the option to segregate.

In doing so, the Court's reasoning informs the ideal and actual society approaches that motivate the argument of this book. First, the Court holds that this kind of political option to segregate is unconstitutional, because the state "indicates that a candidate's race or color is an important – perhaps paramount – consideration in the citizen's choice, which may decisively influence the citizen to cast his ballot along racial lines."[42] The law's "vice lies not in the resulting injury, but in the placing of the power of the State behind a racial classification that induces racial prejudice at the polls."[43] This informs the commitment to the ideal society approach. In a society fully complying with the principles of justice, the race of a candidate for public office should be morally irrelevant. Voters may care about the candidate's party affiliation or their policy proposals or even their character. But in an ideal society, voters would not care about their race. Again, this is why the 2016 Republican Party platform says that "[m]erit and hard work should determine advancement in our society." Taking seriously the idea that merit and hard work and not one's race should matter in society means that it is wrong for Louisiana to mention, let alone list, a candidate's race on the ballot.

Second, the Court acknowledges the "interplay of governmental and private action" in providing this option.[44] The Court references

[40] *Anderson* (1964) at 402.
[41] *Anderson* (1964) at 402.
[42] *Anderson* (1964) at 402.
[43] *Anderson* (1964) at 402.
[44] *Anderson* (1964) at 403.

the actual society approach by recognizing that this kind of disclosure will further racial injustice rather than remedy it. Of course, it is possible that racial disclosure on the ballot could be used to further a more integrated democratic legislative body. After all, if it turns out racial minorities use the designation to vote in more racially diverse legislators, this may serve to remedy racial inequality. In fact, the Court remarks as much, suggesting that in a voting district where blacks predominate, "that race is likely to be favored by a racial designation on the ballot, while in those communities where other races are in the majority, they may be preferred."[45]

Nevertheless, the actual society approach does not engage in how individuals *could* respond to these racial disclosures but rather how they *actually* do so in our society. And that approach to justice reveals that this kind of steering through racial disclosure stands to further racial segregation rather than thwart it. Accordingly, the Court states:

> The 1960 amendment added "race" as the single item of informa-tion other than the name of the candidate. This addition to the statute in the light of "private attitudes and pressures" towards Negroes at the time of its enactment could only result in that "repressive effect" which "was brought to bear only after the exer-cise of governmental power."[46]

The Court recognizes that disclosing the race of the candidate in our actual society makes it easy for voters to act on their prejudicial views by picking representatives that will look like them. Or as Fox puts it, the ballot labels here "had the discriminatory effect of endorsing and facilitating harmful racial discrimination."[47]

This is why the 2016 Democratic Party platform seeks to "fight to end institutional and systemic racism in our society." The actual society approach realizes that racial disclosure in a society where racial inequality, stereotypes, or segregation still exists stands only to further this injustice. Whereas *Anderson* concerns steering in our public or political lives, the argument of this chapter is about steering in our private lives, and in particular the market for gametes. I argue that the

[45] *Anderson* (1964) at 402.
[46] *Anderson* (1964) at 403.
[47] Fox 2009: 1866.

practice at issue here, like the one in *Anderson*, is wrong on both the ideal and actual society approaches to justice.

The Ideal Society Approach

Buyers in this market do not simply buy eggs or sperm on the whim. This decision is one that is arrived at after deliberation and considera- tion. After all, buyers in this market seek to form a biological family. This is a conscious decision, one that requires thought and planning. Choosing the donor is choosing someone who will be, biologically, part of one's family. This is a consequential choice.

According to the ideal society approach, the donor's race would not matter. It would not matter whether our family turned out to be racially homogenous or racially diverse. There would be no stigma, disadvan- tage, or discrimination attached to a racially diverse family. In a well- ordered society, which is fully complying with the principles of justice, a family would be treated the same regardless of the donor's race. In such a society, race would not matter. According to a methodological assumption of full compliance, no one would be selling segregation, because no one would care about a donor's race.

This is why the ideal society approach says that society should treat race as a morally irrelevant characteristic. The practice of selling seg- regation is wrong, because it explicitly invokes a characteristic that should be irrelevant. Reproductive banks plainly violate this moral principle by discriminating against donors simply on the basis of their race. Refusing to contract with donors because the donor is of a different race is the very definition of racism under the ideal society approach.

This does not mean that in a well-ordered society, fully complying with the principles of justice, buyers will be indifferent about possible donors. These buyers may prefer a donor who is an artist. Or perhaps they seek a donor who is a surfer, an author, mountain climber, or a factory worker. They may seek someone who is an athlete or a scholar. Or perhaps they seek a donor who inspires them. The liberty to form a biological family may very well include the ability to choose a donor. After all, a buyer of gametes is seeking to create a future child who will be theirs biologically. Important here is that under an assumption of full compliance, buyers of gametes may care about many characteristics of the donor or none at all, but they would not care about his or her race.

In the same way, in a fully just society, prospective homeowners will not care about the race of their community or neighborhood. A homeowner may care about whether they live near certain kinds of restaurants or stores, schools, landmarks, or public transit options. They may care about whether the community is full of intellectuals or artists. As such, real estate agents may disclose and even steer on the basis of these characteristics. Again, the Realtor Code of Ethics permits realtors to "provide other demographic information."[48] But in a well-ordered society, homebuyers would not seek to segregate. We would not care in an ideal society whether the majority of inhabitants match or do not match our race. It simply would not matter in an ideal society whether the neighborhood is racially homogenous or racially diverse, and so too with families, if we take the ideal society approach seriously.

Reproductive banks also provide buyers information about a donor's appearance, including, for instance, their height or eye color. Buyers can search and filter on these categories too. And it's worth noting that some of these sperm and ova sites include pictures of the donors. The ideal society approach may also say society should treat certain aspects of one's physical appearance, including character-istics such as height or eye color, as morally irrelevant. In a well-ordered society, perhaps buyers would not be discriminating on these cate-gories either. This may suggest that banks act unjustly by allowing buyers to exclude donors on these characteristics as well or even showing buyers photographs of donors. The methodology of the ideal society approach may dictate that result, suggesting that injustice in this market may not simply or only be confined to race. In contrast, as I show below, the actual society approach would likely not dictate that result. So, if we simply adopted the ideal society approach, a just reproductive market may very well be one that does not allow buyers to discriminate on the basis of any characteristics that society should treat as morally irrelevant. But again, this book operates on a moral

---

[48] www.nar.realtor/sites/default/files/documents/2018-Code-of-Ethics-and-Standards-of-Practice.pdf

consensus that looks at what both approaches would agree on. And as I argue below, the actual society approach will treat race differently from height or eye color, creating an overlapping consensus that reproductive banks act unjustly by referencing the race of the donor, and thereby selling segregation.

The Actual Society Approach

By steering us to discriminate on the basis of race, reproductive banks make it easy for many buyers to avoid racially integrating their families. As long as reproductive banks provide us the option to purchase gametes along racial lines and thereby exclude donors on the basis of race, segregation will likely continue through this practice. By encouraging buyers to discriminate on the basis of race, making it easy for us to do so, these reproductive banks encourage segregation. They make it more likely that families will remain racially homogenous. In a society where we need more rather than less racial integration, reproductive banks should not be steering buyers to discriminate on the basis of race. They should not encourage segregation.

Unlike intimacy, the issue here is not about unconscious racism. In the last chapter, I suggested that our romantic desires seem ineffable and often beyond our conscious control; we cannot switch them on or off. Intimacy entails an elusive "X factor," because "[l]ove and identity are beyond the reach of rational judgment."[49] Buyers in the market for gametes, however, are not seeking romantic partners or dates. They are buying genetic materials and often doing so, as outlined above, with deliberation. In fact, this decision is much closer to the one made in the employment context. Just as an employer reviews a range of biographical information in determining whom to hire, so too do prospective buyers in determining which donor to include in their biological family.

Imagine similar language from the Sperm Bank but on a real estate website: "In this spirit we present reasons to consider selecting a neighborhood that looks like you, your partner, and the people who will surround your child as they grow up." Imagine that Movoto.com did not just disclose racial demographics but explicitly encouraged

---

[49] Moran 2003: 14.

prospective buyers to move into racially homogenous areas citing a range of reasons why this would be in the best interest of their families. Such a real estate website would violate federal law by encouraging segregation. In doing so, Movoto.com would be encouraging its users to discriminate against others on the basis of race.

In fact, Article 34 of the old, racist Real Estate Code of Ethics from 1924 made clear that as intermediaries, realtors had an ethical obligation to keep areas or communities racially homogenous:

> A Realtor should never be instrumental in introducing into a neighborhood a character of property or occupancy, members of any race or nationality, or any individuals whose presence will clearly be detrimental to property values in that neighborhood.[50]

In so far as reproductive banks are also intermediaries, connecting buyers to those selling their reproductive material, they steer buyers toward forming racially homogenous families, either explicitly or by simply disclosing the race of the donor. They encourage these buyers to segregate and therefore avoid racial integration of their families. If we take seriously the actual society approach and its emphasis on addressing inequality or segregation, it is wrong for reproductive banks to do so.

Moreover, the methodological assumption of partial compliance suggests that, as a historical matter, race is different from height or eye color or other characteristics that reproductive banks may disclose about the donor. Although those who are taller and slimmer, for instance, have social advantage,[51] these markers simply do not have the salience that race does in our actual society. After all, laws and social institutions have explicitly segregated on the basis of race, not on the basis of height or eye color. Segregation in schools, restaurants, and other places reveals this obvious fact. In 2017 the Court held that the Sixth Amendment's right to an impartial jury may be violated if there is racial bias in the jury verdict, making clear that "racial bias implicates unique historical, constitutional, and institutional concerns."[52] According to the actual society approach, racial inequality or segregation is therefore the relevant and enduring injustice that we should seek

[50] Code of Ethics 1924: 7.
[51] See Kirkland. 2008; Rhode 2010.
[52] *Peña-Rodriguez* v. *Colorado* (2017) at 868.

to address. That informs the idea that in our actual society hair or eye color is not socially significant in the same way as race.

In fact, Seline Szkupinski Quiroga says that the market for gametes "reflect[s] and privilege[s] white kindship patterns and fears about race mixing."[53] She discusses California Cryobank's quality assurance program as a way to reveal this concern with "race mixing." She remarks that as part of that program the bank uses "yellow caps" for Asian donors, "black and brown caps" for black donors, and "white caps" for white donors. "Red caps" refer to "unique ancestry donors" such as "East Indian, American Indian, and Latinos, or to donors who belong to two or more racial groups."[54] According to Quiroga:

> The white kinship system emphasizes genetic relationships with the implicit aim of maintaining cultural whiteness, and biomedical technologies for infertility are one means of perpetuating these racialized kinship systems. Because of the nature of the American racial hierarchy, breeding white children and keeping white identity pure and free from nonwhite influences is vital for the preservation of the white family.[55]

Her argument focuses on racial hierarchy in our actual society and the way the market in gametes furthers this hierarchy through classifying reproductive materials on the basis of race. Banks should not encourage segregation by selling it.

A Discredited View of Race

In disclosing the donor's race, sellers of ova and sperm also reduce race to a simple genetic or biological thing that can be bought or sold. Just as one can buy sperm of someone who is tall, one can buy sperm that is designated as white or black. The fact that the product being bought or sold is reproductive materials reinforces a biological concept of race. Charles Mills, for instance, argues that racial categories often involve, in addition to "bodily appearance," appeals to "ancestry, self-awareness of ancestry, public awareness of ancestry, culture, experience, and self-

---

[53] Quiroga 2007: 143.
[54] Quiroga 2007: 150.
[55] Quiroga 2007: 146.

identification."[56] It is, in part, that experience and culture that racial disclosure in the reproductive market obscures. The reproductive market treats race as simply a genetic or biological thing like being tall or short. This kind of racial disclosure does not signal a capacious view of race but a narrow, discredited view of race as a mere biological or scientific category. It reduces the meaning of racial categories to a crude and essentializing biological fact.

This is problematic because scholars have discredited the view that there is something biological or objectively fixed about racial categories,[57] concluding in fact that there is more biological diversity within the alleged categories of race than among them.[58] And although there is disagreement among philosophers about how to understand the nature of race,[59] Ron Mallon contends there is "now widespread agreement among philosophers, social theorists, anthropologists, and biologists that races do not share . . . biobehavioral essences," defined as "underlying natural (and perhaps genetic) properties that (1) are heritable, biological features, (2) are shared by all and only the members of a race, and (3) explain behavioral, characterological, and cultural predispositions of individual persons and racial groups."[60]

And this is for good reason. After all, it is precisely this discredited idea of race that often underlies the claims of scientific racism and racial eugenics. These claims define race in natural or genetic terms rather than political or social ones. By designating a gamete with a particular race, the reproductive market defines race in just this problematic way, making clear that a prospective parent can pass down a particular race to his or her child. This kind of crude reduction assumes that race is a "biobehavioral essence," which historically has fueled stereotypical claims that one race is superior or inferior to another. Instead of challenging this noxious conception of race, sperm and ova banks validate it.

---

[56] Mills 1998: 50.
[57] Livingstone 1962; Smedley and Smedley 2005.
[58] Lewontin, Rose, and Kamin 1984.
[59] For those who are racial skeptics, see generally Appiah 1995, 1996; Zack 2002. For those who are racial constructionists, see generally Gooding-Williams 1998; Mills 1998; Sundstrom 2002; Taylor 2004. For those who talk about racial population, see generally Andreasen 1998, 2000; Kitcher 2007.
[60] Mallon 2006: 528–529.

Consider that one can objectively measure one's height or weight. These are genuinely aesthetic characteristics. They completely mark out actual physical traits. Now racial categories often correlate with certain physical features (e.g., darker or lighter skin, different facial features). I'm not suggesting that race is entirely unconnected to such features. The important point is that racial categories mean much more. These sites steer on precisely those racial categories that social scientists and legal scholars make clear is a product of legal, social, and political facts, not genetic or natural ones.[61]

By aligning or treating race as just another physical attribute, these sellers obscure the normative and political force that comes with racial categories. Racial categories often mean much more than eye color or height. As Camisha Russell puts it, by "asserting the transmission of racial identity through reproduction as *natural* – rather than *political*," markets that racialize sperm and ova may stand to "normalize existing racialized privilege and inequality."[62] This normalization can occur precisely because race is reduced to a mere commodity or object, to be bought and sold like any other thing.

Suppose these banks adopted a system of categorization based on, what Elizabeth Anderson calls, "minimal race."[63] This kind of category would simply designate clusters of phenotypic traits coupled with geographic ancestry. Anderson suggests that this idea of "minimal race" may categorize individuals without subjecting them to the problematic notions that come with a "biobehavioral" conception of race. Although Anderson may be right when it comes to categorizing *individuals*, a focus on "minimal race" would still be problematic when classifying reproductive materials. It is one thing if these descriptors are used to classify individuals, quite another when used to classify gametes. If what is being sold is the ability to pass down a certain set of genetic traits, any kind of race-based descriptor stands to trigger a crude biological concept of race.

[61] Braman 1999; Haney-Lopez 2006; Hochschild, Weaver, and Burch 2012; Jacobson 1999.
[62] Russell 2015: 609.
[63] Anderson 2013 [2010]: 157–158.

SELLING SEGREGATION IS UNLAWFUL

Selling segregation is not just wrong. It is also unlawful. The law makes it clear that we may not refuse to contract with someone based simply on their race. Section 1981 states that all persons "have the same right in every State and Territory to make and enforce contracts ... as is enjoyed by white citizens."[64] Section 1982 states that we "shall have the same right ... as enjoyed by white citizens ... to inherit, purchase, lease, sell, hold and convey real and personal property."[65] This law prohibits individuals from refusing to contract with someone else simply based on that person's race. And Justice Marshall makes clear in *McDonald* that this law "was meant, by its broad terms, to proscribe discrimination in the making or enforcement of contracts against, or in favor of, any race."[66] As long as a bank denies a donor the private opportunity to donate on the basis of race, the bank violates federal law.

In *Runyon*, the private school sought to keep its school racially homogenous by denying a parent the private opportunity to send their child to that school. According to the Court:

> Just as, in *Jones*, a Negro's ... right to purchase property on equal terms with whites was violated when a private person refused to sell to the prospective purchaser solely because he was a Negro, so also a Negro's ... right to "make and enforce contracts" is violated if a private offeror refuses to extend to a Negro, solely because he is a Negro, the same opportunity to enter into contracts as he extends to white offerees.[67]

The private school violated the law by denying someone a private opportunity based simply on their race. This is why the Court goes on to say that this case involves a "prohibition of racial discrimination

---

[64] 42 U.S. Code § 1981.
[65] 42 U.S. Code § 1982.
[66] *McDonald* (1976) at 296.
[67] *Runyon* (1976) at 170.

that interferes with the making and enforcement of contracts for private educational services."[68] This kind of restriction

> furthers goals closely analogous to those served by § 1981's elimination of racial discrimination in the making of private employment contracts and, more generally, by § 1982's guarantee that "a dollar in the hands of a Negro will purchase the same thing as a dollar in the hands of a white man."[69]

That means that society may not deny individuals a private opportunity based simply on their race. The school could have refused to enter into a contract with the parent, because the family could not afford the school or because the parent's child did not perform well on a particular test. Those refusals would not have been based on race.

Taking that legal prohibition seriously means that reproductive banks violate the law if they deny or refuse prospective donors the opportunity to donate based simply on their race. In *Perez v. Commissioner* (Tax 2015), the federal tax court ruled that compensation to egg donors was considered income for tax purposes. In that case, the donor signed two contracts: "one with the [reproductive bank] and one with the anonymous intended parents."[70] I do not know whether this particular bank discriminated on the basis of race in creating these contracts.

But if banks such as the ones mentioned above enter into these contracts only with individuals of a particular race, they treat donors unequally, subverting the requirement that individuals not discriminate on the basis of race. The private school in *Runyon* violated this requirement, because it refused to contract with black parents. Now it may be that some reproductive banks contract with donors of one race while another only contracts with donors of a different race. But again, the law applies to any denial in "the making or enforcement of contracts against, or in favor of, any race."[71]

---

[68] *Runyon* (1976) at 179.
[69] *Runyon* (1976) at 179.
[70] *Perez* (Tax 2015) at 4.
[71] *McDonald* (1976) at 296.

A CONTRACT TO SEGREGATE IS UNENFORCEABLE
UNDER THE CONSTITUTION

It is not only that selling segregation is unlawful. I also argue that a private agreement to sell segregation should be unenforceable. I support this argument by drawing on *Shelley* v. *Kraemer* (1948), a case where the Court held that private agreements to segregate are unenforceable under the Constitution.

Shelley v. *Kraemer* (1948)

In *Shelley,* the Court held that private agreements to exclude on the basis of race are not enforceable under the Constitution. In that case, the agreement was a restrictive racial covenant. It read:

> [A]s a condition precedent to the sale of the same, that hereafter no part of said property or any portion thereof shall be, for said term of Fifty-years, occupied by any person not of the Caucasian race, it being intended hereby to restrict the use of said property for said period of time against the occupancy as owners or tenants of any portion of said property for resident or other purpose by people of the Negro or Mongolian Race.[72]

This agreement was a covenant that ran with the property so that when a homeowner sold their house, the new homeowner would also be subject to the exclusionary agreement. This contract was a way to ensure that homeowners would keep their community racially homogenous.

And *Shelley* arose because one of the homeowners to the agreement went to court to enforce it. *Shelley* held that it is unconstitutional for a state to enforce this kind of private racial agreement to exclude. The Court realized that this would not stop individuals from segregating.[73] If individuals desire to live together with only those of another race, society may be unable to stop this. "But [according to the Court] here there was more. These are cases in which the purposes of the agreements were secured only by judicial enforcement by state courts of the

---

[72] *Shelley* (1948) at 4–5.
[73] *Shelley* (1948) at 13.

restrictive terms of the agreements."[74] Whereas society may not be able to ensure that individuals integrate, it can at least ensure that courts not enforce private agreements to segregate.

That is why the Court says:

> These are not cases, as has been suggested, in which the States have merely abstained from action, leaving private individuals free to impose such discriminations as they see fit. Rather, these are cases in which the States have made available to such individuals the full coercive power of government to deny to petitioners, on the grounds of race or color, the enjoyment of property rights in premises which petitioners are willing and financially able to acquire and which the grantors are willing to sell.[75]

Even though the agreement or contract to exclude was private, once the state seeks to enforce that agreement, it now runs afoul of the Constitution.

And the Court is explicit that it does not matter whether the homeowners seeking to enforce such an agreement to segregate are black or white. The Court concedes that the "parties have directed our attention to no case in which a court, state or federal, has been called upon to enforce a covenant excluding members of the white majority from ownership or occupancy of real property on grounds of race or color. But there are more fundamental considerations."[76] For even if this were an agreement to exclude white individuals, this too would be unconstitutional to enforce. The Court states:

> The rights created by the first section of the Fourteenth Amendment are, by its terms, guaranteed to the individual. The rights established are personal rights. It is, therefore, no answer to these petitioners to say that the courts may also be induced to deny white persons rights of ownership and occupancy on grounds of race or color. Equal protection of the laws is not achieved through indiscriminate imposition of inequalities.[77]

Shelley holds that the Constitution prohibits states from enforcing a private agreement to segregate.

---

[74] *Shelley* (1948) at 13.
[75] *Shelley* (1948) at 19.
[76] *Shelley* (1948) at 22.
[77] *Shelley* (1948) at 22.

Scholars sometimes ponder over how to understand *Shelley*.[78] This is because *Shelley* does not reject the requirement of state action. It does not reject the principle that in order for an action to violate the Constitution, there must be some action by the state or government. Still, *Shelley* holds that enforcing this kind of racially restrictive covenant (which was formed by private individuals) violates the Constitution. How do we reconcile this?

One way to do so is through the distinction between public and private racism. Public racism is unconstitutional. That much is clear. The Equal Protection Clause of the Fourteenth Amendment generally prohibits the state from discriminating on the basis of race. It also prohibits the state from steering, as outlined in *Anderson*. In contrast, the Civil Rights Act of 1964 and the Fair Housing Act of 1968 (in addition to other such laws) are important statutes that prohibit racism in our private lives. We can interpret *Shelley* as saying that even though the Constitution may not prohibit racism in our private lives directly (because there is no state action), it does prohibit the state or government from enforcing these private racial agreements. Once parties to this agreement seek to enforce this contract to segregate, drawing on the state's coercive power for instance, this has now become an issue of public racism. And public racism is unconstitutional. In short, *Shelley* suggests that a private contract to segregate may be an instance of private racism. But once an individual seeks to enforce that contract in court – thereby seeking action by the state – it becomes an instance of public racism where legal enforcement of its provisions would now be unconstitutional.

That means that a contract to sell segregation should also be unenforceable. Even if reproductive banks provide buyers the option to exclude donors on the basis of race and buyers use that option, courts should not enforce that agreement. Suppose a real estate website provided buyers the option to exclude areas on the basis of race. Again, consider that Movoto.com had provided racial demographic information to its users. Suppose then, I use this option on the website, because I seek to find an area or neighborhood where most if not all of the residents match my race. After moving to this place, I discover that

[78] See, e.g., Rosen 2007, Tushnet 1988.

it is not racially homogenous but racially diverse. The website made a mistake in providing the racial information. I then sue the website for breach of contract and for money damages to enforce our agreement. According to that agreement, the website failed to exclude areas or neighborhoods on the basis of race. Consequently, I have to move out and find another place to live. According to *Shelley*, the Constitution should not permit individuals to enforce that kind of contract in court. Even if all the parties agreed to it, that private agreement to provide buyers the option to exclude areas or communities on the basis of race should be unenforceable. That principle should apply in the market for gametes as well.

Cramblett v. *Midwest Sperm Bank* (N.D. Ill. 2017)

In December 2011, Jennifer Cramblett was artificially inseminated with sperm delivered by Midwest Sperm Bank. In purchasing sperm from the bank, she had requested sperm from a white donor. Cramblett admitted that she was "raised around stereotypical attitudes about people other than those in her all-white environment."[79] According to Cramblett:

> When the receptionist [of the sperm bank] returned for the second time, she asked Jennifer if she had requested an African American donor to which she replied, "No, why would I request that? My partner and I are Caucasian."[80]

Eventually, Cramblett learned that she had been inseminated with sperm from Donor No. 330 (who was black) and not from Donor No. 380 (who was white).[81] Cramblett thought she had purchased sperm from a white donor but the sperm bank delivered sperm from a donor who was black. The reason for the error was that the sperm bank's records are kept in "pen and ink."[82] The person who sent Cramblett the vials of sperm thought "the number '380' looked like '330.'"[83] On August 21, 2012, Cramblett "gave birth to Payton,

[79] *Cramblett* v. *Midwest Sperm Bank* (Ill. Cir. Ct. 2014), Complaint.
[80] *Cramblett* (Ill. Cir. Ct. 2014) at 4, complaint.
[81] *Cramblett* (Ill. Cir. Ct. 2014) at 4–6, complaint.
[82] *Cramblett* (Ill. Cir. Ct. 2014) at 5, complaint.
[83] *Cramblett* (Ill. Cir. Ct. 2014) at 6, complaint.

a beautiful, obviously mixed baby girl."[84] Cramblett lives in a "small, homogenous" town "which she regards as too racially intolerant."[85] All of Cramblett's therapists and experts "agree that for her psychological and parental well-being, she must relocate to a racially diverse community with good schools."[86]

As a result, Cramblett sued Midwest Sperm Bank in federal court for fraud, misconduct, and negligence and damages of more than $150,000.[87] (The federal court has stayed that proceeding, because Cramblett has a similar claim pending in state court.[88]) In her complaint in federal court, Cramblett says that she is facing "numerous challenges and external pressures associated with an unplanned transracial parent-child relationship for which she was not, and is not, prepared."[89] In consulting with a sociologist and a therapist, they agree that both Cramblett and her daughter will "require long-term individual and family counseling as well as a change of domicile to a place that is more racially and culturally diverse."[90] She currently lives in a racially homogenous area, and according to her complaint "[f]amily members, one uncle in particular, speaks openly and derisively about people of color."[91] This is why Cramblett sought out a donor who matched her race.

There was no question that Cramblett's child was biologically her own. That is, this was not a case where the Sperm Bank did not fulfill their contractual obligation in helping Cramblett form a biological family. She exercised her liberty to form a biological family with her partner by buying sperm from the reproductive bank. The bank provided her gametes that resulted in a biological child. In so far as Cramblett sought to exercise a liberty to form a biological family and pass down her genetic material, the bank provided her that opportunity. The bank breached the contract by failing to provide her sperm from someone who was white. By making a mistake in providing the racial information, the bank failed to exclude racially diverse donors.

---

[84] *Cramblett* (Ill. Cir. Ct. 2014) at 6, complaint.
[85] *Cramblett* (Ill. Cir. Ct. 2014) at 6, complaint.
[86] *Cramblett* (Ill. Cir. Ct. 2014) at 7, complaint.
[87] www.dailyherald.com/article/20160427/news/160428804/
[88] *Cramblett* v. *Midwest Sperm Bank* (N.D. Ill. 2017).
[89] *Cramblett* (N.D. Ill. 2017) at 868.
[90] *Cramblett* (N.D. Ill. 2017) at 868.
[91] *Cramblett* (Ill. Cir. Ct. 2014) at 6, complaint.

Cramblett is suing to enforce that private agreement with the bank to exclude donors on the basis of race. The foregoing analysis suggests that the court should have dismissed this case, because this agreement should be unenforceable under the Constitution. The reproductive bank agreed to exclude donors on the basis of race. Enforcing that private agreement violates the principle articulated in *Shelley*. It also regrettably puts reproductive banks on notice that they must not make any mistakes in selling segregation.

DESEGREGATING THE FAMILY

I have argued that the practice of selling segregation is wrong, unlawful, and should be unenforceable under the Constitution. In doing so, this chapter has effectively expanded the boundary of racial justice to include the family. Enforcing the moral and legal prohibition on the sale of segregation may be one way to desegregate the family. In suggesting this, I follow feminist political theory in treating the family as a possible site or space for injustice.[92] This is what it means to take seriously the idea that the personal is the political. According to this logic, the family is not some separate space that is outside the boundary of justice. Feminist political theory rejects that narrow or parochial view of justice and so does this book. As outlined in Chapter 1, even Rawls speaks of the family as a major social institution within the basic structure and hence within the boundary of justice.

We should therefore consider desegregating the family just as we consider desegregating other social institutions and spaces. What would that look like in the market for gametes? Heath Fogg Davis proposes a thought experiment of "racial randomization" in the adoption context that helps answer this question. Davis says:

> Imagine an adoption system consisting solely of centralized public adoption agencies within individual states. This system is the only option available to those who wish to become adoptive parents. In

[92] See, e.g., Allen 1988, 79–80; Kelly 2003; MacKinnon 1987; McClain 1995; Okin 1989, 1989a; Pateman 1989, 118–140.

this adoption system, applicants must undergo a screening process during which each is informed of the agency's policy of discounting race as a permissible preference in being matched with a child who needs a home. If an applicant agrees to this policy, he or she continues the screening process for a minimum level of parental fitness. If all goes well, then he or she is approved to become an adoptive parent. In the randomization process, some white applicants will be matched with white children, while some from both groups will end up adopting children of the same racial classification as their own. Whites are statistically likely to be matched with a black child through a system of racial randomization. And it is probable that a small number of white children will be placed with black parents.[93]

According to Davis, this thought experiment "pushes us to imagine nondiscrimination as a comprehensive moral principle applied to all aspects and stages of adoption."[94] Davis states that the adoption of "white children by black parents would be a beneficial consequence of racial randomization because it would ... call into question the racist presumption that interracial care is unidirectional in family life, that whites adopt black children but black adults can only care for white children as domestic workers."[95] Davis recognizes the "possibility that racial randomization would match some black parents with white children."[96] He views this as a reason to favor this kind of thought experiment because it "forces us to confront some of the race-based expectations we collectively hold about which people belong together in a family."[97] This randomization system stands to challenge such stereotypes. And, Davis goes on to say that we should extend this randomization "to reproductive decisions in the market for new reproductive technologies, because like adoption, these processes necessitate third-party meditation."[98]

We can extend a similar randomization policy relatively easily to our current reproductive market. Reproductive banks, as third-party

[93] Fogg Davis 2002: 78.
[94] Fogg Davis 2002: 83.
[95] Fogg Davis 2002: 78.
[96] Fogg Davis 2002: 79.
[97] Fogg Davis 2002: 79.
[98] Fogg Davis 2002: 87.

mediators, already provide buyers a range of information about donors, including their height, weight, family history, health, and educational/ professional background. These banks also let buyers know other information such as whether the donor prefers to remain anonymous or not. We can imagine that banks continue to provide much of this information but are not allowed to classify and then disclose the donor's race, in line with the moral and legal prohibition on selling segregation. If reproductive banks could not classify donors on the basis of race, buyers would be unable to exclude donors on the basis of race. A market in gametes that is set up in this way would allow us to pass down our genetic material or the material of our partner or spouse in forming a biological family. This market would also allow us to exclude donors based on a range of characteristics or information but not on the basis of race. A market set up in this way, where race is in effect randomized, means that reproductive banks would sell sperm and ova without also selling segregation. In this kind of market, we could not ensure that our family would remain racially homogenous. Some of us are likely to have a biological family that is racially diverse, because we would not have the option to exclude donors simply on the basis of race.

Would this kind of randomized policy applied to the market for gametes generate resistance? Davis believes there would be resistance in the case of his hypothetical adoption system. He thinks that there would be "large-scale defection" from his racial randomization policy.[99] And if there is, he suggests that this tells "us something about the limits of racial integration."[100] Would something similar happen in the market for gametes? How many buyers would object to enlarging the boundary of racial justice to include the family? Or put more directly, how many buyers would prefer a market where reproductive banks also sell segregation?

On the one hand, almost all families are racially homogenous. According to data by the Pew Research Center, in 1970, "among babies living with two parents, only 1% had parents who were different races from each other."[101] As of 2015, when the survey was taken, 7 percent of US adults are now multiracial. Multiracial Americans are those adults who

[99] Fogg Davis 2002: 87.
[100] Fogg Davis 2002: 87.
[101] www.pewsocialtrends.org/2015/06/11/multiracial-in-america/

come from a biological family that is racially diverse or, as the Center puts it, "have at least two races in their background, including themselves, their parents or their grandparents."[102] That means almost 93 percent of adults still come from families that are racially homogenous.

On the other hand, the data found that 60 percent of multiracial Americans say that they are "proud of their mixed racial background,"[103] even though 50 percent have been "subjected to racial slurs or jokes" and about "one-in-four have felt annoyed because people have made assumptions about their racial background."[104] The same study revealed that one in five multiracial Americans found it to be advantageous to come from a biological family that was racially diverse; only 4 percent said it was disadvantageous to do so; and 76 percent said it did not make a difference.[105] This suggests that overall desegregation of the family can have positive consequences for those who grow up in a racially diverse family.

So, I'm not sure if or how many buyers would thereby leave the market if society enforced a ban on selling segregation. But I do know that enlarging the boundary of racial justice has historically met with resistance. As noted in Chapter 1, Bork and others who objected to civil rights resisted the idea of enlarging this boundary, of desegregating our private schools, our stores, our workplace, our restaurants, movie theaters, and our other social institutions. These are important places in the private sphere. In so far as they were segregated, there was resistance to desegregation. That resistance to enlarging the boundary may arise here too just as it did in *Shelley* where individuals sought to keep their social spaces such as their neighborhoods and communities racially homogenous. That does not change the fact that justice, defined by the moral consensus outlined in this book, portends the desegregation of the family along with these other social spaces and institutions.

How will we know we have moved in the direction of desegregating the family? Perhaps a good sign will be when we don't care whether our families are racially diverse or racially homogenous. That may also be a sign that we are living in a society that is more racially just.

---

[102] www.pewsocialtrends.org/2015/06/11/multiracial-in-america/
[103] www.pewsocialtrends.org/2015/06/11/multiracial-in-america/
[104] www.pewsocialtrends.org/2015/06/11/multiracial-in-america/
[105] www.pewsocialtrends.org/2015/06/11/multiracial-in-america/

CONCLUSION: PRIVATE INJUSTICE

This book has focused on racism in our private lives. In doing so, I have sought to expand the boundary of racial justice. Along the way, I have suggested ways we can address racial injustice in the private sphere. I hope it will begin rather than end the conversation about the way in which racial discrimination can further racial inequality and stereotypes not just in our public or political life but also in our private one.

Generally, conclusions or concluding chapters do not make new arguments but rather summarize the existing one. This conclusion breaks from that practice (at least somewhat), because I hope this book will spur a conversation that goes beyond racism to talk about enlarging the boundary of justice for other inequalities. After all, we face economic and social inequalities in our private lives that are not only about race. There are other kinds of private injustice besides private racism.

To jumpstart that conversation, this conclusion will focus on two additional types of private injustice: private homophobia and private economic injustice. These arguments are preliminary ones, meant to flag these issues but not decide them in some definite way. I focus on just these two because the Court has recently discussed the first and because scholarly work in political philosophy discusses the latter. I show that this book can provide intellectual support for the conclusion that homophobia and economic injustice in our private lives are also wrong.

PRIVATE HOMOPHOBIA

Cases such as *Romer* v. *Evans* (1996) support the idea that public homophobia is wrong. In that case, the state of Colorado passed an amendment that held that "neither the State of Colorado, through any of its branches or departments, nor any . . . political subdivisions . . . shall enact . . . any statute . . . whereby homosexual, lesbian or bisexual orientation . . . shall constitute or otherwise be the basis of or entitle any person or class of persons to have or claim any . . . protected status or claim of discrimination."[1] The Court invalidated the state amendment under the Equal Protection Clause of the Fourteenth Amendment, reasoning that it was based on "animus toward the class it affects."[2]

In particular, the Court held that the Amendment raised

> the inevitable inference that the disadvantage imposed is born of animosity toward the class of persons affected. "[I]f the constitutional conception of 'equal protection of the laws' means anything, it must at the very least mean that a bare . . . desire to harm a politically unpopular group cannot constitute a legitimate governmental interest."[3]

It is not simply the disadvantage imposed by the law that did the constitutional work. *Romer* also says that such disadvantage is "born of animosity," that such disadvantage is based on hostility against gays and lesbians. *Romer* concludes that public homophobia is unconstitutional.

The Court reinforced this conclusion in *Obergefell* v. *Hodges* (2015). In that case, it held that it's unconstitutional for a state to deny marriage licenses to gay couples. *Obergefell* recognizes that public homophobia is a form of injustice:

> The nature of injustice is that we may not always see it in our own times. The generations that wrote and ratified the Bill of Rights and the Fourteenth Amendment did not presume to know the extent of freedom in all of its dimensions, and so they entrusted to future generations a charter protecting the right of all persons to enjoy liberty as we learn its meaning. When new insight reveals discord

[1] *Romer* (1996) at 624.
[2] *Romer* (1996) at 632.
[3] *Romer* (1996) at 634.

between the Constitution's central protections and a received legal stricture, a claim to liberty must be addressed.[4]

This case reveals the way in which society has come to realize that it is wrong for government or the state to discriminate against gays and lesbians. This is why Congress passed legislation repealing the Don't Ask Don't Tell Policy in 2010, a policy that barred service members from being openly gay or lesbian.[5] Prior to this repeal, a federal court had ruled that the policy was unconstitutional.[6]

These cases inform the idea that public homophobia is wrong. It's wrong for the state to discriminate on the basis of sexual orientation. We can draw on the ideal and actual society approaches to enlarge the boundary of justice to argue that private homophobia is also wrong. According to the ideal society approach, we can treat sexual orientation as a morally irrelevant characteristic. Just as those in the Original Position would abstract away from their race, it stands to reason that they would also abstract away from their sexuality. In an ideal society fully complying with the principles of justice, one's sexual orientation would not matter in the distribution of rights and opportunities. This would include both public and private opportunities. As such, discrimination against gays and lesbians in private is also wrong.

According to the actual society approach, gays and lesbians often experience discrimination based on stereotype or stigma. It can be difficult for individuals to find goods and services based on their sexual orientation given this kind of stigma in our actual society. This too is wrong for many of the same reasons that racial inequality in private is wrong. Both methodologies of justice can support the conclusion that private homophobia is an instance of private injustice.

Nevertheless, Congress has not sought to enforce this moral consensus. For instance, it has not amended its key civil rights statutes regulating the private sphere to include sexual orientation. There is a pending bill (the Employment Non-Discrimination Act (ENDA)) that would do so, but Congress has not passed it.[7] Still, some states do

---

[4] *Obergefell* (2015) at 2598.
[5] U.S.C. § 654. 2010. Policy concerning homosexuality in the armed forces.
[6] *Log Cabin Republicans* v. *United States* (C.D. Cal. 2010).
[7] www.congress.gov/bill/113th-congress/senate-bill/815

enforce this consensus by banning discrimination against gays and lesbians in finding housing, employment, and other such private goods and services.

This moral consensus came to a head with *Masterpiece Cakeshop* v. *Colorado Civil Rights Commission* (2018), a case where Jack Phillips refused to bake a wedding cake for a gay couple. Colorado prohibited individuals such as Phillips, who operated a wedding cake business, from discriminating on the basis of sexual orientation in serving customers. His refusal was based on religious reasons about the sanctity of marriage as a union between a man and a woman. He argued that the First Amendment's free exercise clause should permit him to discriminate in this way. In a narrow opinion, the Court sided with the baker but did not decide definitively whether we should enlarge the boundary of justice for private homophobia in the same way society has done for private racism.

Some do not want to enlarge the boundary in this kind of case. Ryan Anderson argues that "sexual orientation and gender identity are not like race."[8] Although he accepts an enlarged boundary for racial justice, he rejects it in the case of these other private injustices. For instance, he does not think that Congress should pass ENDA. According to Anderson, while

> race implies nothing about one's actions, sexual orientation and gender identity are frequently descriptions for one's actions: "gay" denotes men who engage in voluntary sex acts with other men, "lesbian" denotes women who engage in voluntary sex acts with other women.[9]

This line of reasoning suggests that a baker should have the liberty to discriminate against gays and lesbians on the basis of their religious beliefs.[10] Private homophobia is different from private racism. Again, at oral argument both the lawyer for the baker and the US Solicitor General (who argued to support the baker's argument) said that "race is different."[11] This is why the counsel for the respondent remarked

---

[8] Anderson 2015.
[9] Anderson 2015.
[10] See, e.g., McConnell 2018, Anderson 2018.
[11] www.supremecourt.gov/oral_arguments/audio/2017/16-111 (p. 22, 32).

that "both Petitioner [the baker] and the United States recognize that these results [acts of discrimination] are unacceptable with respect to race."[12] They, in turn, "suggest that [the Court] draw a distinction between race discrimination and sexual orientation discrimination and the state's ability to protect it."[13]

But others have argued that we should treat these private injustices the same.[14] This logic suggests that we should treat the restaurant owner in *Piggie Park* like the baker in *Masterpiece Cakeshop*. Even if the baker may not want to attend a gay wedding, he may not deny private services or goods to individuals simply because of their sexual orientation.

Linda McClain's forthcoming book *The Rhetoric of Bigotry* suggests that these two types of injustice – private racism and private homophobia – may not be all that different. She draws on history, jurisprudence, and politics to consider how both may be instances of bigotry. In so doing, she importantly points out that the NAACP amicus brief in *Masterpiece Cakeshop* observed that "'the religious beliefs' of Mr. Bessinger, the owner of Piggie Park 'were relatively mainstream' and he was not viewed as 'fringe or disingenuous.'"[15] McClain goes on to conclude that "these religious beliefs were not marginal, but sincerely and widely-held, [making] the Court's ruling all the more significant."[16] The Court condemned private racism even though many individuals supported racial discrimination or segregation on religious grounds. By treating private homophobia alongside private racism, McClain's book suggests that there may be important similarities that would consider both of these as instances of bigotry.

This book has argued that individuals should have the same obligations as the government or state not to discriminate on the basis of race. If we take that expansive view of justice seriously, perhaps individuals should also have the same obligation as the government or state not to discriminate on the basis of sexual orientation – in which case, perhaps the Court should condemn private homophobia even though some

---

[12] www.supremecourt.gov/oral_arguments/audio/2017/16-111 (p. 76).
[13] www.supremecourt.gov/oral_arguments/audio/2017/16-111 (p. 75).
[14] See NeJaime and Siegel 2018.
[15] McClain forthcoming: chapter 8: 376
[16] McClain forthcoming: chapter 8: 376.

individuals support discrimination against gays and lesbians on religious grounds. After all, if we take seriously the overlapping moral consensus of this book, it may very well dictate that we treat both private homophobia and private racism as forms of private injustice.

PRIVATE ECONOMIC INJUSTICE

In addition to private homophobia, we can also consider private economic injustice. Although G.A. Cohen does not characterize his argument in this exact way, I suggest that he too seeks to enlarge the boundary of justice by focusing on private injustice. His article "Where the Action is: On the Site of Distribute Justice"[17] represents an important contribution to political theory, because he seeks to enlarge the boundary of justice. Instead of discussing private racism or homophobia, Cohen discusses private economic injustice.

Cohen focuses on what he calls "high-flying marketeers."[18] These are individuals who are particularly talented in society and can therefore command high salaries. Cohen argues that the difference principle, the idea that economic inequalities should benefit the least advantaged, should apply to these individuals. In effect, he seeks to enlarge the boundary of economic justice to include not just what the government or state must do but also what individuals must do. He argues that individuals who are self-seeking high fliers have some moral obligation to apply principles of justice in their private economic life. This may mean, for instance, that they should take a lower-paying job if doing so will benefit the least advantaged.

In crafting this argument, Cohen also draws on feminist political theory. He says that we "can distinguish between the substance and the form of the feminist critique of standard ideas about justice."[19] The form of this critique is his "prime concern."[20] He draws on that critique to enlarge the boundary of justice to cover economic decisions in our

---

[17] Cohen 1997.
[18] Cohen 1997: 5.
[19] Cohen 1997: 3–4.
[20] Cohen 1997: 4.

private lives. He too begins his paper with the idea that "the personal is political."[21]

If we assume that the government must redistribute in order to benefit the least advantaged (and therefore comply with the difference principle), Cohen argues that individuals such as the "high-flying marketeers" must do the same. This is because the "justice of a society is not exclusively a function of its legislative structure, of its legally imperative rules, but also of the choices people make within those rules."[22] Just as individuals should not discriminate on the basis of race in their private lives, those who are particularly talented should do the same with regard to the difference principle.

In so enlarging the boundary of justice, Cohen's focus is not on discrimination (even though he surely would find racism unjust). In an interesting way, Cohen's argument goes beyond the arguments made in this book about private racism and even private homophobia. Enlarging the boundary of justice in these cases means that individuals should not discriminate on the basis of race or sexual orientation, respectively. Just as the government may not discriminate in certain ways, so too should individuals not discriminate. Private racism and private homophobia are about what individuals may not do.

Cohen's argument, in contrast, is not about discrimination but about redistribution. This means that individuals, those "high-flying marketeers," have an obligation to redistribute their personal resources so as to benefit the least advantaged. I'm not concerned here with working out what this obligation would entail in any particular case. Suffice to say, it requires that these individuals give up or forsake some of their resources or additional income in order to comply with the difference principle. In effect, this means that individuals and not just the government have an obligation to redistribute. Enlarging the boundary of economic justice in this way imposes a positive obligation on individuals to do just that.

Although he does not deploy the ideal and actual society approaches as I have outlined them here, we can seek to support his argument from both methodologies. First, according to the ideal society approach,

---

[21] Cohen 1997: 3.
[22] Cohen 1997: 9.

a fully just society would be one where individuals are also complying with the principles of justice. Cohen instructively characterizes this as an "ethos of justice," arguing that a "society that is just within the terms of the difference principle, so we may conclude, requires not simply just coercive rules, but also an ethos of justice that informs individual choices."[23] For Cohen, an ideal society is one where there is such an ethos that "goes beyond one of obedience to just rules."[24]

Second, in our actual society there is economic inequality. This inequality limits what individuals may do in their private lives. It makes it more difficult for those who are poor to find various private goods and services. If we take seriously the idea that we should address that kind of injustice, perhaps we should consider placing redistributive obligations on certain well-placed individuals as well.

Cohen's argument has also met with resistance.[25] Perhaps this is because Cohen's argument imposes not just negative obligations on individuals but positive ones that require us to remedy inequality in our personal lives. Still, this book's argument about enlarging the boundary of racial justice may help in supporting the idea of private economic injustice. This book has argued that individuals should have the same obligations as the government or state not to discriminate on the basis of race. If we take that expansive view of justice seriously, perhaps individuals should also have the same obligation as the government or state to remedy or address economic inequality.

★★★

By making an argument about private racism, this book has sought to focus our attention on the boundary of justice. Whether we adopt the ideal or actual society methodology of justice, I have argued that both methodologies push us to enlarge this boundary. And once we do so, perhaps we should consider enlarging this boundary in other ways as well. In suggesting two additional ways we may do so; this conclusion hopes to continue the conversation not just about private racism but about private injustice more generally.

---

[23] Cohen 1997: 10.
[24] Cohen 1997: 18.
[25] See generally Cohen 2008: 373–411.

REFERENCES

Abizadeh, Arash. 2007. "Cooperation, Pervasive Impact, and Coercion: On the Scope (Not Site) of Distributive Justice," *Philosophy & Public Affairs* 35(4): 318–358.

Ackerman, Bruce. 2014. *The Civil Rights Revolution, Volume 3: We the People.* Cambridge, MA: Belknap Press.

Ackerman, Bruce. 1991. *We the People, Volume 1: Foundations.* Cambridge, MA: Belknap Press.

Allen, Anita L. 1988. *Uneasy Access: Privacy for Women in a Free Society.* Totowa, NJ: Rowman & Littlefield.

Almeling, Rene. 2011. *Sex Cells: The Medical Market for Eggs and Sperm.* Berkeley, CA: University of California Press.

American Society for Reproductive Medicine. 2013. "Access to Fertility Treatment by Gays, Lesbians, and Unmarried Persons: A Committee Opinion." Ethics Committee.

Anderson v. Martin, 375 U.S. 399 (1964).

Anderson, Elizabeth. 2013 [2010]. *The Imperative of Integration.* Princeton, NJ: Princeton University Press.

Anderson, Elizabeth. 2000. "Why Commercial Surrogate Motherhood Unethically Commodifies Women and Children," *Health Care Analysis* 8: 19–26.

Anderson, Elizabeth. 1999. "What Is the Point of Equality?" *Ethics* 109(2): 287–337.

Anderson, Elizabeth. 1990. "Is Women's Labor a Commodity?" *Philosophy & Public Affairs* 19(1): 71–92.

Anderson, Ryan T. 2018. "Disagreement Is Not Always Discrimination: On Masterpiece Cakeshop and the Analogy to Interracial Marriage," *Georgetown Journal of Law & Public Policy* 16(1): 123–146.

Anderson, Ryan T. 2015. "Sexual Orientation and Gender Identity Are Not Like Race: Why ENDA Is Bad Policy," *Public Discourse: The Journal of the Witherspoon Institute.* www.thepublicdiscourse.com/2015/03/14649/

Andreasen, Robin. 2000. "Race: Biological Reality or Social Construct?" *Philosophy of Science* 67: S653–S666.

Andreasen, Robin. 1998. "A New Perspective on the Race Debate," *British Journal of the Philosophy of Science* 49: 199–225.

Appiah, Anthony. 1996. "Race, Culture, Identity: Misunderstood Connections," in *Color Conscious*, Anthony Appiah and Amy Gutmann (eds.), Princeton, NJ: Princeton University Press.

Appiah, Anthony. 1995. "The Uncompleted Argument: DuBois and the Illusion of Race," in *Overcoming Racism and Sexism*, L. Bell and D. Blumenfeld (eds.), Lanham, MD: Rowman & Littlefield.

Ayres, Ian, Mahzarin Banaji, and Christine Jolls. 2015. "Race Effects on eBay," *Rand Journal of Economics* 46(4): 891–917.

Balfour, Lawrie. 2014. "Integration, Desegregation and the Work of the Past," *Political Studies Review* 12(3): 347–352.

Balkin, Jack M. and Reva B. Siegel. 2003. "The American Civil Rights Tradition: Anticlassification or Antisubordination?" *University of Miami Law Review* 58: 9.

Bany, J. A., B. Robnett, and C. Feliciano. 2014. "Gendered Black Exclusion: The Persistence of Racial Stereotypes among Daters," *Race and Social Problems*, 6(3): 201–213.

Barry, Brian. 1973. "John Rawls and the Priority of Liberty," *Philosophy & Public Affairs* 2: 274–290.

Bartholet, Elizabeth. 1999. *Nobody's Children: Abuse and Neglect, Foster Drift, and the Adoption Alternative*. Boston, MA: Beacon Press.

Bartlett, Katharine T. and Mitu Gulati. 2016. "Discrimination by Customers," *Iowa Law Review* 102: 223–257.

Batzel v. *Smith*, 333 F.3d 1018 (9th Cir. 2003).

Bedi, Sonu. 2014. "The Scope of Formal Equality of Opportunity: The Horizontal Effect of Rights in a Liberal Constitution," *Political Theory* 42(6): 716–738.

Bedi, Sonu. 2013. *Beyond Race, Sex, and Sexual Orientation: Legal Equality without Identity*. New York, NY: Cambridge University Press.

Bedi, Sonu. 2010. "Expressive Exclusion: A Defense," *Journal of Moral Philosophy* 7(4): 427–440.

Bedi, Sonu. 2009. *Rejecting Rights*. Cambridge: Cambridge University Press.

Bedi, Suneal. 2017. "Fully and Barely Clothed: Case Studies in Gender and Religious Employment Discrimination in the Wake of Citizens United and Hobby Lobby," *Hastings Bus Law Journal* 12: 133.

Benhabib, Seyla. 2004. *The Rights of Others: Aliens, Residents, and Citizens*. Vol. 5. Cambridge: Cambridge University Press.

Benhabib, Seyla. 1992. *Situating the Self*. New York, NY: Routledge.

Bertrand, Marianne and Esther Duflo. 2017. "Field Experiments on Discrimination," Chapter 8 in *Handbook of Economic Field Experiments*, Abhijit Vinayak Banerjee and Esther Duflo (eds.) (Vol. 1), Amsterdam: North-Holland (an imprint of Elsevier).

Bertrand, Marianne and Sendhil Mullainathan. 2004. "Are Emily and Greg More Employable than Lakisha and Jamal? A Field Experiment on Labor Market Discrimination," *The American Economic Review* 94(4): 991–1013.

Bob Jones Univ. v. *United States*, 461 U.S. 574 (1983).

Bork, Robert. 1963. "Civil Rights: A Challenge," *New Republic*, August 31, 1963.

Bowen, James. 1988. "Cultural Convergences and Divergences: The Nexus between Putative Afro-American Family Values and the Best Interests of the Child," *Journal of Family Law* 26: 487–544.

Boy Scouts of America v. *Dale*, 530 U.S. 640 (2000).

Brake, Elizabeth. 2010. "Minimal Marriage: What Political Liberalism Implies for Marriage Law," *Ethics* 120(2): 302–337.

Braman, Donald. 1999. "Of Race and Immutability," *University of California, Los Angeles Law Review* 46: 1375.

Brettschneider, Corey. 2007. "The Politics of the Personal: A Liberal Approach," *The American Political Science Review* 101(1): 19–31.

Brighouse, Harry and Ingrid Robeyns. (eds.). 2010. *Measuring Justice: Primary Goods and Capabilities*. New York, NY: Cambridge University Press.

Brown, William III, 2003. "Discrimination dot com: Racially Biased Interaction in the Online Gay Male Community," *The McNair Scholars Journal of the University of California, Davis* 6: 22–29.

Brown v. *Board of Education of Topeka*, 347 U.S. 483 (1954).

Browning v. *Slenderella Systems of Seattle*, 341 P.2d 859 (Wash. 1959).

Burwell v. *E. Air Lines, Inc.*, 633 F.2d 361 (4th Cir. 1980).

Carpenter, Dale. 2001. "Expressive Association and Anti-Discrimination Law after Dale: A Tripartite Approach," *Minnesota Law Review* 85: 1515–1590.

Chandra A, G.M. Martinez, W.D. Mosher, J.C. Abma, and J. Jones. 2005. "Fertility, Family Planning, and Reproductive Health of U.S. Women: Data from the 2002 National Survey of Family Growth National Center for Health Statistics," *Vital Health Stat* 23(25).

Chicago Lawyers' Committee for Civil Rights under the Law, Inc. v. *Craigslist, Inc.*, 519 F.3d 666 (7th Cir. 2008).

Chicago Lawyers' Committee for Civil Rights under the Law, Inc. v. *Craigslist, Inc.*, 461 F.Supp. 2d 681 (N.D. Illinois 2006).

Cohen, C.J. 1999. *The Boundaries of Blackness: AIDS and the Breakdown of Black Politics*. Chicago, IL: University of Chicago Press.

Civil Rights Cases, 109 U.S. 3 (1883).

Clarke, Averil Y. 2011. *Inequalities of Love: College-Educated Black Women and the Barriers to Romance and Family*. Durham, NC and London: Duke University Press.

Claybrooks v. *ABC, Inc.*, 898 F.Supp. 2d 986 (M.D. Tenn. 2012).

Clover Hill Swimming Club v. *Goldsboro*, 47 N.J. 25 (N.J. 1966).

Coeytaux, Francine, Marcy Darnovsky, Susan Berke Fogel et al. 2011. "Assisted Reproduction and Choice in the Biotech Age: Recommendations for a Way Forward," *Contraception* 83(1): 1–4.

Code of Ethics. 1924. National Association of Real Estate Boards.

Code of Federal Regulations. 29 C.F.R. Section 1604.2 Sex as a bona fide occupational qualification.

Cohen, G.A. 2008. *Rescuing Justice and Equality*. Cambridge, MA: Harvard University Press.

Cohen, G.A. 1997. "Where the Action Is: On the Site of Distributive Justice," *Philosophy & Public Affairs*, 26 (1): 3–30.

Cohen, Jean. 2002. *Regulating Intimacy: A New Legal Paradigm*. Princeton, NJ: Princeton University Press.

Coleman, Nathaniel. 2011. "What? What? In the (Black) Butt," *Newsletter on Philosophy and Lesbian, Gay, Bisexual, and Transgender Issues* 11 (1): 12–15.

Cramblett v. *Midwest Sperm Bank*, 230 F.Supp. 3d 865 (N.D. Ill. 2017).

Cramblett v. *Midwest Sperm Bank, LLC*, No. 2014-L-010159 (Ill. Cir. Ct. filed September 29, 2014), 2014 WL 4853400 (complaint).

Crenshaw, Kimberlé. 1989. "Demarginalizing the Intersection of Race and Sex: A Black Feminist Critique of Antidiscrimination Doctrine, Feminist Theory and Antiracist Politics," *University of Chicago Legal Forum* 1 (8): 139–167.

Curran v. *Mt. Diablo Council of the Boy Scouts of Am.*, 952 P.2d 218 (Cal. 1998).

Daniels, Cynthia R. and Erin Heidt-Forsythe. 2012. "Gendered Eugenics and the Problematic of Free Market Reproductive Technologies: Sperm and Egg Donation in the United States," *Signs* 37 (3): 719–747.

Daniels, Norman. 2003. "Democratic Equality: Rawls's Complex Egalitarianism," in *The Cambridge Companion to Rawls*, Samuel Freeman (ed.), Cambridge: Cambridge University Press.

Diaz v. *Pan American World Airways, Inc.*, 442 F.2d 385 (5th Cir. 1971).

Doleac, Jennifer L. and Luke C.D. Stein. 2017. *The Visible Hand: Race and Online Market Outcomes* (revised March 23, 2017) (unpublished manuscript), http://ssrn.com/abstract=1615149.

Dresser, Rebecca. 2000. "Regulating Assisted Reproduction," *Hastings Center Report* 30: 26.

Equal Employment Opportunity Commission (E.E.O.C) 2006. Compliance Manual Section 625.1 2006 WL 4672772.

Edelman, Benjamin, Michael Luca, and Dan Svirsky. 2017. "Racial Discrimination in the Sharing Economy: Evidence from a Field Experiment," *American Economic Journal: Applied Economics, American Economic Association* 9 (2): 1–22, April.

Emens, Elizabeth F. 2009. "Intimate Discrimination: The State's Role in the Accidents of Sex and Love," *Harvard Law Review* 122: 1307.

Eng, David L. 2001. *Racial Castration: Managing Masculinity in Asian America*. Durham, NC: Duke University Press.

Edelman, Benjamin and Michael Luca. 2014. "Digital Discrimination: The Case of Airbnb.Com." Working Paper, Harvard Business School. *SSRN Electronic Journal*, January 1, 2014. https://doi.org/10.2139/ssrn.2377353.

Epstein, Richard A. 1992. *Forbidden Grounds: The Case against Employment Discrimination Laws*. Cambridge, MA: Harvard University Press.

Equal Employment Opportunity Commission (EEOC) 2011. Guidelines on Discrimination Because of Sex. Part 1604.

Ertman, Martha. 2010. "The Upside of Baby Markets," in *Baby Markets: Money and the New Politics of Creating Families*. New York, NY: Cambridge University Press.

Estlund, David. 1996. "The Survival of Egalitarian Justice in John Rawls's Political Liberalism," *Journal of Political Philosophy* 4 (1): 68–78.

Ewens, Michael, Bryan Tomlin, and Liang Choon Wang. 2014. "Statistical Discrimination or Prejudice? A Large Sample Field Experiment," *Review of Economics and Statistics* 96 (1): 119–134.

The 2018 Fair Housing Trends Report.

Fair Housing Council of San Fernando Valley v. *Roommates.com, LLC*, 521 F.3d 1157 (9th Cir. 2008) (*Fair Housing I*).

Fair Housing Council of San Fernando Valley v. *Rommates.com, LLC* 666 F.3d 1216 (9th Cir. 2012) (*Fair Housing II*).

Farrelly, Colin 2007. "Justice in Ideal Theory: A Refutation," *Political Studies* 55: 844–864.

Feliciano, Cynthia, Belinda Robnett, and Golnaz Komaie. 2009. "Gendered Racial Exclusion among White Internet Daters," *Social Science Research* 38(1): 39–54.

Fleming, James E. 1993. "Constructing the Substantive Constitution," *Texas Law Review* 72: 211.

Fogg Davis, Heath. 2002. *The Ethics of Transracial Adoption.* Ithaca, NY: Cornell University Press.

Fox, Dov. 2009. "Racial Classification in Assisted Reproduction," *The Yale Law Journal* 118 (8): 1844–1898.

Freeman, Samuel. 2007. *Rawls.* New York, NY: Routledge Press.

Galster, George and Erin Godfrey. 2005. "By Words and Deeds: Racial Steering by Real Estate Agents in the U.S. in 2000." *American Planning Association. Journal of the American Planning Association* 71 (3) (Summer): 251–268.

Geuss, Raymond. 2008. *Philosophy and Real Politics.* Princeton, NJ: Princeton University Press.

Gladstone Realtors v. *Bellwood*, 441 *U.S.* 91 (1979).

Gooding-Williams, Robert. 1998. "Race, Multiculturalism and Democracy," *Constellations* 5 (1): 18–41.

Habermas, Jürgen. 2001. "Remarks on Legitimation through Human Rights," in *The Postnational Constellation: Political Essays*, Max Pensky (trans. and ed.), Cambridge: Polity Press.

Han, Chong-suk and Kyung-Hee Choi. 2018. "Very Few People Say 'No Whites': Gay Men of Color and the Racial Politics of Desire," *Sociological Spectrum*, 38(3): 145–161.

Han, Chong-suk. 2008a. "No Fats, Femmes, or Asians: The Utility of Critical Race Theory in Examining the Role of Gay Stock Stories in the Marginalization of Gay Asian Men," *Contemporary Justice Review* 11(1): 11–22.

Han, Chong-suk. 2008. "A Qualitative Exploration of the Relationship between Racism and Unsafe Sex among Asian Pacific Islander Gay Men," *Archives of Sexual Behavior* 37(5): 827–837.

Haney-Lopez, Ian. 2006. *White by Law: The Legal Construction of Race.* New York, NY: New York University Press.

Hanson, Andrew and Zackary Hawley. 2011. "Do Landlords Discriminate in the Rental Housing Market? Evidence from an Internet Field Experiment in US Cities," *Journal of Urban Economics* 70(2): 99–114.

Harney, Kenneth R. 2016. "Don't expect realty agents to answer loaded questions about neighborhoods," *Washington Post*. 3/6/2106 (www.washingtonpost.com/rea lestate/dont-expect-realty-agents-to-answer-loaded-questions/2016/03/15/ 16b1727e-ea0c-11e5-a6f3-21ccdbc5f74e_story.html?noredirect=on&utm_term= .a52fa39a6ad8)

Harney, Kenneth R. 2014. "Some realty sites describe neighborhoods' racial and ethnic makeup; is that legal," *Washington Post*. 6/20/2014 (www.washingtonpost .com/realestate/some-realty-sites-describe-neighborhoods-racial-and-ethnic-makeup-is-that-legal/2014/06/19/58a7cdfc-f587-11e3-a3a5-42be35962a52_story .html?noredirect=on&utm_term=.4194b2e19212)

Harris, John. 2007. "Reproductive Choice," *Encyclopedia of Life Sciences*. Hoboken, NJ:John Wiley & Sons, Incorporated.

Hart, H.L.A. 1989. "Rawls on Liberty and Its Priority," in *Reading Rawls: Critical Studies on Rawls' A Theory of Justice*, Norman Daniels (ed.), Stanford, CA: Stanford University Press, pp. 230–252.

Hayat, Norrinda Brown. 2017. "Accommodating Bias in the Sharing Economy" *Brooklyn Law Review* 83: 613.

Hayward, Clarissa. 2013. *How Americans Make Race: Stories, Institutions and Spaces*. New York, NY: Cambridge University Press.

Heart of Atlanta Motel, Inc. v. *United States*, 379 U.S. 241 (1964).

Herman, Melissa R. and Mary E. Campbell. 2012. "I Wouldn't, But You Can: Attitudes toward Interracial Relationships," *Social Science Research* 41: 343–358.

Hochschild, Jennifer L., Vesla M. Weaver, and Traci R. Burch. 2012. *Creating a New Racial Order: How Immigration, Multiracialism, Genomics, and the Young Can Remake Race in America*. Princeton, NJ: Princeton University Press.

Howe, Ruth-Arlene. 1997. "Transracial Adoption (TRA): Old Prejudices and Discrimination Float under a New Halo." *Boston University Public Interest Law Journal* 6: 409–472.

Hurley v. *Irish American Gay, Lesbian, and Bisexual Group of Boston*, 515 U.S. 557 (1995).

Hwang, Wei-Chin. 2013. "Who Are People Willing to Date? Ethnic and Gender Patterns in Online Dating," *Race and Social Problems* 5(1): 28–40.

Jacobson, Matthew Frye. 1999. *Whiteness of a Different Color*. Cambridge, MA: Harvard University Press.

Jakobsson, Niklas and Henrik Lindholm. 2014. "Ethnic Preferences in Internet Dating: A Field Experiment," *Marriage & Family Review* 50 (4): 307–317.

Jain, Tarun and Mark D. Hornstein. 2005. "Disparities in Access to Infertility Services in a State with Mandated Insurance Coverage," *Fertility and Sterility* 84 (1): 221–223.

Jane Doe No. 1 et al. v. *Backpage.com, LLC*, 817 F.3d 12 (1st Circuit 2016).

Jones v. *Alfred H. Mayer Co.*, 392 U.S. 409 (1968).

Kau, James B., Donald C. Keenan, and Henry J. Munneke 2012. "Racial Discrimination and Mortgage Lending," *The Journal of Real Estate Finance and Economics* 45(2): 289–304.

Keehn, Jason, Eve Holwell, Ruqayyah Abdul-Karim, Lisa Judy Chin, Cheng-Shiun Leu, Mark V. Sauer, and Robert Klitzman. 2012. "Recruiting Egg

188 References

Donors Online: An Analysis of in Vitro Fertilization Clinic and Agency Websites' Adherence to American Society for Reproductive Medicine Guidelines," *Fertility and Sterility* 98 (4): 995–1000.

Kelly, Kristin A. 2003. *Domestic Violence and the Politics of Privacy*. Ithaca, NY: Cornell University Press.

Kennedy, Randall. 2003. *Interracial Intimacies: Sex, Marriage, Identity, and Adoption*. New York, NY: Vintage Books.

Kirkland, Anna. 2008. *Fat Rights: Dilemmas of Difference and Personhood*. New York, NY: New York University Press.

Kitcher, Philip. 2007. "Does 'Race' Have a Future?" *Philosophy and Public Affairs* 35(4): 293–317.

Knight v. *Nassau Cty. Civil Serv. Comm'n*, 649 F.2d 157 (2d Cir. 1981).

Koppelman, Andrew. 2004. "Should Noncommercial Associations Have an Absolute Right to Discriminate?" *Law and Contemporary Problems* 67 (4): 27–57.

Krysan, Maria and Kyle Crowder. 2017. *Cycle of Segregation: Social Processes and Residential Stratification*. New York, NY: Russell Sage Foundation.

Ksiazkiewicz, Aleksander and James Hedrick. 2013. "An Introduction to Implicit Attitudes in Political Science Research," *PS: Political Science & Politics* 46(03), 525–531.

Ladd, Helen F. 1998. "Evidence on Discrimination in Mortgage Lending," *The Journal of Economic Perspectives* 12 (2): 41–62.

Lawrence, Charles R. 1987. "The Id, the Ego, and Equal Protection: Reckoning with Unconscious Racism," *Stanford Law Review* 39: 317.

Leigh, Suzanne. 2006. "Reproductive 'Tourism,'" USA TODAY, May 3, 2006, at 7D.

Leong, Nancy and Aaron Belzer. 2017. "The New Public Accommodations: Race Discrimination in the Platform Economy," *The Georgetown Law Journal* 105: 1271.

Lewontin, Richard. 1997. *Critical Race Theory: Essays on the Social Construction and Reproduction of Race*, E. Nathaniel Gates (ed.) (vol. 1). New York, NY: Routledge Press.

Lewontin, Richard C., Steven Peter Russell Rose, and Leon J. Kamin. 1984. *Not in Our Genes: Biology, Ideology, and Human Nature*. New York, NY: Pantheon Books.

Lichter, Daniel T., Domenico Parisi, and Michael C. Taquino. 2015. "Toward a New Macro-Segregation? Decomposing Segregation within and between Metropolitan Cities and Suburbs," *American Sociological Review* 80(4): 843–873.

Lin, Ken-Hou and Jennifer Lundquist. 2013. "Mate Selection in Cyberspace: The Intersection of Race, Gender, and Education," *American Journal of Sociology*, 119(1), 183–215.

Livingstone, Frank. 1962. "On the Non-Existence of Human Races," *Current Anthropology* 3.

Loevy, Robert D. 1990. *To End All Segregation: The Politics of the Passage of the Civil Rights Act of 1964*. Lanham, MD: University Press of America.

Log Cabin Republicans v. *United States*, 716 F.Supp.2d 884 (C.D. Cal. 2010).

MacKinnon, Catharine A. 1987. *Feminism Unmodified: Discourses on Life and Law.* Cambridge, MA: Harvard University Press.

Mallon, Ron. 2006. "Race: Normative, Not Metaphysical or Semantic," *Ethics* 116 (3): 525–551.

Mann, Ronald J. and Seth R. Belzley. 2005. "The Promise of Internet Intermediary Liability," *William and Mary Law Review* 47: 239.

Marketdata Enterprises. 2013. U.S. Fertility Clinics & Infertility Services: An Industry Analysis. November 5, 2013.

Masterpiece Cakeshop, Ltd. v. *Colorado Civil Rights Commission*, 584 *U.S.* ___ (2018).

Mayer, Gerald. 2011. Selected Characteristics of Private and Public Sector Workers, Congressional Research Service. July 1, 2011.

McClain, Linda C. Forthcoming. *The Rhetoric of Bigotry.* Oxford University Press.

McClain, Linda C. 2011. "Involuntary Servitude, Public Accommodations Laws, and the Legacy of Heart of Atlanta Motel, Inc. v. United States," *Maryland Law Review* 71: 83.

McClain, Linda C. 1995. "Inviolability and Privacy: The Castle, the Sanctuary, and the Body," *Yale Journal of Law and Humanities* 7: 195–241.

McClintock, Elizabeth Aura. 2010. "When Does Race Matter? Race, Sex, and Dating at an Elite University," *Journal of Marriage and Family* 72(1): 45–72.

McConnell, Michael W. 2018. "Dressmakers, Bakers, and the Equality of Rights," to be published in *Religious Freedom, LGBT Rights, and the Prospects for Common Ground* (William N. Eskridge, Jr. and Robin Fretwell Wilson, eds.) Stanford Public Law Working Paper. Available at SSRN: https://ssrn.com/abstract=3128373

McDonald v. *Santa Fe Trail Transp. Co.*, 427 *U.S.* 273 (1976).

Mendelsohn, Gerald A., Lindsay Shaw Taylor, Andrew T. Fiore, and Coye Cheshire. 2014. "Black/White Dating Online: Interracial Courtship in the 21st Century," *Psychology of Popular Media Culture* 3(1): 2.

Michelman, Frank I. 2003. "Rawls on Constitutionalism and Constitutional Law," in *The Cambridge Companion to Rawls*, Samuel Freeman (ed.), Cambridge: Cambridge University Press.

Milkman, Katherine L. Modupe Akinola, and Dolly Chugh. 2012. "Temporal Distance and Discrimination: An Audit Study in Academia." *Psychological Science* 23 (7): 710–717.

Mills, Charles W. 2017. *Black Rights/White Wrongs.* New York, NY: Oxford University Press.

Mills, Charles W. 2015. "*The Racial Contract* Revisited: Still Unbroken after All These Years," *Politics, Groups, and Identities* 3 (3): 541–557.

Mills, Charles W. 2014. "White Time: The Chronic Injustice of Ideal Theory," *Du Bois Review* 11 (1): 27–42.

Mills, Charles W. 2008. "Racial Liberalism," *PMLA* 123 (5): 1380–1397.

Mills, Charles W. 1998. *Blackness Visible: Essays on Philosophy and Race.* Ithaca, NY: Cornell University Press at 50.

Mills, Charles W. 1997. *The Racial Contract.* Ithaca, NY: Cornell University Press.

Mills, Charles. 1994. "Do Black Men Have a Moral Duty to Marry Black Women?" *Journal of Social Philosophy*, 25th Anniversary Special Issue, 131–153.

Moran, Rachel F. 2003. *Interracial Intimacy: The Regulation of Race and Romance.* Chicago, IL: University of Chicago Press.

Mutcherson, Kimberly M. 2012. "Welcome to the Wild West: Protecting Access to Cross Border Fertility Care in the United States," *Cornell Journal of Law and Public Policy* 22 (2), Article 3.

Nagel, Thomas. 2003. "Rawls and Liberalism," in *The Cambridge Companion to Rawls*, Samuel Freeman (ed.), Cambridge: Cambridge University Press.

Nardinelli, Clark and Curtis Simon. 1990. "Racial Discrimination in the Market for Memorabilia: The Case of Baseball," *The Quarterly Journal of Economics* 105 (3) (August): 575–595.

NeJaime, Douglas and Siegel, Reva B. 2018. "Religious Exemptions and Antidiscrimination Law in Masterpiece Cakeshop," *Yale Law Journal Forum* 128: 201.

Nelson, Eric. 2008. "From Primary Goods to Capabilities Distributive Justice and the Problem of Neutrality," *Political Theory* 36(1): 93–122.

Newman v. *Piggie Park Enterprises, Inc.*, 390 *U.S.* 400 (1968).

Note. 1994. "Racial Steering in the Romantic Marketplace," *Harvard Law Review* 107: 877.

Nussbaum, Martha C. 2013. *Political Emotions: Why Love Matters for Justice.* Cambridge, MA: Harvard University Press.

Nussbaum, Martha C. 2005. "Women's Bodies: Violence, Security, Capabilities," *Journal of Human Development* 6 (2): 167–183.

Nussbaum, Martha C. 2003a. "Rawls and Feminism," in *The Cambridge Companion to Rawls*, Samuel Freeman (ed.), Cambridge: Cambridge University Press.

Nussbaum, Martha C. 2003. "Capabilities as Fundamental Entitlements: Sen and Social Justice," *Feminist Economics* 9 (2–3): 33–59.

Nussbaum, Martha C. 2001. *Women and Human Development: The Capabilities Approach.* Cambridge: Cambridge University Press.

O'Connor v. *Village Green Owners Ass'n*, 662 P.2d 427, 431 (Cal. 1983).

Obergefell v. *Hodges*, 135 S.Ct. 2584 (2015).

Okin, Susan Moller. 1989a. "Justice and Gender," *Philosophy and Public Affairs* 16: 42–72.

Okin, Susan Moller. 1989. *Justice Gender, and the Family.* New York, NY: Basic Books.

Palmore v. *Sidoti*, 466 *U.S.* 429 (1984).

Papcke, Luise. 2018. "Reaching a New Balance in Freedom of Association: The Good Approach," *Polity* 50 (3): 366–397.

Parents Involved in Cmty. Sch. v. *Seattle Sch. Dist. No. 1*, 551 *U.S.* 701 (2007).

Pateman, Carole. 1989. *The Disorder of Women: Democracy, Feminism and Political Theory.* Cambridge: Polity.

Peña-Rodriguez v. *Colorado*, 137 S.Ct. 855 (2017).

Perez v. *Commissioner*, 144 *T.C.* 4 (Tax 2015).

Pittsburgh Press Co. v. *Human Relations Comm'n*, 413 *U.S.* 376 (1973).

Post, Robert C. and Reva B. Siegel. 2000. "Equal Protection by Law: Federal Antidiscrimination Legislation after Morrison and Kimel," *Yale Law Journal* 110 (3): 441–526.

Prasso, Sheridan. 2005. *The Asian Mystique: Dragon Ladies, Geisha Girls, & Our Fantasies of the Exotic Orient*. New York, NY: Public Affairs.

Quiroga, Seline Szkupinski. 2007. "Blood Is Thicker Than Water: Policing Donor Insemination and the Reproduction of Whiteness," *Hypatia* 22 (2): 143–161.

Radin, Margaret Jane. 2000. *Contested Commodities*. Cambridge, MA: Harvard University Press.

Ragin v. *New York Times* 923 F.2d 995 (2nd Cir. 1991), cert denied 502 U.S. 821 (1991).

Rawls, John. 2001. *Justice as Fairness: A Restatement* (ed. Erin Kelly). Cambridge, MA: Belknap Press.

Rawls, John. 1999 rev. [1971]. *A Theory of Justice*. Cambridge, MA: Belknap Press.

Rawls, John. 1997. "Social Unity and Primary Goods," *Frontier Issues in Economic Thought* 3, 276–280.

Rawls, John. 1996 [1993]. *Political Liberalism*. New York, NY: Columbia Press.

Rhode, Deborah L. 2010. *The Beauty Bias: The Injustice of Appearance in Life and Law*. New York, NY: Oxford University Press.

Roberts v. *United States Jaycees*, 468 *U.S.* 609 (1984).

Robinson, Russell. K. 2007a. "Structural Dimensions of Romantic Preferences," *Fordham Law Review* 76: 2787.

Robinson, Russell K. 2007. "Casting and Caste-Ing: Reconciling Artistic Freedom and Antidiscrimination Norms," *California Law Review* 95 (1): 1–73.

Robinson, Russell K. and David M. Frost. 2018. "LGBT Equality and Sexual Racism," *Fordham Law Review* 86: 2739.

Robnett, Belinda and Cynthia Feliciano. 2011. "Patterns of Racial-Ethnic Exclusion by Internet Daters," *Social Forces* 89(3): 807–828.

Romer v. *Evans*, 517 *U.S.* 620 (1996).

Rosen, Mark D. 2007. "Was Shelley v. Kraemer Incorrectly Decided: Some New Answers," *California Law Review* 95: 451.

Rosenberg, Gerald. 2004. "Substituting Symbol for Substance: What Did *Brown* Really Accomplish?" *PS: Political Science & Politics* 37 (2): 205–209.

Rotary Club of Duarte v. *Bd. of Dirs.*, 224 Cal. Rptr. 213, 221–26 (Cal. Ct. App. 1986).

Rudder, Christian. 2014. *Dataclysm*. New York, NY: Crown Publishers.

Rumsfeld v. *Forum for Academic and Institutional Rights*, 547 *U.S.* 47 (2006).

Runyon v. *McCrary*, 427 *U.S.* 160 (1976).

Russell, Camisha. 2015. "The Race Idea in Reproductive Technologies: Beyond Epistemic Scientism and Technological Mastery," *Journal of Bioethical Inquiry* 12 (4): 601–612.

Sandel, Michael. 2012. *What Money Can't Buy*. New York, NY: Farrar, Straus, and Giroux.

Sandel, Michael. 2009. *The Case against Perfection*. Cambridge, MA: Harvard University Press.

Sandel, Michael. 2000. "What Money Can't Buy: The Moral Limits of Markets," *Tanner Lectures on Human Values* 21: 87–122.

Schmidt, Christopher W. 2013. "Defending the Right to Discriminate: The Libertarian Challenge to the Civil Rights Movement," in *Signposts: New Directions in Southern Legal History*, Sally E. Hadden and Patricia Hagler Minter (eds), Athens, GA: University of Georgia Press.

Schuette v. Coal. to Defend Affirmative Action, Integration & Immigrant Rights & Fight for Equal. By Any Means Necessary (BAMN), 572 U.S. 291 (2014).

Selden v. Airbnb, Inc., 16-cv-00933 (D.C. 2016).

Shelley v. Kraemer, 334 U.S. 1 (1948).

Shelby, Tommie. 2016. *Dark Ghettos: Injustice, Dissent and Reform.* Cambridge, MA: Harvard University Press.

Shelby, Tommie. 2014. "Integration, Inequality, and Imperatives of Justice: A Review Essay," *Philosophy and Public Affairs* 42 (3): 253–85.

Shelby, Tommie. 2004. "Race and Social Justice: Rawlsian Considerations," *Fordham Law Review* 72 (5): Symposium: Rawls and the Law: 1697–1714.

Shue, Henry. 1975. "Liberty and Self-Respect," *Ethics* 85: 195–203.

Smedley, Audrey and Brian D. Smedley. 2005. "Race as Biology is Fiction, Racism as a Social Problem Is Real: Anthropological and Historical Perspectives on the Social Construction of Race," *American Psychologist* 60(1): 16.

Smith, Jesus. 2014. "Getting Off Online: Race, Gender, and Sexuality in Cyberspace," in *Illuminating How Identities, Stereotypes and Inequalities Matter through Gender Studies*, Demetrea Nicole Farris, Mary Ann Davis, and R. D'Lane (eds.), Springer Netherlands.

South Dakota v. Wayfair, 138 S.Ct. 2080 (2018).

Sundstrom, Ronald. 2002. "Racial Nominalism," *Journal of Social Philosophy* 33: 193–210.

Stevens v. Optimum Health Inst., 810 F. Supp. 2d 1074 (S.D. Cal. 2011).

Sylvain, Olivier. 2018. "Emerging Threats: Discriminatory Designs on User Data," Knight Institute.

Taylor, Paul C. 2004. *Race: A Philosophical Introduction*, Cambridge: Polity Press.

Taylor, Robert. 2004. "Self-Realization and the Priority of Fair Equality of Opportunity," *Journal of Moral Philosophy* 1 (3): 333–347.

Thorsby, Devon. 2015. "What Your Real Estate Agent Can't Tell You," US News. 12/ 14/2105 (https://realestate.usnews.com/real-estate/articles/what-your-real-estate-agent-cant-tell-you).

Todisco, Michael. 2015. "Share and Share Alike: Considering Racial Discrimination in the Nascent Room-Sharing Economy," *Stan. L. Rev. Online* 67: 121.

Trafficante v. Metropolitan Life, 409 U.S. 205 (1972).

Tsunokai, Glenn T., Allison R. McGrath, and Jillian K. Kavanagh. 2013. "Online Dating Preferences of Asian Americans," *Journal of Social and Personal Relationships* 31(6): 796–814.

Tushnet, Mark V. 2001. "The Redundant Free Exercise Clause?" *Loyola University Chicago Law Journal* 33: 71–94.

Tushnet, Mark V. 1998. "Shelley v. Kraemer and Theories of Equality," *New York Law School Law Review* 33: 383.

United States v. *Hunter*, 459 F.2d 205 (4th Cir. 1972), cert denied 409 U.S. 934 (1972).

United States v. *Hunter*, 324 F.Supp. 529 (D. Md. 1971).

Valentini, Laura. 2012. "Idea vs. Non-Ideal Theory: A Conceptual Map," *Philosophy Compass* 7 (9): 654–664.

Walzer, Michael. 1983. *Spheres of Justice: A Defense of Pluralism and Equality.* New York, NY: Basic Books.

White, Jaclyn M., Sari L. Reisner, Emilia Dunham, and Matthew J. Mimiaga. 2014. "Race-Based Sexual Preferences in a Sample of Online Profiles of Urban Men Seeking Sex with Men," *Journal of Urban Health* 91 (4): 1–8.

Wiens, David. 2012. "Prescribing Institutions without Ideal Theory," *Journal of Political Philosophy* 20 (1): 45–70.

Young, Iris Marion. 1990. *Justice and the Politics of Difference.* Princeton, NJ: Princeton University Press.

Yuracko, Kimberly A. 2016. *Gender Nonconformity and the Law.* New Haven, CT: Yale University Press.

Zack, Naomi. 2002. *Philosophy of Science and Race.* New York, NY: Routledge.

Zheng, Robin. 2016. "Why Yellow Fever Isn't Flattering: A Case against Racial Fetishes," *Journal of the American Philosophical Association* (2016): 400–419.

Zivi, Karen. 2011. *Making Rights Claims: A Practice of Democratic Citizenship.* New York, NY: Oxford University Press.

Zuch v. *Hussey*, 394 F.Supp. 1028 (E.D. Mich. 1975).

INDEX